Laws and Explanation
in the Social Sciences

Laws and Explanation in the Social Sciences

Defending a Science of Human Behavior

Lee C. McIntyre

WestviewPress

A Division of HarperCollins*Publishers*

For my mother and father

Copyright © 1996 by Westview Press, Inc., A Division of HarperCollins Publishers, Inc.

Published in 1996 in the United States of America by Westview Press, Inc., 5500 Central Avenue, Boulder, Colorado 80301-2877, and in the United Kingdom by Westview Press, 12 Hid's Copse Road, Cumnor Hill, Oxford OX2 9JJ

A CIP catalog record for this book is available from the Library of Congress.
ISBN 0-8133-2828-4

This book was typeset by Letra Libre, 1705 14th St., Suite 391, Boulder, Colorado, 80302

The paper used in this publication meets the requirements of the American National Standard for Permanence of Paper for Printed Library Materials Z39.48-1984.

10   9   8   7   6   5   4   3   2   1

Contents

The only foundation for the knowledge of the natural sciences is the idea that the general laws, known or unknown, which regulate the phenomena of the Universe, are necessary and constant; and why should that principle be less true for the intellectual and moral faculties of man than for the other actions of nature?

—Condorcet

Preface

Are there laws in social science? If so, can they be used for the explanation of human behavior? This issue has been at the heart of the philosophy of social science since its inception. The emulation of the models of explanation drawn from natural science has long framed the aspirations of social scientists. In the philosophy of natural science, Carl G. Hempel and others have made a case for the role of laws in the explanation of scientific phenomena. Of course, there has been controversy over the adequacy of specific accounts. But in the philosophy of social science what has been most controversial is the attempt to extend nomological models to explanation in the social sciences.

The status of laws in the explanation of human behavior is *the* methodological question in the philosophy of social science. To what extent can social science make use of laws in the explanation of social events? Are there barriers preventing such laws? Can they be overcome?

These issues have been much discussed (though little developed) in the literature. For it is usually antecedently believed that social science *cannot* use laws, and the nature of the debate about them has largely—in recent years—consisted of disagreement over the adequacy of each attempted inference to the best explanation for why there are in fact no social scientific laws. The issue, therefore, doesn't seem to be whether there are or could be laws. Rather, the debate is over finding the right peg upon which to hang the failure of social scientists to produce them. The concern is whether we have isolated the correct reason for why they could not be given. So the argument about the barriers to nomological explanation in the social sciences comes for the most part after the fact and is concerned with justifying an antecedent belief that laws are either impossible, impractical, or irrelevant. And no matter what the outcome of this debate, many believe the result will be the same: Laws will not be forthcoming.

By and large, since roughly the time of John Passmore's announcement of the "death of positivism" in his article in *The Encyclopedia of Philosophy,* a defense of social scientific laws has been out of fashion; we have stopped believing in the feasibility of social scientific laws, and it has become an academic exercise to find the cause of their failure. The Doctor of Philosophy arrives too late to save the patient, but he is happy to perform the postmortem.

In this book I aim to reevaluate the course of this debate and to show that the reason most of the arguments against the possibility, practicality, or relevance of laws in social science miss their mark is that the premise they are starting from is dubious. That is, I hope to defend the status of nomological explanation in the social sciences and to show that we have been far too hasty in our abandonment of the nomological ideal in the social sciences. Indeed, the failure of social scientists to produce unequivocal laws has been equalled only by the failure of philosophers of social science to produce good reasons for believing that such laws are unattainable.

In large part this failure stems from adherence to a highly idealized view of nomologicality, allegedly drawn from the natural sciences, but which only doubtfully could be realized there either. When compared to this standard, it is true that the social science perform poorly. However, the last thirty years of the philosophy of science have involved a rethinking of the applicability of such standards throughout the sciences without giving up the centrality of laws to scientific explanation. In light of this, it is time to reexamine the epistemological similarities and differences between the natural and social sciences. I seek, therefore, to reconsider the status of laws in the explanation of human behavior and to demonstrate that there is reason to be optimistic about the prospects for nomological explanation in the social sciences.

But before I proceed in this task, I would first like to acknowledge those who have been most influential in helping me to shape the ideas that are presented here. My interest in the relationship between natural and social science began while I was an undergraduate at Wesleyan University, where I had the good fortune to have Richard Adelstein, Howard Bernstein, and Brian Fay among my teachers. Indeed, it was Rich Adelstein's comment in a class on introductory economics in the Spring of 1981 that first sparked my interest in this topic. Over the years I still feel myself responding to the challenges he has set for me. My interest deepened during graduate school at the University of Michigan, while writing a dissertation on problems in the philosophy of social science, where I benefitted immensely from the advice and comments given by Jaegwon Kim, Peter Railton, Lawrence Sklar, and Hal Varian. Since then, while putting my thoughts together into a book, I have enjoyed the opportunity to benefit from the comments of many of the top scholars in my discipline, including Harold Kincaid, Daniel Little, Michael Martin, Alexander Rosenberg, and Merrilee Salmon. Contributions made in conversation by Mary Williams and Stephen J. Gould, though briefer, helped me in ways that they could not have imagined, as have the comments of many of my colleagues at Colgate.

My debt to Michael Martin and Alex Rosenberg, however, is of an altogether different order of magnitude, for each read the complete book manuscript and made numerous critical comments. I am grateful to them both.

For this and much else, I am fortunate to have been a colleague of Michael Martin while I was a Research Fellow at the Center for the Philosophy and History of Science at Boston University and to have enjoyed his friendship. In addition to his commentary and advice, he has always been unfailing in his encouragement and has helped me by his example as a philosopher in more ways than he may realize. Alex Rosenberg, both in his written works and in conversation, has also served as a source of inspiration to me and an example of true intellectual honesty. I cannot name a philosopher whose opinions are in general farthest from my own, but whom I respect more.

The debt I owe to those who originally inspired me in this project, Lady Barbara Wootton and Carl G. Hempel, is much harder to pin down. Each provided me with words of encouragement when I was first beginning to develop my thoughts on these issues over ten years ago. I was fortunate to have benefitted from the kindness of Lady Wootton over the ensuing years as she continued our correspondence.

For their assistance in actually helping this project to see the light of day, I would like to acknowledge several others: Spencer Carr, Allison Sole, and Cindy Rinehart at Westview Press, Jon Brooks and Andrew Davis at Letra Libre, Ed Freedman for the enormous job of proofreading and preparing the index, and Deborah Wilkes for her sound advice along the way. In this regard, I would also like to mention Robert Cohen, without whose kind support I never would have had the freedom to complete the original manuscript. For financial assistance, I am grateful to the Research Council and to the Dean of the Faculty's Office at Colgate University.

Finally, especially at the end of such a project, one realizes that there are others, all of whom have in their own way contributed to its development. To my family and friends, I cannot begin to express my thanks for their patience and support as I have been working on this project. My grandmother in particular took a special interest in seeing me finish, providing me with suitable admonishment when she thought I might be slacking off. My daughter, Louisa, has had a different agenda entirely, helping me to realize that what is dearest in life, even for a philosopher, is not ideas but people. My closest friend, Chuck Schneider, has been with me every step of the way as well. But to my wife, Josephine, goes perhaps my greatest thanks of all—for she has contributed herself and her ideas to this book in more ways than I will ever begin to realize. Indeed, I have written it for her, with and for whom all things are possible.

Despite incurring so many debts in completing this book, the choice for its dedication was easy. I dedicate this book to my mother and father, Drena and Frank McIntyre, whose patience and guidance over the years has made me who I am.

Lee C. McIntyre

1

The Nomological Ideal

What it demands is that the sociologist put himself in the same state of mind as the physicist, chemist, or physiologist when he probes into a still unexplored region of the scientific domain. When he penetrates the social world, he must be aware that he is penetrating the unknown; he must feel himself in the presence of facts whose laws are as unsuspected as were those of life before the era of biology; he must be prepared for discoveries which will surprise and disturb him.

—Emile Durkheim

It has long been debated whether we can use the same method of inquiry in social science that has been used in natural science. Central to this debate has been the question of the role of laws in the explanation of human behavior. Many philosophers and social scientists alike have felt that the social sciences deal with phenomena so disparate from that of the natural sciences that fruitful inquiry requires a kind of methodological independence.[1] Specifically, many have thought that the unique subject matter of the social sciences forces a break in the kind of explanatory accounts one could use in social inquiry, suggesting that law-like explanation is here impossible or impractical to pursue. Moreover, some have made the stronger claim that the difference in subject matter is bound up with the fact that we want something different explained *about* human behavior than we want explained about natural phenomena, which laws, even if available, could not capture. Nomological explanations on this account are thereby held to be irrelevant. Despite their surface diversity concerning the scope of these implications, however, it is important to note that all of these claims are rooted in a commitment to the uniqueness of the subject matter of social science and purport to militate against the explanatory value of social scientific laws on these grounds.[2]

But can one nevertheless defend the use of laws in the explanation of human behavior against its critics? Have the arguments concerning the complexity of social phenomena, the openness of human systems, and the non-repeatable and non-controllable aspects of social experimentation really shown that there is a difference "in kind" between the subject matters

1

of natural and social science, thus requiring a correspondingly different type of explanation? If not, what *do* such considerations imply about our ability to use law-like explanations when investigating human behavior? Do they impose potential restrictions or limitations, or otherwise significantly hamper us, in devising law-like accounts? Does the cumulative effect of such factors impose special constraints in the case of social science? And would we even *want* nomological explanations in social science should they be available? What account of explanation is appropriate in social science in the face of these considerations?

In this book I will deal with the above issues by considering some of the most prevalent arguments against the use of law-like explanation in social science rooted in the alleged intractability of its subject matter.[3] I will examine not only those arguments that purport to have shown that the goal of law-like explanation is impossible, but also those that have attempted to show that, even if law-like explanation is not in principle impossible, there are factors endemic to social inquiry that so severely restrict the use of laws as to render them effectively useless and undesirable for social scientific explanation. In short, I will attempt to defend the use of law-like explanations in social science against those arguments that purport to show that, due to certain unique features of its subject matter, such laws are impossible, impractical, or irrelevant. But before I launch into a dispute with such views, it is first important to be clear about the position that they are attacking. What is "law-like explanation," and how might it be employed in practice?

There are, of course, a whole constellation of possible criteria for nomologicality: a law has been variously held to be a well-confirmed general regularity, that is embedded in a theory, confirmable by its instances, that supports its counterfactuals, and that is used for explanation. Moreover, some also have held that laws must reflect exceptionless regularities, immutable over time and place, that are universal in scope, and capture non-contingent relationships. Some have also held that laws should be derivable from larger regularities, must yield predictions, and unify diverse phenomena.

Naturally, there are few examples even within physics that may fit all of these criteria, and there has been an interesting and heated debate in the philosophy of science concerning what the proper criteria may be.[4] But the question I will be concerned with in this book is not whether any one or combination of these factors properly define what we may legitimately call "social scientific laws." Instead, I will focus on the arguments that purport to show that no matter which criteria correctly define the conditions for nomologicality in natural science, social science cannot live up to them. That is, I am not interested in defending any particular view of a social scientific law, hoping to show that if we pick out a suitably restricted set of criteria we are in business. Rather, I seek to determine whether social scientific explanation can live up to the standards for what has been extensionally deemed a "law" in natural scientific explanation.

In order to understand the nature of such a comparison, however, we must first examine the role that laws play in scientific explanation. What is the role of laws in natural science? A variety of different rationales have been given for laws. It has been argued, for instance, that laws are useful because they: (1) help us to unify diverse phenomena, (2) aid us in the identification of causal mechanisms, (3) serve an instrumental role in accounting for observed regularities, or (4) fulfill our desire for explanation by satisfying the criterion of "nomic expectability."[5] It is not my intent here, however, to adjudicate the dispute about the role of laws in scientific explanation, but only to suggest that laws have a potentially important role to play in the explanation of scientific phenomena. That is, just as it is not my interest to defend any particular view of what a law *is*, my task does not require me to choose between alternative accounts of what role laws play in the explanation of scientific phenomena.

It *is* important, however, to examine in more detail the view that has been historically most influential in the debate about the status of laws in social science and that has captured the imagination of so many social scientists. In their 1948 paper "Studies in the Logic of Explanation,"[6] Carl Hempel and Paul Oppenheim outline the classic version of what was later to be called the "covering law model" of scientific explanation.[7] Roughly, the idea put forth is that one has not fully explained an event until one has shown that it could be derived from a set of scientific laws and antecedent conditions; that is, one aims to show that the phenomena to be explained was "to be expected" (and could have been predicted) on the basis of the covering laws, if the laws and antecedent conditions had been known in sufficient detail in advance.[8] The goal therefore is to show that the event to be explained is merely an instantiation of some larger general regularity, and thus one seeks to account for it by describing the regularity and showing that the event to be explained is a consequence of it.

Of course, there has been great controversy during the last several decades of the philosophy of science over the internal adequacy of Hempel and Oppenheim's model and its applicability to natural scientific explanation.[9] The logical symmetry between explanation and prediction, for example, has been singled out for much criticism, as have various other aspects of the model, such as its ability to contend with probabilistic phenomena and the adequacy of Hempel's account of "explanation sketches."[10] But although it is important to be aware of the controversy that has surrounded the adequacy of the covering law model in capturing what goes on in natural scientific explanation, it is also true to say that despite these problems, the covering law model has nevertheless framed the aspirations of those social scientists who have sought to bring their methods of explanation up to the standards of rigor represented in natural science. Thus, I will focus on the question of whether or not there would be problems in trying to employ covering laws in social scientific explanation, while leaving aside the question of what refinements would be necessary before Hempel's account of them might adequately capture the role that laws play in scientific explanation. For one thing seems clear: whatever the status of any particular model of natural scientific explanation, it is widely agreed that natural science does indeed make use of laws.[11] Those who have criticized Hempel's version of the covering law model of natural scientific explanation have not, for the most part, denied that laws play a role in the explanation of natural phenomena but instead have questioned whether Hempel's version of the model adequately captures what that role in fact is. However, for all the disagreement, it is important to remember that the classic version of the covering law model captures at least the spirit of the crucial role that laws play in scientific explanation.[12] And to the extent that its critics remain committed to some version (albeit revised) of the covering law model, the arguments provided by those who have argued that the model is not appropriate in *social* science would hardly differentiate between different versions of it.[13]

Thus, whether Hempel's model adequately captures what goes on in detail in natural scientific explanation is for our purposes a side issue. The issue immediately before us is whether or not social science can make any use of laws at all—whether it can do whatever it is that natural science has done in explanation, not whether Hempel's account of nomological explanation is fully adequate in all of its detail. Indeed, it is important to note that it is the *intuition* behind the covering law model, rather than its detail, that has captured the imagination of social scientists. The nomological ideal has proven to be a powerful prototype for social scientific explanation. And even if the ideal picture sketched out in any particular version of it is somewhat problematic, the saliency of the practical success of laws in natural scientific explanation has lent this ideal tremendous credibility in the eyes of social science. Perhaps through an example we might better understand the nature of its appeal.

Before Newton's derivation of Kepler's Laws from his theory of universal gravitation, astronomers were unsure how best to explain the small perturbations in the orbit of the planets. According to Kepler's first law, the path of each planet around the sun should be an ellipse, with the sun at one focus. Yet it was later found that the actual paths of the planets deviated slightly from this predicted route. After Newton presented his law of universal gravitation, however, which holds that not only the sun but also "every body in the universe attracts every other body," one could explain these perturbations as a result of the small attractive force (when compared with the sun's) between each of the planets. Indeed, given Newton's law of universal gravitation, such perturbations are *to be expected*.

In testament to the success of this explanation we note that it was on the basis of Newton's account that Adams and Leverrier were able to predict the existence and path of the planet Neptune. The inability to account for the perturbations in the orbit of the planet Uranus as a function of the attractive forces of the known planets led them to posit the existence of an eighth planet, which was later found, close to the place predicted.[14]

Within this account we can begin to see the elegant way in which nomological models have been instrumental in helping us to explain scientific phenomena. The search for an explanation of the perturbations in the orbit of the planets, for instance, is answered when one can subsume it under a more general regularity; one hopes to be able to show that this previously anomalous and puzzling phenomenon is actually an expected outcome of a well-ordered regularity. We therefore aim at subsuming such events under a causal law—we strive to *explain* them by accounting for the laws and initial conditions from which they inevitably result.[15] In the simplest terms, we want to show that the occurrence of the thing to be explained was "no accident."

The desire to repeat the success enjoyed by this paradigm has long informed the methodology of social inquiry. It has been hoped since the time of the early positivists that by imitating the successful components of natural scientific methodology, one might arrive at accurate predictions and lawlike explanations of human behavior. The success of natural scientific explanations, through the use of nomological models, has provided the social sciences with a "nomological ideal" to which they might aspire. But what is behind such a desire for a "successful" social science? In part, it is simply the goal of providing better explanations. But a significant impetus has also been the conviction that there is something terribly wrong with the social world as we now find it, and that through the emulation of the nomological model of explanation in natural science we can better move towards increased knowledge of how to improve human affairs.[16]

It is no secret that as far as our ability to foresee—and therein move towards control over—the tragedies of our social world, we have not been very successful. We live in a world where war, crime, and poverty are accepted by many as incurable ills, inflicted upon us by factors beyond our control or comprehension. Many have accepted the status quo, either openly or tacitly, and have supposed that our power to change such things is either minuscule or, perhaps, dangerous.[17] Yet others have thought that at the root of such social problems might be our inadequate knowledge of what causes them. Is it possible to repeat the success of the natural sciences by employing a broadly similar methodology of explanation in the study of social behavior?

The ability of physical scientists to arrive at the sort of knowledge that resulted in the Industrial Revolution, when humans first began to assert their control over nature on a vast scale, must have made the nomological paradigm quite attractive to early social scientists. Indeed, the ability to predict or explain riots, strikes, depressions, and revolutions would go far towards helping us to alleviate many of the social problems that we currently suppose to be insoluble. Yet even while recognizing the attractiveness of such a worldview, we do not want to make the error of supposing that nomological inquiry would somehow magically cure the evils that afflict our world.[18]

Certainly the positivistic philosophy of Auguste Comte had behind it such an idealistic goal. Comte and his followers in the early nineteenth century were pioneers in campaigning for the significant advantages that the use of a physical scientific paradigm could have in our social inquiry.[19] Indeed, Comte's view presupposed that the social world was constituted similarly to the natural one and therefore validated his presumption that nomological inquiry was also possible there. Comte's own statement on this point is unambiguous: "I shall bring factual proof that there are just as definite laws for the development of the human race as there are for the fall of a stone."[20] And the spirit of Comte's vision has continued to influence many philosophers even to the present day.[21]

Yet despite the historical importance of Comte's worldview, it would be unwise for us to dwell on it here any longer, for it is clear that his original position has been superseded and reinterpreted by many later thinkers. Some have reformulated and extended his worldview and have thought that it may be possible to groom the social sciences by following the methodology employed in natural science. These thinkers hold that political and personal bias in data interpretation, overly generalized and non-testable explanations, and the reliance on outmoded descriptions and vocabulary for investigating human behavior have impeded the progress of the social sciences in their proper task of searching for the covering laws that govern human behavior. For our purposes, however, we need not enter the complex debate over just where the modern "naturalist" orthodoxy finds itself in relation to Comte's original work. Rather we need only define in broadest terms the characteristics of the "naturalist" view.

In philosophy, "naturalism" has been used in many different ways. In ethics, for instance, it represents the view that ethical facts are "nothing but" natural facts. It is here a type of "metaphysical" thesis, which points out the continuity or connectedness between these two realms. But there is also sometimes a *methodological* component to such a view. Naturalism, in the methodological sense, is the idea that (perhaps because of ontological kinship) two domains are amenable to inquiry using broadly similar methods. In social science it is naturalism in the second sense that has been most controversial.[22] Namely, the debate over naturalism in the philosophy of social science concerns the thesis that it is both possible and desirable to use the same methodology and canons of explanation in examining social behavior that have been used in the investigation of natural scientific phenomena. Is it true that one can use a nomological prototype in the explanation of social scientific phenomena? It is naturalism in this sense that I will be examining in this book.

Yet despite the attraction one might feel toward such an account, many have suggested that it will not work to employ a law-like model of explanation in the social sciences.[23] The claim made here is either that one cannot find the laws that would be needed for such social explanation or that such explanation is inappropriate to the task we face in social science. At base, it is suggestive to think of such criticism as divisible into two general types of claims: that the subject matter of social science is intractable and would therefore prevent us from finding social scientific laws, versus the claim that we want something different explained *about* human behavior than we do about natural phenomena, which laws could not capture. The former view has been used to ratify the belief that even if one thought that laws in social science would be explanatory, they are just impossible to have (social scientific laws do not exist) or they are impractical to obtain (we could not find them anyway). The second claim, however, would seem to be more radical. Here it is emphasized that social scientific laws are irrelevant to the explanation of human behavior (so we would not want them) irrespective of the difficulties one might have in obtaining them. On this view laws are thought to be unexplanatory, and whether they are possible or practical is just moot.

It is interesting to note, however, that the break between these views is not as clean as one might think. Upon close examination, for instance, we realize that all of the above claims rely, at least implicitly, on a commitment to the idea that the difference in social scientific methodology is due to its differing subject matter. Surely, it is clear that this is true of the first claim. But even the second—that we want something different explained *about* human behavior—seems firmly rooted in the idea that nomological explanation would be irrelevant precisely because it does not do justice to what we have understood the subject matter of social science to be.[24] At base, this claim is surely one about the proper subject matter of social science.

Similarly, the division between claims about possibility and relevance are not so neat as one might hope. For certainly some who claim that social scientific laws are irrelevant also think that they are impossible and indeed may believe that they are irrelevant for the same reason that they are impossible.[25] Indeed, what is the claim of irrelevance if not just that at some important level we desire an explanation, but laws just do not exist there or cannot be found?

Of course it is also true that there are others who contend that social scientific laws are indeed irrelevant (and unexplanatory), but who do not hold any commitments about the possibility of laws—for them the issue of the possibility of laws is moot in light of their inappropriateness. On this view we could well allow for the possibility of laws but nevertheless would hold that they just would not explain what it is that we find interesting about human behavior. Thus, it is important to realize that not all of those who profess that social scientific laws are irrelevant believe this for the same reason.

So what might be our strategy in examining these arguments? First, one sees that it would be fruitful to admit at the outset that the focus will be on those arguments that purport to show that because of the unique nature of the subject matter of social science, we cannot have, or would not want, social scientific laws. Since all of the above arguments rely implicitly on the belief that any difference in methodology of explanation is due, at base, to a difference in subject matter, these matters are best investigated at this level. Second, our efforts in examining each of the particular arguments can be consolidated a bit; those who believe that social scientific laws are irrelevant for the same reason that they are impossible can be dealt with when we consider the general claim of irrelevance, for despite potentially different commitments about the possibility of laws, we should focus here on what irrelevance arguments have in common—the idea that social scientific laws would be unexplanatory in light of what we have taken the subject matter of social science to be. Third, it is important to notice that many of the arguments that purport to show that social scientific laws are *impossible* are also used to show that they are *impractical*; by and large, these arguments are the same, the difference being in the scope of their implications.

In this book, therefore, I will consider those arguments that purport to show that social scientific laws are either impossible, impractical, or irrelevant due to the intractability of the subject matter of social science. Specifically, I will examine the arguments from the complexity of human phenomena, the openness of human systems, and the claims behind "interpretivism" and "physicalism" in an effort to defend the nomological status of social science against some of the most important objections that have been offered against it.[26] It will serve us later to have a more specific typology of what such arguments purport to imply about the status of social scientific laws, so I will detail one below. I will start with the views concerning "possibility" and "practicality":

1a. There are no laws in social science. It is impossible, therefore, to give law-like explanations of human behavior. The subject matter of social science is so radically distinct from that found in natural science that it constitutes a difference "in kind," and thus enjoins the use of law-like explanations. Whereas in natural science we are dealing with systems that are well-isolated, stationary, and recurrent, in the social sciences we are dealing with those that undergo constant change.[27] Therefore, given the "complex" and "open" character of human systems, we could not hope to ascertain the laws that would be needed for nomological explanation (because there are none).

1b. Even if there *are* laws governing our social behavior, we could not find them.[28] The phenomena are probably part of an open system and are at least prohibitively complex, and so we cannot use laws in our explanations of human behavior. For all intents and purposes we ought to treat human phenomena as if it were impossible to formulate laws about them given the enormous practical barriers which stand in our way.

1c. The problem is not that we could not find *any* laws in social science, but that we cannot find any that are *interesting* enough (i.e., non-truistic) to be explanatory. This claim is allied with (1b) above but is more subtle. The complaint here is that we cannot find any laws that are precise enough to do justice to the phenomena *at the level at which we desire to have them explained*.[29] There seems to be a tension at work: where laws are possible, it is only at a level at which the phenomena are described so simply that any regularities are truistic and, thus, not explanatory. But at a level at which the phenomena are described in such a way that any regularities *would* be explanatory, the phenomena are too complex for us to find them. So the impracticality of our task still serves as a barrier to law-like explanation even though we are *not* here defending the stronger claim, made in (1b), that we cannot find *any* social scientific laws.

We must now consider, however, a second class of implications. Whereas the foregoing claims have all centered around the idea that although laws *would be explanatory*, perhaps, they are just not possible or practical to pursue, we must now explore those views that hold that laws are *irrelevant* to the task of explanation in social science. These claims are often associated with the "interpretivist" school of thought, which holds that it is the task of social explanation to interpret the meaning behind intentional human action, in lieu of documenting its regularity. Human behavior is seen here as purposive, and so given this characterization, we desire an account of explanation that will do justice to the unique character of human action. The method we ought to pursue, it is argued, is that of *verstehen*—the empathetic understanding of human action achieved by attempting to rethink the thoughts of the person. And nomological inquiry, for these purposes, is simply moot.

But, as I have mentioned, there seem to be two different versions of this "irrelevance" critique of nomological inquiry, which I will outline below:

2a. Laws are not relevant to the task of social explanation and are also impossible to have. Indeed, law-like explanation is irrelevant for the same reason that it is impossible—because the subject matter of social science is intentional human action, and laws cannot be given about, and would be irrelevant to, human action as understood in this sense. Therefore, we will need to pursue a type of explanation that is more sensitive to the intentional components of our behavior.[30]

2b. Whether laws are possible/practical is moot. Even if we could find laws governing human behavior, they would not tell us what we fundamentally want to know about human action. The commitment here is to the idea that laws are unexplanatory—irrespective of their possibility or practicality—given the fact that in social inquiry we are just not interested in finding out what the deterministic forces are that lie behind our behavior, but instead we are interested in the "thought behind it." At any level of explanation, laws are simply uninteresting and uninformative.[31]

Finally, one must also consider those arguments that are purportedly sympathetic to the nomological ideal in explaining human behavior but not within the context of social science. These claims—such as those of the physicalist—indeed support the idea that laws are an important tool in the explanation of human action, even while denying that they can be constituted in a way that can meaningfully be called "social scientific." This view ratifies the idea that nomological explanations of human behavior are relevant, and even available, but that they cannot be offered in a context that is continuous with the practice of social science.

I contend, however, that all of the above arguments fail to show that social scientific laws have no role in the explanation of human behavior. The arguments from complexity and openness fail to show that social scientific laws are either impossible or impractical; the claim behind "interpretivism" fails to show that they are irrelevant; and the argument behind "physicalism" fails to show why laws would only be available outside of the domain of social inquiry. In the chapters that follow, I intend to show why each of the arguments in turn fail, and I will provide reasons for being optimistic about the prospects of nomological explanation in social science in light of an analogy with an example drawn from natural science.

In Chapter 2, I will examine the claim that because of the radically different subject matter studied in social science, it would be impossible to use the same method of explanation as has been used in the natural sciences. Namely, because of the alleged complexity and openness of human systems some have thought that social scientific laws are impossible. I hope to demonstrate, however, that one cannot show, on a priori grounds, that this is true.

Yet certainly there *is* a sense in which complexity and openness are important in determining the constraints imposed on the kind of explanations we can give in social science. Once we are past the rather glib statement that these factors make law-like explanation impossible, it is important to ask precisely what limitations they might impose on our explanatory accounts. In Chapter 3, I will explore what these limitations might be and will consider the argument that in light of them social scientific laws are rendered *impractical*.

In Chapter 4, I will turn to the consideration of an example drawn from natural science, in an effort to see what we might be able to learn from those disciplines that have successfully employed nomological explanations, even in light of some of the same constraints that are thought to preempt their efficacy in social science. This analogy between natural and social science, I will argue, has been obscured by reliance on an overly idealized conception of the role that laws play in natural scientific explanation and the conditions required for its success.

In Chapter 5, it will then be important to consider other arguments against social scientific laws, which have purported to show that any analogy between natural and social science is inappropriate, given the fact that we want to have something different explained about human phenomena, which laws cannot capture. The claim that nomological explanations are irrelevant to social scientific inquiry will be examined here. Moreover, it is here that we will consider the claim made by the physicalist—that even if laws *are* taken to be relevant, they cannot be given in terms of social science.

In Chapter 6, I will consider the metaphysical status of my prior epistemological claims in order to determine what sort of ontological assumptions might lie behind a defense of nomological social scientific explanation.

Finally, in Chapter 7, I will sum up the preceding considerations and will assess the implications of our analysis for the defense of social scientific laws. Here I will consider the prospects and limitations of nomological explanation in the social sciences with respect to the arguments explored in previous chapters.

Notes

1. By "social science," I mean such disciplines as economics, sociology, anthropology, political science, psychology, and history. By "natural science," I mean such

disciplines as physics, chemistry, astronomy, geology, meteorology, and biology (including evolutionary).

2. There are, of course, other arguments against the use of social scientific laws on other grounds, such as political or normative arguments, or religious ones. But my focus here will be on those arguments that purport to enjoin the use of law-like explanation in social science on the grounds that its subject matter is intractable. For defense of the claim that relevance arguments are indeed rooted in claims about the subject matter of social science, see note 24 below.

3. These are arguments such as those that claim human systems are inherently open; that human phenomena are prohibitively complex; that human systems are non-controllable and present situations that are non-repeatable; and the claims that stand behind the argument in favor of "interpretation."

4. Peter Achinstein, in his *Law and Explanation: An Essay in the Philosophy of Science,* has commented that there in fact probably isn't a tidy set of necessary and sufficient criteria that can be given at all (Oxford: Oxford University Press, 1971), p. 1.

5. For an excellent discussion of these alternative positions, one might look at Wesley Salmon's article, "Four Decades of Scientific Explanation," in P. Kitcher and W. Salmon, eds., *Minnesota Studies in the Philosophy of Science,* Vol. 13 (Minneapolis: University of Minnesota Press, 1989), pp. 3–219.

6. *Philosophy of Science,* Vol. 15, pp. 135–175.

7. It was William Dray who first used the term "covering law." It is important to note, though, that whereas Dray uses it to describe only deductive-nomological explanations, Hempel uses it to describe inductive-statistical explanations as well.

8. Carl G. Hempel, "The Function of General Laws in History," reprinted in *Aspects of Scientific Explanation* (New York: The Free Press, 1965), p. 235.

9. For a useful discussion of this controversy see Wesley Salmon's article "Four Decades of Scientific Explanation," cited in note 5 above.

10. Discussion of the controversy over the symmetry between prediction and explanation can be found in Van Fraassen's *The Scientific Image,* and also in Scriven's article "Explanation and Prediction in Evolutionary Theory." A general discussion of the problem, with excellent references, can be found in Salmon's "Four Decades of Scientific Explanation." An excellent discussion of the problems with Hempel's "Inductive Statistical" model of explanation, and an attempt to provide a nomological account that can contend with probabilistic phenomena, is Peter Railton, "A Deductive-Nomological Model of Probabilistic Explanation," *Philosophy of Science,* Vol. 45, pp. 206–226.

11. Of course, there are dissenters. For instance, J. L. Aronson, "Explanation Without Laws," *Journal of Philosophy,* Vol. 66 (1969), pp. 541–557.

12. W. Salmon, "Four Decades," *passim.*

13. Merrilee H. Salmon, "Explanation in the Social Sciences," in P. Kitcher and W. Salmon, eds., *Minnesota Studies in the Philosophy of Science,* Vol. 13 (Minneapolis: University of Minnesota Press, 1989), p. 387.

14. Douglas Giancoli, *Physics* (Englewood Cliffs, N.J.: Prentice-Hall, 1980), p. 78.

15. Cf. Lee Brown, "The Sufficiency of Nomological Subsumption for the Explanation of Events" (Ph.D. dissertation, The University of Michigan, 1986).

16. Brian Fay, *Social Theory and Political Practice* (London: George Allen and Unwin, 1975), Ch.2, *passim*.

17. See, for example, Hayek's political writings against the merits of "planning." But, for a counterbalance, one might also examine Barbara Wootton's *Freedom Under Planning*.

18. Even if we could control human affairs better, it is not necessarily true that they would improve. Knowledge of how best to understand and control the causes behind our behavior may be necessary for improvement, but perhaps is not sufficient. I will not in this book, however, address this issue. I will be dealing solely with the question of whether the discovery of laws in social science is possible, practical, or relevant, not whether such laws, if we could have them, would inevitably result in an improved state of the human condition.

19. Auguste Comte, *The Positive Philosophy of Auguste Comte*, H. Martineau, trans. (London: Kegan Paul, Trench, and Trubner, 1875).

20. Lewis White Beck, *Philosophic Inquiry: An Introduction to Philosophy* (New York: Prentice-Hall, 1952), p. 183.

21. See, for example, George Lundberg's positivist polemic *Can Science Save Us?* (New York: Longmans, Green, and Co., 1961).

22. In the Introduction to his *Philosophy and the Human Sciences, Vol. 2*, Charles Taylor contends that the "man is a part of nature" thesis is relatively uncontroversial, and that it is the methodological thesis that has been the subject of the greater debate in the philosophy of social science. It would be wrong to assume, however, that choosing either side of the methodological debate compels a specific corollary view in the metaphysical debate. For instance, one needn't believe in physicalism or reductionism in order to be a naturalist about the methodology of explanation appropriate to social science.

23. As mentioned, some have also argued that this model does not work, either, in the natural sciences. But I will not be dealing with these claims here.

24. The idea here is that the claim that laws are irrelevant to what we want explained about human behavior is closely related to the claim that we have understood the subject matter of social science to be something about which laws would be uninformative. For instance, if we take the proper subject matter of social science to be meaningful human behavior, and the thoughts and purposes that stand behind it, then it is felt that laws would be irrelevant to revealing what it is that we want to know about it. Indeed, some have also used this view to argue that social scientific laws are therefore conceptually impossible, as a corollary to the relevance thesis, but I will not be examining this issue here.

25. Cf. Charles Taylor, "Interpretation and the Sciences of Man," *Review of Metaphysics*, Vol. 25, No. 1 (Sept, 1971), p. 49, for an example. This is just such a case where one might feel that the special nature of the subject matter of social science demonstrated both why laws were irrelevant and impossible—because no laws could capture its meaningful content.

26. The account of interpretivism that I will be examining is the one given by such thinkers as Charles Taylor and Clifford Geertz. This account will be dealt with in Chapter 5.

27. Cf. Karl Popper, *Conjectures and Refutations*, p. 399, and also Richard Adelstein, "Institutional Function and Evolution in the Criminal Process," *Northwestern University Law Review*, Vol. 76, No. 1 (March 1981), pp. 46–51.

28. It is interesting here to ask, however, what it would mean to say that there were laws that we were not aware of. Do laws exist in nature or in the mind of the theoretician? Perhaps it is best to say that although laws are *dependent* upon relationships that exist in the world, they are relative to the way these relationships have been described in the theory and vocabulary of the scientist. Laws do not cover the phenomena as such, then, but the phenomena as described. What impact this would have on the debate over whether any laws would exist even if we could not find them would then best be settled as a question of metaphysics.

29. The notion of a "level of description" or a "level of explanation" is meant to indicate that there are alternative "modes of categorization" for one and the same social event—that there is a distinction between the phenomena themselves and the language that we have chosen to capture them. Although such talk about "levels" may seem to have unwanted implications of hierarchy, though imperfect it is the preferred way of expressing this idea, since one often does feel that we compare alternative descriptions or explanations in terms of their completeness or subtlety.

30. Cf. note 25 above.

31. As already mentioned, despite the subtle differences between (2a) and (2b) on the extent of their commitment to the impossibility of laws, they will be considered together for the purpose of critical analysis in Chapter 5, because they both make a claim about the irrelevance of laws that is virtually identical. Their differences on whether this specific stance on the irrelevance of laws is coextensive with the claim that they are also impossible, I think, is only a semantic issue and involves how each side would describe its commitments, even though they in fact share very similar beliefs. This issue is dealt with more fully in Chapter 5.

2

Fundamental Objections
to Social Scientific Laws

At the threshold of this enquiry we are met by an objection, which, if not removed, would be fatal to the attempt to treat human conduct as a subject of science. Are the actions of human beings, like other natural events, subject to invariable laws? ... [The subject of social science is] the most complex and most difficult subject of study on which the human mind can engage.

—John Stuart Mill

There are many arguments which purport to show that social scientific laws are impossible. Most often, these claims are made in terms of the intractability of the subject matter with which social scientists must contend.[1] It is popularly held by some critics of social scientific laws that there is a fundamental difference "in kind" between the subject matter of natural and social science, and that this is what precludes the use of laws in the explanation of human behavior. It is argued that while natural scientific phenomena are well-isolated, stationary, recurrent, and simple, human phenomena are, on the contrary, interactive, variable, singular, and complex.[2] Given such differences, it is thought to be a hopeless task to attempt to discover social scientific laws.

But are such accounts persuasive? Do they serve to demonstrate that it is impossible to find laws in the social sciences? It is my thesis that they do not. In this chapter I will explore two of the most influential arguments that have been based on the claim that there is a difference in the subject matter of the social and natural sciences sufficient to guarantee the impossibility of laws that govern social phenomena. I will then attempt to show why these arguments have failed to demonstrate that such laws are impossible.

But what are the arguments? There are myriad claims that allege to pinpoint just what the difference in subject matter is—the source of the intractability—that prevents us from having social scientific laws. Various accounts have tried to isolate this difference by characterizing it as due to:

"uniqueness," "instability," "variability," "flux," "dynamism," "singularity," "historicism," "interactiveness," "complexity," and the problems with performing controlled or repeatable experiments in the social realm. But such notions together produce a hodge podge of cause and effect, and merely detail different aspects of—or worse, different names for—what is basically the same problem.[3] Is there a common theme behind such claims?

We probably cannot, without remainder, hope to reduce *all* of the specific claims that jointly define the class of arguments against social scientific laws, due to the intractability of its subject matter, to one or two discrete and exhaustive claims.[4] Yet, it is clear that most of the above objections do have in common an emphasis on the more general assertion that, in contradistinction to the situation in natural science, in social science we are dealing with a subject matter that is undergoing *constant change,* and that this will have radical implications for the possibility of formulating nomological explanations of human behavior.[5] As we have seen, this constant change can produce repercussions that may hamper the search for laws, such as the inability to perform controlled or repeatable experiments. But what is the *source* of such difficulties? What is it that stands behind them? The most prevalent and comprehensive versions of the arguments that stand behind such claims are (1) the argument from the complexity of human phenomena, and (2) the argument from the openness of human systems.[6] These two arguments will be the subject of analysis in the remainder of this and the following chapter.

The problem is this: in order to come up with laws, we need some type of regularity or stability in the phenomena under investigation. But if human systems are either open or prohibitively complex, it is argued, we just will not have the conditions necessary to discern such patterns. It is thought that openness or complexity would be sufficient to preclude social scientific laws, either because there are no laws at all (because human systems are open), or because we cannot find them (due to complexity). Thus, these arguments seek to establish the assertion that because of the distinctive subject matter faced in social scientific research, we will be enjoined from discovering the regularity or stability in the relationship between the variables that would be needed to formulate laws of human behavior.

In the next two chapters of this book, it will be my task to focus on these two key notions: complexity and openness (and their attendant repercussions, such as problems in experimentation), in order to see what impact they have on the search for laws in social science. Can they show that social scientific laws are impossible? In the present chapter, I will examine the implications of the argument from complexity and the argument from openness for what they reveal about the *possibility* of social scientific laws. In Chapter 3, I will examine their implications for the *practicality* of social scientific laws.

So we here start by asking, "What *is* the claim made about complexity or openness? Does either show that laws are impossible?" We will start with the argument from complexity.

The Argument from Complexity

The argument from complexity purports to show that it is either impossible or impractical to have social scientific laws because the phenomena dealt with in social science are so complicated that they would prevent us from ever finding them. This is a general claim about the difficulty of deriving laws, rooted in the intractability of the subject matter. In this section I will provide an account of the argument from complexity, and I will focus on its implications for the possibility of social scientific laws.

Complexity claims are ubiquitous. In almost every discussion of why it seems to be that social scientists have not yet been able to find laws of human behavior, one reason offered is that the subject matter of social science is so complex that it precludes their discovery. The general claim is that there are just too many critical influential variables behind human action, and the interaction between them is too intricate, for us ever to be able to capture them in a comprehensive theory. Consequently, we are prevented from finding social scientific laws.[7]

But there are two versions of the complexity argument: the "naive" and the "sophisticated."[8] What I will call the naive view, which is advocated by such thinkers as F. A. Hayek and Morris Cohen, contends that there is a sort of fundamental difference in the subject matter of social versus natural science *as such*. Behind this claim is an assertion that human phenomena, from any perspective, are too complicated for us to find laws governing human behavior; it is a claim that the subject matter of social science is *inherently* complex.

In support of such a view, it is often asserted that there is some sort of a fundamental limitation on the ability of human beings to process information, and that given this limitation, it will just be impossible for us to capture the full compass of human diversity in a comprehensive system of laws. There are simply too many interactions between the variables, and things change too quickly, for us ever to hope to be able to pin things down long enough to discover laws. No matter how hard we may try, or how many different theories we may use, there are always elusive elements that will resist subsumption under a law. So human phenomena are thought to be inherently complex. Cohen writes, "the subject matter of the social sciences is inherently more complicated in the sense that we have more variables to deal with than in physics. ... Social phenomena, though determined, might not to a finite mind in limited time display any laws at all."[9]

Such a position usually also maintains that the phenomena studied by natural science are relatively simple. Here we find fewer variables and more direct relationships between them.[10] But these are rare systems, it is held, and we are lucky that the phenomena here are simple enough that they do not frustrate our desire for laws.[11] But in the social sciences we have not been so lucky. Indeed, our failure to find social scientific laws thus far is taken to be testament to the tremendous complexity of human social interaction.

Thus, we see that this account attempts to isolate a fundamental distinction between the subject matters—and so the methods of explanation—of natural and social science. Advocates have argued that there seems to be a difference in *kind* at work. But how to motivate this, given the fact that any difference in the level of complexity looks like a difference in degree? Defenders of the naive complexity view attempt to characterize this difference in complexity as absolute by making the point that complexity seems omnipresent at all levels of inquiry, and from all points of view, because of the limitations of human mental capacity; the difference in degree of complexity between the phenomena is of such magnitude that it effectively constitutes a difference in kind between the subject matter of natural and social science, and thus provides a fundamental limitation on the possibility of social scientific laws. Hayek explains,

> The practical limits determined by the impossibility of ascertaining all the relevant data lie so far inside the logical limits that the latter have little relevance to what in fact we can do.[12]
>
> The number of separate variables which in any particular social phenomenon will determine the result of a given change will as a rule be far too large for any human mind to master and manipulate them effectively. In consequence our knowledge of the principles by which these phenomena are produced will rarely if ever enable us to [discover laws covering] any concrete situations.[13]

It is felt that the subject matter of social science will always prove to be too complex for us to discover any law-like regularities behind human behavior.

But what kind of an argument could stand *behind* such a claim? Surely it would not be enough merely to rely on the claim that the complexity of human phenomena is due solely to our limited mental capacity, for this would make the problem merely one of the quantity of calculations that one would need to perform in order to come up with social scientific laws; one is here viewing the complexity of the phenomena as relative to our incapacity to understand it. But this argument would surely fail, then, to support the alleged *inherentness* of the complexity of social scientific phenomena, since it suggests that the complexity derives not simply from the phenomena itself but from the phenomena as we are capable of understanding it. In turn, we can see that this would fail to show that social scientific laws were impossible *in principle*. If the goal is to show the impossibility of social scientific laws, based on a claim that the phenomena are inherently complex, one must offer an argument that is stronger.

Here one might posit that there are perhaps two different kinds of complexity: combinatorial (linear) versus reciprocal (non-linear).[14] One might usefully think of complexity as due to amplification—the idea that one small change can have effects far beyond itself, in potentially large measure. With combinatorial complexity we are indeed talking about the effects resulting from a kind of amplification—for instance, the fact that one vote can change the outcome of an election, which in turn can have a huge effect on the direction of human history. But it is important to remember that with combinatorial complexity, we are talking about an amplification that is unidirectional. There are innumerable such chains of causal influence out there, and we cannot keep track of them all. Our minds are too limited to get a handle on the complexity that is produced as even one small change in the influence over human systems radiates its effects successively outward, falling like rows of dominoes from a central point.

But as we now realize, this problem—no matter how daunting it may seem—is merely one of quantification and is not strong enough to underlie a claim that social scientific laws are impossible in principle. If the kind of complexity that lay behind human systems were only of this variety, one might hope that someday a sufficiently powerful computer could keep up with it. And while the absence of such cognitive capacity (either human or technological) may represent a very real barrier to the production of laws, it certainly does not suggest that the complexity is inherent, nor does it show that laws are impossible. Therefore, we are in need of a stronger version of the argument from complexity.

Here one might consider a complexity that purports to be of a different order. According to such a notion, the complexity of human systems is not due simply to the fact that we cannot do the necessary computing (it is not due merely to the quantity of the calculations), but instead has to do with the nature of the interaction between the underlying variables. The relationships between the critical influential variables that stand behind human action are undergoing constant change as we interact with one another. The kind of complexity one is talking about is not linear; it is not akin to tracing out the consequences of an initial change. Rather, the complexity is due to the amplification of human decisions, as they feed off of one another, which results from human consciousness. The decision one person makes can influence the response of a second, which may in turn cause the first to reevaluate his position, and so on. So, the interaction here is not *linear* but is instead *reciprocal* or *reflexive*. It is as if the dominoes are now weighted—each one potentially different—and we can never tell just by looking at their size which one or combination will be sufficient to knock down another one (or row). Worse, it is as if the dominoes can now *change their weights* as a result of each interaction and stand upright again, ready to interact once more.

We are now facing a type of complexity that is non-linear and allegedly unlike that found elsewhere in nature. Human systems are constantly changing due to the fact that, as conscious beings, we affect and are affected by one another. The relationship between the variables that underlie our action is constantly being defined and redefined by the nature of our interaction itself. And this constant realignment of the critical influential variables—which results from the reciprocal amplification of our actions— allegedly produces a complexity of a different order. Consequently, it is argued that human systems will never stay still long enough to pin down the exact relationship between the variables; once we think we have it, the system has had time to change. Which variables are critical will change over time. Thus, the complexity of human systems is held to be genuinely inherent in virtue of the nature of the relationship between the variables, and not their mere number, and makes it impossible for us to formulate social scientific laws.

Schematically, the argument might look like this:

1. To find laws, we need to be able to discover regularity in the phenomena under investigation and to try to account for this regularity by understanding the nature of the relationship between the critical influential variables that lie behind it.

2. Laws depend, therefore, not merely on regularity (in terms of pattern recognition), but also on *stability* in the relationship between the variables which produce it.

3. But, if we are prevented from understanding the nature of this stability or regularity, we will not be able to come up with any laws.

4. In social science, there are a large number of critical influential variables, and the relationship between them undergoes *constant* change.

5. Because of human consciousness, the influence of one idea can be amplified well beyond what we might imagine (this is sometimes referred to as the "butterfly wing effect"). This leads to complexity in the nature of the influence on human ideas.

6. But, there is not merely a problem in trying to quantify these effects— to trace out all of the repercussions. It is not merely a combinatorial problem, where we are somehow prevented from performing all of the calculations that would be needed to comprehend the nature of the interaction (although this is a genuine practical problem, it doesn't show that laws would be impossible).

7. For our consciousness is *reflexive*, and we not only cause ideas in other people, but are influenced by them too. And, these ideas feed off of one another. The amplification of our ideas and decisions, therefore, works in both directions, in a way that is reciprocal, rather than linear.

8. Thus, there is constant realignment in what the critical influential variables will be, in any given social interaction. The network of causal influence is constantly being defined and redefined by our interaction with one another. This produces a complexity of a different order than mere linear (combinatorial) complexity.

9. This non-linear complexity (when coupled with linear complexity) presents us with a situation where we are just not able to pin down the relationship between the critical influential variables. The system just will not stay put long enough for us to determine the nature of the causal influence, in a way that would allow us to produce laws.

10. Human systems, therefore, while they may be *ordered*, are not stable enough over time for us to understand the relationship between the underlying variables, due to constant realignment in the network of underlying influences. This presents us with a deep epistemological problem in social science, where even though a system may be orderly and causal, it does not exhibit the stability needed to produce laws because of complexity.

11. Therefore, it is impossible to have laws about social phenomena because we cannot have the required stability that is needed to find them. Social systems are just not the type of things about which one can have laws, due to the complexity of the systems caused by the reciprocal amplification of social interaction that results from human consciousness.

This argument, if cogent, would truly imply the impossibility of social scientific laws. The claim is that there are so many things to consider, and so many factors to hold constant, that it is very difficult to imagine how any laws of social science could be more than mere caricatures of the actual principles by which humans operate. Moreover, the constant realignment of the relationship between the variables that stand behind our action would just about guarantee that by the time we had worked out any stability in their relationship, they would have changed by the time we got back to them. Here one is not denying that there is a certain order to human affairs, or that there are indeed causal influences behind them, but rather one is merely claiming that because of the epistemological difficulties caused by the instability of human systems, we will be prevented from producing laws of social science. Karl Popper sums up the position nicely when he observes that: "Even if there were immutable sociological uniformities, like the uniformities in the field of physics, we might very well be unable to find them, owing to ... complexity. But if we cannot find them, then there is little point in maintaining that they nevertheless exist."[15] It is thereby reiterated that social scientific laws are impossible due to the inherent complexity of human phenomena.

But we can now begin to critique the naive version of the argument from complexity and show that it does not establish the impossibility of social scientific laws. The argument does not go through. Why not? For one thing, the naive complexity view is not at all sensitive to the fact that social phenomena are not complex *as such*, but only *as described and defined* by a given level of inquiry. Surely the complexity of human phenomena, like all other phenomena, depends crucially on the level of description and investigation we are using, and the subject matter is thereby shaped by the nature of our engagement with it. A subject matter does not arise fully formed from certain phenomena—questions do not magically jump out begging to be asked. Instead, the way that we have described the phenomena, and the things we are interested in knowing about it, shape and frame the methods and modes of explanation that we will be able to use in our investigation of a set of phenomena.

The subject matter is defined by the questions that we ask about the phenomena we see. So if we choose to describe them by using natural kinds and categories that do not reveal the nature of any regularities, we may find that laws elude us. But at a different level of inquiry, they may not be so difficult to find. We cannot say that at *any* level the phenomena are too complex for us to find laws, for complexity just is a function of the level of inquiry and descriptions we are using.

It is a mistake to argue, then, that there is a fundamental difference in subject matter between natural and social science on the grounds of complexity for we have been facing a possible confusion about what a "subject matter" is. It is not merely an ontological issue. We cannot treat a subject matter as if it marks off a natural kind in the world, and we come upon it fully formed. Instead, both the phenomena in the world, and the level of our interest and engagement with them, contribute to what becomes our "subject matter." At the ontological level the subject matter is just "matter"; it is only when we begin to ask questions about it that a "subject" first arises. A subject matter is not so much discovered as it is *defined* by the questions we ask about the phenomena we are interested in having explained. The possibility of law-like explanation within a particular field of investigation will be a function not of the phenomena as such, but of that phenomena as defined by our questions about it.[16] For explanation, after all, is of the phenomena *as described*, not as such.

So we see that the complexity of human phenomena is *not* inherent, but is derivative. It is a function of the nature of our engagement with it. The possibility of finding social scientific laws, therefore, is dependent on the level of our inquiry. Moreover, complexity at any one level of inquiry (using certain natural kinds and descriptions) does not necessarily guarantee complexity at all others. Thus, the absence of laws at one level of investigation cannot be used to rule out the possibility of laws at all others.

We can clearly see the nature of the problem with the naive complexity view by considering what might happen in the natural sciences if it were true. What might be said about the possibility of laws in the natural sciences if we insisted that there was only a single level of description available?[17] The phenomena of physical science, per se, are just phenomena, in the same way as are social events. It is only at the level of description, explanation, and inquiry that a particular type of investigation requires that any distinctions begin to arise between the two. In physical science we use those categories and theories that help to reveal for us the law-like regularities that lie behind the phenomena. But what if we were not free to determine these for ourselves, feeling rather that the phenomena themselves dictated certain categorizations that happened to obscure the underlying laws? Would we then hold that the phenomena of natural science were inherently complex? Or would we, more probably, be tempted to continue inquiry at a different level of description?

The issue of simplicity and complexity only makes sense with reference to a level of description and explanation. And, to a certain extent, the ability of some physical scientists to come up with laws has been partially due to the efficacious level at which natural scientific phenomena have been investigated. But if a different level of investigation had been chosen, would this render natural scientific laws impossible because of complexity? Certainly not. There is no reason to suppose that complexity at any one level somehow precludes nomological inquiry at all others, nor is there even any good reason to suppose that complexity at a particular level would preclude the later formulation of laws even *at that level*.[18]

We are led to reject the naive complexity view, therefore, for the same reason that we would reject the conclusions of a physicist who, choosing only to inquire at the sub-atomic level, concluded that all of physics was therefore non-predictive. The possibility of social scientific laws is crucially dependent upon how the phenomena are framed by our level of engagement with them. It is narrow to say that the subject matter of social science is inherently more complicated than that faced in natural science and thus precludes the possibility of social scientific laws, for we now see that complexity is relative to the level of description of the phenomena we are using. The complexity of the subject matter is a continuum, and we choose our place upon it by the level of description and investigation we undertake. The possibility of inquiry at different levels thus holds out the prospect of social scientific laws.

It is now important to consider a somewhat stronger and more sophisticated version of the argument from complexity. Someone might object, in response to the above account, that the prospect of inquiry at a different level is not adequate to the task before us in social science, for in response to the criticism just leveled at the naive view, it can be argued that in no area of inquiry do we really have a "choice" of the level at which we are going to inquire. Certain phenomena just seem interesting to us and, whether we like it or not, we *just are interested* sometimes in investigating phenomena at a level at which we are enjoined from discovering laws.[19] So, it is not as if we may simply choose to investigate at another level of inquiry, where laws may be possible. That would be to let the tail wag the dog.

It is easy to see that such a position is more sophisticated than the previous one. The naive complexity view held that at any level of investigation the phenomena will be too complex for us to discover laws. We saw this view come to grief upon the idea that we cannot infer, based on the difficulty of obtaining laws at one level, that they will be impossible at all others. But the sophisticated view goes beyond this and holds that *at* the level at which we are interested in having human phenomena explained to us, the phenomena are too complex to yield laws. At precisely *this* level laws seem precluded.

We see here the subtlety of this view, in that it takes into account the idea that complexity is a function of the level of description and investigation we are using and admits that complexity is derivative. But, this view holds, at precisely the level at which we wish to frame our inquiry, complexity forbids laws. This account does not, therefore, attempt to rule out the possibility of truistic laws, pursued at other levels of investigation. But what it does rule out is the possibility of laws that are *explanatory* because it argues that at any level at which laws are possible, the phenomena are described in such simple terms that laws at that level would not be explanatory. Furthermore, at a level at which the phenomena are engaged in such a way that laws would be explanatory, things are too complex for us to discover them. In short, the phenomena are complex at precisely the level at which laws, if possible, would be explanatory.

The most developed version of this argument has been offered by its chief advocate, Michael Scriven. Scriven rounds out the above argument by making a case for the idea that the situation faced by the early physicists was comparatively easy, compared to that faced by today's social scientists, and that people like Galileo were lucky that they were not facing a field of such intractable complexity that there were no laws to discover. In the social sciences, he claims, we face a task far more difficult than we do in physics. He explains this by arguing that in social science all of the easy laws have been skimmed off by long non-formal reflection on human affairs, and poaching by other fields (such as literature). Social science, in contrast to a popular myth, is not young at all, but rather is among the oldest areas of inquiry. Consequently, after millennia of observation into human affairs, the social scientists are left with all of the hardest problems; they are stranded with a subject matter that is complex, because we demand explanation at a level of description and investigation where we have no good reason to suppose that we will ever be able to find laws. Scriven admits that the subject matter of social science is derivatively complex, but, given our interest in a particular level of inquiry, we are left with the dilemma of choosing between truism and the absence of laws in the face of complexity. At precisely the level where we would find laws to be explanatory, the subject matter is too complex to yield them. Consequently, the social scientist faces a hopelessly difficult task. Scriven writes: "The difference between the scientific study of human behavior and that of physical phenomena is thus partly due to the relatively greater complexity of the *simplest phenomena we are concerned to account for* in a behavioral theory."[20] The social sciences, he contends, face a situation far worse than that of even the most complicated natural science; for the search for social scientific laws is limited by the complexity of the phenomena at the most basic level of inquiry at which social science proceeds.

Such observations have led Scriven to claim that it is merely good fortune that in the natural sciences we, in the main, happen to be interested in a level of investigation that does not fatally frustrate the search for laws; but in the social sciences we have not been so fortunate. Scriven holds that "if it were the case that the problems of predicting astronomical positions involved predicting the behavior of the planets to within a micron or an inch, astronomy would be in its infancy."[21] Yet, given our interest in social phenomena, there is little we can do. Scriven is willing to accept the fact that the complexity of certain subjects may well be a matter of an inefficacious level of description—of "bad luck"—but given the level of our interest in social scientific explanation, laws will continue to elude us. He sums up the situation aptly:

> One is inclined to respond to comments of this kind by saying that this is surely no different from the situation in physics. We know what happens to falling bodies in a vacuum, but, when it comes to the way bodies behave when we drop them in air, we are not able to say very precisely what they will do. And, when it comes to the question of how a particular leaf falls from a particular tree on a particular autumn day, we are almost helpless. This is true, but nobody feels that it is very important to be able to predict the behavior of a leaf. If this were the kind of crucial problem in physics then it would be the case that physics would always be a subject of a very unsatisfactory kind.[22]

The unfortunate situation for social science, however, is that we *have* been concerned to know how a "particular leaf falls from a particular tree."[23]

If this argument goes through, it would imply that social scientific laws are impossible, not merely because we think that all human phenomena are complex, but because at the level at which our descriptions of human behavior are "social"—and it is at such levels that we wish to have the phenomena explained—the subject matter is too complex to be captured in law-like form. So, in contradistinction to the naive claim, this argument implies the impossibility of laws not at *all* levels, but at a *particular* level. Yet it is precisely the level at which we would find social laws, if possible, to be explanatory that complexity proves to be a barrier.

But what interpretation is Scriven using here of "complexity"? What is it about the phenomena *at* this particular level that would *make* them complex, and so would prevent social scientific laws? On his account, Scriven makes it sound as if the complexity is merely a function of the level of precision or accuracy demanded in social scientific explanations—as if one is simply demanding too much of social science, because of the level of our interest. But is this interpretation adequate? Surely, in order to motivate an argument for the *impossibility* of social scientific laws, there must be more to it than this. For this is to talk about complexity as if it were merely a combinatorial problem—as if it were only a problem of performing enough calculations to get the level of precision that would be required in order for social scientific explanations to be explanatory. The idea here would be that in some areas of inquiry, we are satisfied with a level of description that is suitably lax, such that laws are possible, but in other areas we are not. And, social science just happens to be one of those areas of inquiry in which we are interested in the phenomena at a level of explanation at which the degree of rigor required will prevent laws.

But could this be all there is to the argument? If so, it is not clear why the sophisticated version of the argument from complexity purports to show that social scientific laws are impossible. For if it is only the precision and accuracy of our descriptions that are standing in the way of nomological explanation, then one suspects that the kind of complexity being discussed here is only different in degree from that encountered in natural science. But would linear (combinatorial) complexity be thought to show that social scientific laws were impossible in principle? We have already seen that this endeavor would fail. The kind of complexity that is needed to back up a claim of impossibility must be about something more than that which could be fixed merely by lowering our standards for explanation. Does Scriven really believe that if we just had more precision in our descriptions of the phenomena, we could have social scientific laws? Is the only difference between the kind of complexity that prevents us from predicting the weather and predicting human behavior that we are relatively over-demanding in our standards of accuracy in the latter case? If so, it is obvious that this kind of complexity would fail to imply the impossibility of laws. So, if one hopes to show this, one must look for a stronger interpretation of "complexity" than Scriven describes. Will his account accommodate a stronger reading of what is meant by "complexity" than the one he offers?

What could be the problem of complexity? It is *not* that the level of precision and accuracy demanded at the level of description at which we wish to conduct social science makes the phenomena complex, but rather is due, perhaps, to the very nature of the natural kinds and descriptive terms used to characterize the phenomena *at* this level of inquiry. The notion is that given the kinds and categories that we use to capture the phenomena *at* the level at which we are interested in conducting social science, there is no reason to expect that we will have laws *of any degree of precision whatsoever*. It is not as if the phenomena are complex as a matter of happenstance (because of the level of precision and accuracy we demand of them), but instead because of the way in which we have described the phenomena, and the natural kinds we use, at the level at which we are investigating them. The complexity we encounter here alleges to be of an order of magnitude that would prevent laws all together.

Indeed, at this level of precision—using the descriptive terms that we do—precision may well be an ill-defined notion. The complexity is so great, one might argue, that we cannot even begin to grasp what it might mean to talk about laws with any degree of precision at all. In natural science, we have a fairly good idea of what we mean when we talk about needing explanations that are "more precise." But in social science, this view holds, we are not even sure that the natural kinds and descriptions that we are using will yield any laws at all, let alone ones with any particular degree of precision. The descriptive terms do not necessarily capture any features of social science that we could have laws about. The complexity, therefore, is felt to threaten not merely the *accuracy* of laws, but their very existence.

This stronger interpretation of complexity ties in here with the earlier account given of non-linear complexity. In order to justify a claim that social scientific laws are impossible (and not merely difficult to get), we saw, one must try to show that the complexity dealt with is different in kind from that found in those areas in which one can produce laws. The idea is that the complexity found in human systems is due to the reciprocal amplification of our ideas, and their influence over our action, and causes instability in the relationship between the variables that produce it, thereby undermining our efforts to find laws. Thus, on this stronger interpretation of what may be meant by "complexity," one sees that the sophisticated version of the argument from complexity could genuinely aspire to show the impossibility of social scientific laws. The claim that at the level at which we would desire to have social scientific explanations, we face a complexity which purports to thwart the very prospect of laws—due to the descriptive terms used to capture the phenomena at this level—presents a powerful argument against the possibility of nomological social scientific explanation. One here faces the highest rung on the dialectic of complexity arguments.

And yet such an argument, at least in its attempt to show the impossibility of social scientific laws, fails. We saw that the naive view foundered because it overlooked the important notion of investigating at different levels of inquiry. The view that human phenomena are too complex at *any* level of description for there to be laws belies the fact that at some levels of investigation, we do have fairly accurate generalizations available. Of course, the sophisticated view objects here, and tells us that such generalizations are not genuine laws. But the sophisticated view fails for a similar reason—for it is no more reputable to claim that laws will always fail at a *given* level, than it is to say that laws will always fail at *all* levels. For who is to say what is possible or not even *at* a particular level of description (even given a specific set of kinds and categories)? In principle, it is always possible that even using the descriptive terms required, we could nevertheless come up with a nomological relationship between the phenomena.[24] Perhaps one might think that this would be unlikely, but it is important to realize that there is nothing in the argument from complexity that rules it out as impossible. The sophisticated complexity argument does not show that laws are impossible at even the most detailed levels of description.

Indeed, what guarantee do we have that the dividing line between simple and complex phenomena will always remain where it is today? What is simple and what is complex changes over time, and is dependent not just on the level of our inquiry, but also on the concepts and theoretical tools available to us at any given time. Has the division between simple and complex phenomena always been as it is now? Will it always be so? Rollo Handy has observed that "physical phenomena that now seem simple probably struck the original investigators as bafflingly complex."[25] To think otherwise, and maintain that what is today regarded as the dividing line between simplicity and complexity will always be so, is a position that others have been forced to abandon in the face of scientific advancement. The extension of the set of complex phenomena is not absolute; it is relative to scientific progress.

In any field of inquiry, there are conceptual and technological breakthroughs that change the face of the order of complexity with which science can contend and render a previously complex subject matter suitable for nomological inquiry. Look, for example, at the important role that computers have played in the advancement of space exploration. Before the computer, one questions whether the ambition of space travel also appeared to be so complex that it was considered to be impossible. We simply could not process the information in such a way as to untangle the enormous complexity. And it is not just a matter of the computer doing more quickly what we ourselves might be able to do if just given the time; the time itself becomes an issue. The role of computers in monitoring interdependent on-board systems, and performing nearly instantaneous self-correction of or-bital path, is an example of an operation that humans could not have done at all before the computer afforded such fast and accurate calculations.

We must not overlook, either, the role that conceptual breakthroughs can have in helping us to simplify once "complex" operations. Even before the development of the computer, the growth of human knowledge played a crucial role in rendering once complex phenomena simple, thereby al-lowing prediction and nomological explanation in a previously forbidden field. The conceptualization of the epicycle by Ptolemy or the ideal gas law by Boyle allowed later scientists to make predictions that had previously been thought to be impossible. The field of chemistry must truly have been a wilderness before the development of the periodic table by Mendeleev. This advance allowed later chemists to predict the weight and structure of certain elements sometimes even before those elements had been discov-ered. Surely such an innovation must have advanced the frontier of the order of complexity with which scientists could contend. We see, then, that the distinction between simple and complex phenomena is not absolute, but rather depends on both our technological and conceptual advances, as well as the level of description and inquiry with which we are involved. To preclude the possibility of laws at any one level of inquiry, then, is to ally oneself with an intrinsically tenuous position, for it is subject to constant revision in light of the progress of science.

Moreover, it would seem rash to say that it is just the case that the natu-ral sciences have been "luckier" in the development of these conceptual or technological tools than have the social sciences, or that they were fortu-nate to start with a "simpler" subject matter to begin with. Scriven has consistently underestimated the complexity with which many natural sci-entists contend, and the ingenuity that has been used to overcome it. In-deed, it is wrong even to say that the kind of complexity faced in natural science is merely of a single kind—for certainly there are examples through-out the natural sciences of efforts to overcome even non-linear complexity with nomological models.[26] Rather, it seems that in natural science we make our luck, and that the harder we work, the luckier we get! We have already seen that we do not just choose an arbitrary place to begin our inquiry, and it just happens that we have chosen a good field for nomological explana-tion. Although this does happen sometimes, at other times we make our luck by the constant erosion of the barriers that stand in our way, by build-ing up comprehensive theories slowly through painstaking work in collat-eral fields and by the refinement of our definitions and descriptive catego-ries used to cover the phenomena that we desire to have laws about. There are two ways to have a clear path: One is to follow the smoothest trail through the natural landscape, and the other is to remove the obstacles that lie before us. Natural science has proceeded along both routes.

In short, we should note here that the natural sciences too have faced a diversity of problems of enormous complexity. J. O. Wisdom has argued that many "complexity" arguments against social scientific laws, such as Scriven's, have not taken seriously the complexity of the phenomena with which natural scientists must contend. If one thinks that physics deals exclusively with simple phenomena, he chides, one just has not done much physics.[27] It is not all eclipses and the theory of gravity—this is a myth perpetuated by social scientists. Similarly, it would be naive to claim that all of the multifarious types of complexity faced in evolutionary biology, meteorology, volcanology, and geology are merely "combinatorial." The upshot is that complexity could not serve as an absolute barrier to the establishment of laws; the history of science has shown that such factors as "complexity" are negotiable in the face of nomological ambitions. And it would just be *ad hoc*, Wisdom claims, to say that every field of inquiry that can use laws is simple, and every field that cannot is complex.[28]

Indeed, at some level Scriven himself seems to realize this, as he is fond of comparing the situation faced by the social sciences with that of "fringe" physical sciences like volcanology and meteorology, where we are also often held back by enormous complexity at the level at which we wish to predict and explain. He admits that certain natural sciences also face complexity due to inquiry at a particularly precise level of investigation.

But overtly Scriven has not yet come to terms with the implications of this admission. For the concession that certain natural sciences face complexity presents him with a dilemma: If his claim is that sciences like meteorology and volcanology are in the same boat as social science, where complexity proves to be a barrier to the possibility of laws, why make a claim that there is any demarcation in terms of the differing subject matter between natural and social science at all? Recall here Scriven's explanation that the reason we do not have laws in social science is because of the complexity of the simplest phenomena we are concerned to explain in social science, as compared with the relative simplicity of our task in physical science. Yet if some *physical* sciences are also precluded from discovering laws because of complexity at the level at which we demand explanation, it would seem that any distinction in terms of *subject matter* is unmotivated. Why all of the fuss, earlier, over the "situation faced by social scientists," if some physical scientists face it too? Why maintain that there is any type of clear distinction?

Indeed, any distinction here would not be one of subject matter at all, but would be between simple and complex *phenomena*.[29] But, as noted earlier, why think that even *this* distinction will hold up over time in the face of scientific progress? What can possibly motivate a belief that the division between fields of simple versus complex phenomena will always remain as it has? It may turn out to be the case that in meteorology, for instance, we will be able to overcome complexity and arrive at accurate and law-like explanations. And, in principle, the same may be true for social science. Scriven, after all, admits that it is possible for there to be regularities at "truistic" levels of inquiry. But this is to hold open the future possibility that there may be regularities to uncover at other levels as well, and one must hold out the possibility that these might someday be formulated at a level of description that we would find explanatory.[30] Barbara Wootton has noted that:

> It is agreeable to think that what is unknown to us in our day and generation is also unknowable. The advance of knowledge has, however, constantly shown how false such an assumption might have been in the past: forewarned by this, we should be wise to presume that this assumption is not less dubious now.[31]

In the face of complexity, we may well have to satisfy ourselves for awhile with relatively simple, possibly unsatisfying, explanations. But, as our knowledge and technological abilities grow, who can foresee what developments might still result from our advances into a field of complex phenomena?

Indeed, if Scriven has meant to ally social science with meteorology and volcanology, he has inadvertently shown that there is no *in principle* barrier to laws even *at* a particular level of description, for certainly chemistry, for instance, was once in a situation similar to the one that meteorology is now in. If the social sciences are in the same boat as those natural sciences that face the problem of complexity, there is reason to be optimistic. For certainly this emphasizes not a break between subject matters, but rather a continuum in the degree of complexity faced. And, as such, it provides no in principle barrier to the possibility of laws even in the most "complex" fields. Indeed, it may yet encourage us to hold out hope that even the practical barriers standing in the way of laws might yet be overcome.[32] At the very least, it demonstrates that any barriers are borne of a difference in degree, and are not rooted in a difference in kind. As such, it undercuts the belief that social scientific laws are impossible.

But, Scriven would also face difficulties if he meant to argue that the social sciences were *not* in the same boat as such sciences as meteorology and volcanology. That is, perhaps Scriven never meant to imply, by invoking the example of complexity in meteorology, that it was in the *same situation* as the social sciences. Maybe he meant that while meteorology and volcanology indeed face complexity, it is a different kind of complexity, so there is reason to think that they have a better chance of overcoming it. Or, he might mean that the difference in *degree* of complexity is so great that it effectively constitutes a difference in kind and therefore precludes the possibility of law-like explanation of human behavior but not in meteorology. In short, Scriven may wish to preserve the difference between the social and natural sciences, despite the fact that each has areas where complexity is encountered.

Certainly such a belief would be bolstered by noting that even though there is complexity facing certain fields of inquiry like meteorology and volcanology, inquiry in these fields is not stagnant. Have they given up prediction and nomological explanation, as ideals, as Scriven has advocated for the social sciences?[33] Certainly not. Perhaps they are not as successful in finding laws as are the practitioners of cosmology, but this does not mean that laws in volcanology and meteorology are somehow impossible or fundamentally forbidden, as they are thought to be in the social sciences. Why believe that we will never have laws at the level at which we wish? In such fields they are ever refining models and attempting to arrive at more comprehensive theories and accurate predictions; they are making progress. And while we might remain skeptical about the practical barriers standing in the way of the degree of success that has been enjoyed in physics or chemistry, we can find no reason to think that meteorology or volcanology are in the same boat as social science. Here there is no limit on the possibility of laws. The degree of complexity faced is not great enough to provide such a stringent limitation on the possibility of laws. And, yet, despite the relatively advantageous position of these sciences, as compared to social science, we have not yet found accurate laws due to complexity. That is, even in some *relatively simple* fields—like meteorology—we don't yet have laws. Such an admission serves as testament to the probable intractability of the barriers facing laws in social science; for if we cannot succeed in the relatively straightforward task of finding laws in fields where we have made some progress in eroding complexity, what hope do we have of achieving laws in a field like social science, where the problem of complexity is even more formidable?[34]

But, if this is Scriven's position, and he means that there is indeed still some difference in *kind* between the situation faced in social science as compared to that faced in meteorology, he faces the slippery problem of trying to explain how it could be that two separate fields of inquiry both face the problem of complexity, and one gets around it while another cannot. What is there to motivate such a distinction—to convince us that complexity has differential implications for the possibility of laws in these two cases? Why think that in one case complexity is not an in principle barrier (it wouldn't show that laws were impossible), but in another it would? How much complexity is too much? Or, could it be that there is indeed a difference in the kind of complexity facing each field? If so, what could it be?—the distinction between linear versus non-linear complexity? But surely the issue of the "fringe" natural sciences again presents a problem for this point of view—for certainly there are some examples from the natural sciences where we face the same kind of (non-linear) complexity that allegedly faces social science. Perhaps this complexity is produced through different *mechanisms* than we find in social systems (since natural scientific systems are not "reflexively self-conscious"), and yet some of the effects produced may be the same. The kind of "dialogue" that exists in evolutionary biology between the environment and a species, for instance, is a good example of how such complexity might be produced. The selection for certain masking techniques in response to the threat of a predator species, and the subsequent evolutionary changes of the predator in response to this, provides a simple example of how such reciprocal amplification could be produced in natural systems.[35]

But couldn't one, then, just group the categories differently, insisting that social science be grouped with the "fringe" natural sciences, which also face non-linear complexity, on the one hand, as against those harder natural sciences, which do not, on the other hand? This division would have the virtue of standing on a well-conceived distinction between the two groups (even if it is not the more common one between natural and social science), and would purport to preserve the semblance of a difference in kind. But there would still be problems for this view. For it remains unclear how one can account for the lingering differences between the situations faced by social science and the "fringe" natural sciences that are now grouped together. If fields like meteorology could possibly erode the barrier of complexity, there is no good reason to think that there are other than merely practical barriers preventing economics and political science from doing the same. We are again faced with the problem of how to account for the differential implications in such fields, when facing the same type of complexity; in social science, one holds that laws remain impossible in principle, yet in meteorology and evolutionary biology, one may legitimately contend that—despite practical problems—the nomological ideal is intact.[36]

Either way, then, it appears that Scriven faces problems. He has not been able to justify his relative pessimism regarding the ability of fields that now face the barrier of complexity to overcome it, nor has he been able to motivate any kind of key distinction between the situation faced in natural versus social science. Each horn of the dilemma is potentially fatal to the attempt to show that social scientific laws are impossible. The allegedly fundamental distinction between simple and complex phenomena herewith collapses.

It is now clear, then, that the sophisticated version of the argument from complexity fails to show that social scientific laws are impossible. There is no coherent argument that denies the possibility of laws on the grounds of a difference in the complexity of the subject matter. A difference in *degree* would fail to show that laws were impossible, and a difference in *kind* seems unmotivated in light of the problems encountered in trying to find a non-arbitrary place to draw such a distinction. Scriven has shown us why the achievement of laws under such unfavorable circumstances may be *difficult*, but he has not shown that they are *impossible*. And so, with the failure of both the naive and the sophisticated version of the argument from complexity to imply the impossibility of social scientific laws, we here note that the argument that the subject matter of social science is too complex to support the discovery of laws at all levels, or even any particular one, does not work.

In the last few pages, however, we have seen that in certain "complex" fields, laws may yet be quite difficult to get, even if it cannot be shown that due to complexity they are impossible in principle. Will it work to follow the lead of fields like meteorology in an attempt to develop the theoretical tools needed to achieve laws? Or are the problems insurmountable? Perhaps the argument from complexity does point out a very genuine *practical* difficulty in coming up with laws at the level of description at which we require explanations in social science. It is an interesting question whether the sophisticated complexity argument, for instance, provides reason for thinking that there is a formidable (and potentially impenetrable) *practical* barrier to the search for social scientific laws, even if it does not quite show on conceptual grounds that they are impossible. Here a difference in degree could well be fatal to the achievement of social scientific laws. But does the argument from complexity show this? This question will be taken up in Chapter 3. Our immediate task, however, will be to evaluate whether the argument from the openness of human systems is any more successful in its attempt to show that social scientific laws are impossible.

The Argument from Openness

We are now in a position to ask whether the argument from the openness of human systems works any better than the argument from complexity in its attempt to show that social scientific laws are impossible. The argument from complexity featured problems brought about by the number and intricacy of the relationship between the variables *within* a system; but what about the problems involved with isolating a system from the influence of factors *outside* the system? What about the problem of closure? Certainly the intrusion of "outside" factors is potentially detrimental to any attempt to formulate laws since it would destabilize our attempts to find regularity. We can see how such a state of affairs could be even more troubling than the contention that the relationships within a system are complex.

The argument from openness purports to be more comprehensive than the argument from complexity, and the barrier it provides to laws is allegedly more fundamental. For it is now not just a problem of *discovering* social scientific laws—of trying to formulate them out of the tangle of complexity—instead the claim is that, because of the nature of the influences acting upon social systems, it is conceptually impossible for there to be social scientific laws describing them. The argument from openness is based on the idea that social scientific laws just do not exist because in social science we cannot have the closed systems necessary to support them.[37] Thus, the argument from openness aims to show (1) that human systems are open, and (2) that this openness implies the impossibility of social scientific laws. Yet before we can evaluate this claim, it is important first to explore what is meant by an "open" versus a "closed" system.

A closed system is one in which there are a small number of important variables, which are relatively immune to outside influences (or can be made to be so).[38] The paradigm case for this would be a system which is stationary, repetitive, and insulated. An example of such a closed system is the orbiting of satellites around planets. Initially it was not clear precisely what the influences were that caused a satellite to orbit a planet. Yet, after Newton it became clear that gravitational forces have an important effect on the path of such satellites, and indeed that their paths can be predicted with reference to a law with only a few known variables. In our desire to predict this path, based on subsumption under a law, we are wise to focus on the mass of the satellite, as well as the mass of neighboring bodies, and the distance these bodies are away from the satellite itself. This example represents a *closed system*, in which we are able to formulate a law as a result of our knowledge of the type and relationship of a few known variables, free from outside disturbance. Moreover, in such systems we are usually also able to account beforehand for any errors that might be found in our predictions merely by stating that any bodies over critical value (M), which pass within critical distance (D), will perturb the orbital path of the satellite by (X) amount.[39] Our law is thereby rendered more accurate, and we become confident that we have isolated the key features.

Such a closed system, however, should be distinguished from "open" systems, i.e., those systems where we cannot or do not yet have the knowledge or information that would allow us to come up with a precise general law, because we cannot capture all of the important variables in one system. The system is subject to outside influences. Keep in mind, however, that there are two different types of open systems, which are often confused with one another.

One type of open system, which I shall call "pragmatically open" (or "epistemically open") represents those systems in which it is only our current lack of knowledge of what the critical variables are that is keeping us from the accurate formulation of a law. My intention here is to suggest that such systems might someday become capable of closure as a result of our growing knowledge. For instance, we know that in the science of meteorology there are only a finite number of variables that can affect the weather. These variables, however, are quite numerous and are not all presently known. We already know that certain important variables—such as pressure, the seasons, and local geography—can profoundly affect our weather. However, there may be many other variables, which we may or may not be aware of, that can also affect our weather patterns. These might include disturbance from volcanic eruptions, stellar radiation, or sun spot activity, whose effects are not yet understood in their entirety. In this capacity meteorology does not yet study a "closed" system, but rather one which is pragmatically open. That is, it is assumed to be open relative to human ignorance.[40]

In contradistinction to both "closed" and "pragmatically open" systems, however, there are also those systems that are thought to be "fundamentally open" as well.[41] These systems are unique in that it is not clear that there is any limit or regularity in the number or type of influences exerted upon the system; such systems have an indefinite number of variables influencing them and do not provide a determinate and repetitive pattern of interaction between them.[42] Consequently, we will never be able to insulate these models from the influence of "outside" variables, nor will we be able to isolate the critical variables in every case. There will always be at least one factor that we do not consider, at least one variable that we cannot fit into our model, and at least one disturbing influence that we fail to account for.

But what kind of systems could possibly look like this? Some have thought that human systems are open in precisely this way. It is here that we can begin to see the alleged uniqueness of the subject matter of social science. The argument based on the claim about the "fundamental openness" of human systems purports to show that such openness forbids the presence of social scientific laws. The claim is that it is impossible for us to formulate laws because we can never hope to insulate human systems from influence by "outside" factors, and thus we will never be able to define the "closed system" that would be required to come up with social laws. The idea behind this is that a law requires a closed system, because only in a closed system can we account for the regularity in the interaction and influence of the critical variables that determine human affairs. But, it is argued, it is impossible for us to define such a closed system in social science because which variables are "critical," and what the important patterns of influence are, changes over time. What we would hope to be able to exclude as outside factors continually intrude upon our static model and, since it is subject to constant revision, it becomes virtually impossible to capture all of the important variables that influence human action.[43] Influences from outside the system will always throw us off balance and preempt nomological systematization.

But why is this? What is the nature of this "openness," and why does it occur in human systems? It is rooted in the idea that human action is profoundly influenced by the growth of human ideas and conceptual innovations. But, because our ideas and concepts are constantly changing (and because this change is unpredictable), this web of important influences will be in constant flux, and will frustrate our attempts to capture it in one system. Thus, the growth of human knowledge and the evolution of human ideas will prevent us from formulating the kind of closed system that we would need in order to derive social laws. To the extent that human action is influenced by this growth in our ideas, human systems will remain open. We will never be able to insulate our models from influence by "outside" factors because it will never be possible to know in advance which factors will be "outside" and which will not. In human affairs we are subject to a heady dose of what meteorologists have called the "butterfly wing effect"— the idea that the flap of one butterfly's wings can, through the amplification of its effect, change global weather patterns—for the influence of one small idea can spread and change the course of human history.[44] Our models of human systems never seem to be wide enough to capture all of the subtle influences, and they never seem to be penetrating enough to tell us in advance what we can exclude as irrelevant.

Thus, we see that when one maintains that human systems are "open," it is usually held that they are not just open relative to the current state of our knowledge, but that they are somehow "fundamentally open."[45] The important influence that our knowledge, ideas, and conceptual innovations have over our actions seem to be unique to human systems, and therefore is thought to supply the distinction between fundamentally open versus pragmatically open and closed systems.[46] We can never hope to limit the number of possible influences from outside the system by some artificial means; it must remain indefinite. Thus we see how it is that the subject matter of social science is thought to be unique.[47]

Such an argument has been characterized in many ways.[48] But the most developed version of it has been offered independently by Karl Popper and Charles Taylor, each of whom have argued that the openness of human systems is best illustrated by focusing on the unpredictability of human action as a result of the critical influence and unforeseeable effects that our ideas have over our behavior. In turn, such openness is thought to have profound implications for the possibility of social scientific laws. It is felt by these commentators that there is a strong link between the predictability of human action and the subsumability of human behavior under a covering law.[49] Both depend on the closure of human systems. Thus, if it can be shown that one is in jeopardy, the other is similarly threatened. Such a strategy, involving an indirect attack on the status of social scientific laws, has been defended by Popper.

But before we examine Popper's view in more detail, it is first important to defend its status as a claim about the alleged "openness" of human systems. In the account just given, it is possible to discern three different senses of "openness":

1. Open in the sense that there are more variables that we haven't considered.
2. Open in the sense that the system we are studying can interact with outside environments.
3. Open in the sense that Popper is talking about, where our behavior is affected by the novelty of our ideas.

While it is important to be aware of these different senses of the term "openness," I think it is clear that Popper's usage can be defended as a special case of it, which has kinship with the other two. For, what all of the views have in common is the idea that—in contrast to a closed system, where we know the nature of and interaction between all of the relevant influential variables—in an open system we must allow for the potential influence of variables whose influence we did not, or could not, anticipate. So, Popper's intention in referring to his objection as one about the "openness" of human systems, I think, is to suggest that the novelty of our ideas may potentially destabilize any attempt to account for human behavior in terms of a closed set of variables; the potential influence of any new ideas must mean that human systems are "open" in the sense that they are constantly threatened by the intrusion of other influences, whose consequences we could not foresee.

In the preface to his book *The Poverty of Historicism*,[50] Popper begins to outline what he feels is a logical argument against the possibility of predicting human behavior, based on the openness of human systems. The formal, and indeed "logical," argument in its entirety, however, is only found spread over three books and twenty years of Popper's work.[51] Yet the distillation of his views, given in *The Poverty of Historicism* represents the most important single statement Popper has made on this question. He contends that:

1. The course of human history is strongly influenced by the growth of human knowledge.

2. We cannot predict, by rational or scientific methods, the future growth of our scientific knowledge.

3. We cannot, therefore, predict the future course of human history.[52]

Popper goes on to say that the crucial step in the above argument is number two, which he feels is obvious in and of itself. He tells us that "if there is such a thing as growing human knowledge, then we cannot anticipate today what we shall know only tomorrow."[53] In other words, to predict a conceptual innovation seems to be just to *have* that innovation. And herein Popper has set the foundation for his purportedly "logical" argument, which contends that the prediction of human action is impossible due to the openness of human systems. Because of the influence of our ideas and concepts on our action, he argues, human systems are not capable of closure, and therefore we cannot hope to predict human behavior. The growth of human knowledge will always stand in our way.[54]

We can see the impact of such an argument on the possibility of social scientific laws by noting that the openness of human systems, if true, would seem to preempt subsumption under a law as well as predictability. And here the purported link between prediction and nomologicality becomes explicit. For if we could predict human behavior (based on some theory), then we could also subsume it under a law; similarly, if we can have social scientific laws, then prediction is at least a theoretical possibility.[55] We can now formalize Popper's account, and make explicit its impact for social scientific laws, in the following way:

1. If social scientific laws are possible, then it is theoretically possible to predict human behavior.

2. But human action is strongly influenced by human ideas.

3. Furthermore, the course of our ideas is always changing and cannot itself be predicted.

4. So to the extent that human action is influenced by the growth of human ideas, human action is unpredictable.

5. Therefore, by the contrapositive of (1), we see that it is impossible for there to be laws of human behavior.

But such an account, while it makes explicit the nature of the relationship between prediction and law-like explanation, leaves implicit the important notion that both the possibility of laws *and* predictability depend on the openness of human systems. How best to characterize this openness, and its impact on the possibility of social scientific laws? For this we must turn to the work of someone who builds upon and extends Popper's argument—Charles Taylor.

In his important paper "Interpretation and the Sciences of Man,"[56] Charles Taylor has two tasks. First, he sketches out the blueprint of a hermeneutical alternative to law-like explanation, and the important role that it can play in social research. In the last five pages of his article, however, he attempts to root this "prescription" for the improvement of social explanation in his "diagnosis" of why prediction and laws are impossible in social science. In what follows, I will be concerned exclusively with Taylor's argument about the possibility of laws. My quarrel will be with his argument in the last few pages of his essay.

The development of Taylor's argument, as with Popper's, pays allegiance to the problem of prediction. But, it is easy to see that the case Taylor makes is readily applicable to the possibility of social scientific laws. For hermeneutics, as an alternative to the methods of science, is meant to be seen as an alternative to law-like explanation. It is not meant to compete directly with the goal of prediction.[57] Rather prediction, as an implication of the law-like model, is attacked in Taylor's article as the most developed and vivid offspring of the nomological ideal. Taylor thus attempts to show, through the failure of social scientific prediction, why law-like explanation of human behavior is misguided and impossible, for both depend on a state of affairs that allegedly does not exist in human systems. Although he attacks prediction, his target is the entire nomological paradigm upon which prediction rests.

Near the end of his article he highlights the way in which human systems are "fundamentally open," and demonstrates why this would have a profound impact on the possibility of prediction and laws. He writes,

> [The] most fundamental reason for the impossibility of hard prediction is that man is a self-defining animal. With changes in his self-definition go changes in what man is, such that he has to be understood in different terms. But the conceptual mutations of human history can and frequently do produce conceptual webs which are incommensurable, that is, where the terms can't be defined in relation to a common stratum of expressions. ... Conceptual innovation ... alters human reality.[58]

That is, Taylor is arguing that humans are self-constituting beings and, moreover, that this self-constitution is importantly influenced by our growing conceptual innovations. The growth of these conceptual innovations is unpredictable, however, so we see that it would be impossible to predict the behavior that they effect.

We can see how Taylor's argument builds upon Popper's framework by making explicit the point that our ideas partially constitute the subject matter of social science. In rough outline, Taylor's argument to this point is parallel to Popper's. Yet, it is here most useful to characterize it, in schematic form, as an extension of Popper's account, developed into a direct attack on the status of law-like explanation because of the openness of human systems resulting from the growth of human knowledge:

1. The prediction of human behavior presupposes the formulation of laws of social science.

2. Social scientific laws are only possible if human systems are closed.

3. A closed system presupposes the absence of disruption from outside influences; it requires regularity and stability in the system of influences governing it.

4. Human action is influenced, and at least partially constituted, by self-understanding.[59]

5. This self-understanding, though, is constantly in flux due to its influence by the growth of our ideas and concepts.

6. Our ideas and concepts, in turn, are constantly changing and are unpredictable. We cannot predict a conceptual innovation for this would be simply to *have* that innovation.

7. So to the extent that human action is influenced by the growth of our concepts and ideas, it will *not* be fixed and repetitive. It will change along with our ideas and self-understanding.

8. But this lack of regularity in influence and development means that human action is constantly subject to the "outside" influence of the growth of human knowledge.

9. So human action seems to be part of an open system.

10. Therefore, there can be no laws of social science (and no predictability either).

With this account we can begin to see how the "open" quality of human systems is thought to be a fundamental barrier to the possibility of social scientific laws. Following Popper's lead, Taylor has argued that changes in our ideas are unpredictable and that these ideas importantly influence our action. Yet the quantity or character of our ideas and concepts seem to know no natural limit and therefore seem to constitute an open system. Taylor then roots the impossibility of social laws in the open character of human systems. The growth of human knowledge, and its effect on human affairs, he feels, renders human systems open, and thereby preempts the formulation of laws.[60]

And here, returning to Popper for a moment, we can begin to sketch out the balance of the argument from openness, again concerned here primarily with the predictive aspect of nomologicality. In his article "Prediction and Prophecy in the Social Sciences,"[61] Popper outlines both the source of the idea that the social sciences can be similarly as predictive as the natural sciences, as well as the reasons why such a hope will be frustrated in the face of the openness of human systems. The source of the view that the social sciences can be predictive, Popper contends, arises from a perceived analogy between the ability of astronomers to predict the occurrence of eclipses, and the ability of social scientists to predict revolutions, depressions, and wars. Such a goal, he feels, is necessarily misguided in the face of the *non-repetitive* (and therefore "open") character of social phenomena. Popper states that, "[one can only make predictions if] they apply to systems which can be described as well-isolated, stationary, and recurrent. These systems are very rare in nature: and modern society is surely not one of them."[62] He goes on to assert that one is only able to predict such events as eclipses because our solar system is a stationary and repetitive system.[63] Moreover, its repetitive character is only manifest because of the relative isolation and insulation of the solar systems from other influences—in other words due to its closure. Popper discounts the perceived analogy between these "rare" systems, and the phenomena which are dealt with in social science, by submitting that eclipse prophecies, and other similarly repetitive events, are the result of special circumstances. He writes, "society is changing, developing. This development is not, in the main, predictive. ... The fact that we can predict eclipses does not, therefore, provide a valid reason for expecting that we can predict revolutions."[64] Yet we are curious here to know how Popper can be so sure that development in the social sciences is not repetitive—the answer is that it cannot be.

In the physicist's laboratory we might be able to perform a "controlled experiment," which can be repeated several times, by changing only one variable at a time. But in social science, Popper is denying us precisely this ability to perform a controlled experiment in our historical "laboratory." In this vein, we observe that a ball being thrown into the air in a physicist's laboratory, for instance, does not "learn" something each time this experiment is performed; and therefore perfect repetition is possible.[65] Yet the same cannot be said of our social experiments. Our very ability to *learn* over time, by the fact of our consciousness and influence by concepts and ideas, necessarily forbids us this repetitive and static quality found in closed systems and instead lends our behavior a "historetic" quality. A ball does not learn over time; a human being does. And we often apply what we have learned to subsequent trials, thus effecting the outcome. Human systems are open, therefore, and unpredictable precisely because our growing knowledge does indeed importantly influence our action. The openness of human systems subverts the nomological ideal.

A well known example of the above observations is seen through the so-called "Oedipus effect" (also known as the problem of "reflexive prediction"). Even before Robert Merton coined the famous phrase "self-fulfilling prophecy" it must have been realized that our very offering of a prediction, subsumption under a law, or repetition of an event can influence the behavioral outcome. An individual can become aware of the predictions made about his or her behavior, and therefore can act to confound it if he or she wishes. Surely, such effects are commonplace and widely recognized: witness social psychological experiments involving deception where a "veteran" subject defiantly refuses to offer the predicted response or, similarly, police forecasts of the number of holiday traffic fatalities, which are made precisely because they are trying to capitalize on this "Oedipus effect" by scaring people into driving safely. Humans seem to be unique in that we can take account of the prediction governing us and defy it once we are aware of it.[66]

We can see, therefore, the nature of the argument that human behavior is unpredictable on "logical" grounds. Similarly, it is now obvious that if such an argument goes through, the openness of human systems would forbid the possibility of social scientific laws as well. A law requires a closed system, but closure requires regularity. But due to the non-repetitive growth of human ideas and concepts, and their influence over our behavior, human action will always be subject to disruption by "outside" factors. Thus, due to the openness of human systems we can expect no laws of human behavior.

But is such an argument successful? Does the argument from the openness of human systems really show that human systems are open and, because of this, that social scientific laws are impossible? No. It is now time to examine the shortcomings of such an account. I contend that the argument from openness fails for at least two reasons.

First, how do we know that human systems are indeed open rather than merely very complex? Even if one admits the obvious point that our ideas do have an important influence over our actions, why is it necessary to characterize the problem this entails as one of the *openness* of human systems? That is, why suppose that our previous inability to find laws is due to openness rather than merely to a high degree of complexity? The results, after all, would be similar; in both cases it would be very difficult to formulate laws, and we would have a hard time sorting out the complicated interaction between the variables. But the fact is that the recalcitrance of human behavior to subsumption under a law gives us no reason to assume that human systems are "fundamentally open," rather than just tremendously complex. It is unclear what the special nature of humans systems is that it could not be attributed to complexity. Moreover, it is ill-motivated to attempt to mark off a special class of openness for human systems without sufficient evidence that there is some dimension that cannot be captured within an existing category (i.e., pragmatically open systems). We must not infer more categories than we need.

As in the case of meteorology, for example, we can see that even those systems that are assumed to be fully determinate do not necessarily easily yield the patterns needed for subsumption under a law. But is it legitimate to assume on the basis of the sometimes chaotic and wildly divergent nature of our predictive success in meteorology that the weather is part of a "fundamentally open" system, and that laws there are impossible? No. The existing categories will do, absent strong evidence that there is some unique feature that cannot be accommodated.[67] The evidence only allows us to infer that the task is difficult, not that it is impossible. I submit that the same is true of human systems.[68]

Thus, we see that it is terribly difficult to motivate a claim that we can sharply differentiate between pragmatically and fundamentally open systems. We must infer only as much diversity as the data require. It is perhaps illegitimate to use the alleged fundamental openness of human systems to argue that laws are impossible—for what evidence do we have, besides the fact that laws are difficult to formulate, that suggests that human systems are fundamentally open?

Second, even if human systems *are* fundamentally open, why would this necessarily preclude the existence of laws? The argument that laws necessarily presuppose a closed system just doesn't go through. Indeed, if it did we probably would have very few laws even in the natural sciences.[69] Again it is instructive to consider the example of meteorology. There we face the problem of openness of a system, and yet we are able to trace the regularity of influence between some of the variables, arriving at laws. That is, despite our inability to shield our models and systems from outside influence, we are nevertheless able to formulate some law-like connections because of our ability to see patterns and underlying regularity in the way that the systems change. And even if this cannot be done perfectly in all cases, and outside barriers do often intrude, at least one must admit that the barrier is not a *logical* one and does not preclude the *possible* existence of laws. In short, the openness of meteorological systems does not demonstrate that laws in this science are impossible. So even if human systems are open, why suppose that the implication in this case is any different?[70]

It is true that laws require the presence of an underlying regularity.[71] But it is unclear why this regularity must necessarily be found only in a closed system. Why can't we have open systems in which change occurs in a *regular* way, where we are able to trace out the evolution of the causal relations? Why think that a closed system is the only way to get regularity? As long as change occurs in a regular way, it is in principle possible for there to be laws describing it. So we are here led to question premise number two of the argument from open systems, detailed earlier in this chapter. For why be bound by the belief that law-like expression of underlying regularity must be mediated by closure?[72] The argument from openness does not go through; even if human systems are open, this would not prove that social scientific laws are conceptually *impossible*.

Yet perhaps here an opponent of the possibility of social scientific laws might try a counterargument: One might concede that we don't need a closed system to have laws. But what we do need is a good understanding of which variables are more influential, and in what situations, than others.[73] Similarly, we need to know which variables can be discounted. But this is constantly changing in social science. We just cannot tell in advance what factors will be influential in each case. So even if there is underlying regularity, absent closure we will not be able to find it and thus will be prevented from coming up with laws. True, some open systems are more regular than others. But what we need in social science isn't what we have—we lack the tools to access this regularity. In natural science we happen to be dealing with a subject matter where the system of influences is regular enough, and the number of variables is small enough, that we can come up with laws. The systems are conceptually isolable. But this isn't analogous to the situation faced in social science.[74]

Yet perhaps such a reply is itself readily ripe for criticism—for it apparently gives up on the earlier attempt to show that laws in the social sciences are impossible because of the openness of human systems and instead focuses on their difficulty. The claim now seems to be that there are too many critical variables for us to see a regular pattern of influence between them so that, even if there *is* underlying regularity, we have no guarantee that we will find it. But this is just a restatement of the complexity argument that was dismissed earlier. And we saw that it could not motivate a claim that social scientific laws were impossible.[75] We saw in the last section (on the argument from complexity) that we have no guarantee that the division between simplicity and complexity (or between what we can and cannot do) will always remain where it is. How can we know in advance that we won't be able to come up with some conceptual or technological breakthrough that will allow us to contend with such complexity? Analogously, it is not conceptually incoherent to believe that we may someday be able to formulate laws or even have predictions involving "open," yet regular, systems.[76]

And while the problems involved in doing this may indeed be formidable, and the demands for requisite regularity may be stringent, it is unfortunately true that if either the argument from complexity or the argument from openness were to succeed in showing that social scientific laws are *impossible*, one would need to show on conceptual grounds that such stringent demands were not even theoretically achievable. It is not enough to show that the task is difficult—if one desires to show that social scientific laws are impossible, one must satisfy rigorous standards in demonstrating that the task is in principle insoluble. The argument from openness, like the argument from complexity, has failed to meet these demands.[77]

Conclusion

Where are we left? We have now seen the problems in proposing that we can decide the *possibility* of social scientific laws on the grounds of an allegedly fundamental difference in subject matter between natural and social science. Neither the argument from complexity nor the argument from openness has succeeded in showing that the subject matter of social science is so intractable that it establishes the impossibility of laws. Indeed, such a thing probably cannot be shown a priori. To argue that there is a fundamental difference "in kind" between the subject matters of natural and social science trades on a certain ambiguity in what is meant by a "subject matter." As we saw earlier, a subject matter is not merely an ontological entity—it depends crucially on the level of our investigation and description of the phenomena studied. So it is unclear that in any *logical* or *conceptual* sense there is any difference at all. It is just not an a priori question whether laws are possible or not.[78] Such matters probably cannot be settled on conceptual grounds.

Both natural and social science deal with unique events of varying degrees of complexity, which may or may not exhibit readily apparent regularities that can be easily formulated into a law. But the job of science is to search for such regularities despite surface diversity. And neither the argument from complexity nor the argument from openness has demonstrated that there is a fundamental distinction between the subject matters of natural and social science, which would somehow vitiate the possibility of laws, or the fruitfulness of their search. What I have demonstrated so far is that it cannot be shown that social scientific laws are impossible due to the intractability of its subject matter because the prospects for the future success of science in finding ways to deal with these factors cannot be ruled out in principle.

But, of course, to show that something hasn't been shown to be impossible does not amount to a demonstration that it *is* possible, or that it is something we ought to pursue.[79] We saw at the end of each section that the arguments examined did not show that laws were impossible but only showed why they were, perhaps, difficult to formulate and might not be forthcoming. But isn't this in itself something to contend with? The arguments from complexity and openness are important and have to be reckoned with in our consideration of issues beyond the possibility of social scientific laws. So we are now compelled to ask, "if the arguments from complexity and openness do not show that laws in the social sciences are impossible, what do they show? Do they, perhaps, show that social scientific laws are impractical or infeasible?" This is the question that will be taken up in the next chapter.

The arguments from complexity and openness surely demonstrate that even if there is no difference in kind between natural and social science, certainly there is an important difference in degree that has yet to be dealt with. One must admit that although the problems of nomological social scientific inquiry are to a large extent derivative from the level of our investigation, they are real problems nonetheless. They represent sometimes formidable barriers in our attempt to formulate laws of human behavior, and they impinge on the practical considerations that are everyday faced by the social scientist. The sophisticated complexity view, for instance, is a good example of an argument that, although it does not demonstrate the impossibility of social scientific laws, perhaps presents an important pragmatic obstacle to their generation. Similarly, we just saw that the problem of closed human systems may inhibit our search for regularity and thus may hamper the development of social scientific laws.

In the next chapter, I will evaluate the impact that complexity and openness, and their attendant difficulties, have on the practical considerations involved in formulating laws in social science. This task will be facilitated—in Chapter 4—by a comparison with how certain fields in natural science have dealt with similar problems, in an effort to determine whether the social sciences can benefit from learning how other sciences have attempted to ameliorate the practical difficulties that the problems of complexity and openness provide.

Notes

1. See here Harold Kincaid's discussion of possibility arguments in his paper, "Defending Laws in the Social Sciences," *Philosophy of the Social Sciences*, Vol. 20, No. 1 (March 1990), pp. 56–83. Alexander Rosenberg has also explored the issues surrounding the claim of "intractability" in his book *Philosophy of Social Science* (Boulder, Colo.: Westview Press, 1988).

2. Karl Popper, *Conjectures and Refutations: The Growth of Scientific Knowledge* (New York: Harper Torchbooks, 1963), p. 339.

3. For instance, variability may cause singularity, which in turn means that we will lack the repetitiveness that is required to perform a controlled experiment.

4. For example, there are other claims involving intentionality, which argue that human action is guided by the actor's understanding of the situation. Some have held that the content of the subject matter of social science is basically meaningful and cannot be captured by laws. This argument, although it is indeed a claim about the subject matter of social science, will be dealt with in Chapter 5, when I consider the "relevance" of social scientific laws.

5. For a good discussion of this issue see Richard Adelstein, "Institutional Function and Evolution in the Criminal Process," *Northwestern University Law Review*, Vol. 76, No. 1 (March 1981), pp. 46–51.

6. As mentioned, there are a plethora of ways people have referred to the same set of problems. The notions of "complexity" and "openness," however, capture most comprehensively what seems to be at issue in accounts discussing "uniqueness," "variability," and so on.

7. As a general theory, the argument from complexity can be agnostic on the question of the *existence* of laws, focusing instead on whether or not, if they exist, we could find them.

8. It is useful to think of "naive" complexity as the claim that there are no social scientific laws at any level of description because of the *inherent* complexity of the subject matter. "Sophisticated" complexity, on the other hand, holds that there are no laws at a *particular* level, due to the *derivative* complexity of investigation at that particular level.

9. Morris R. Cohen, *Reason and Nature: An Essay on the Meaning of Scientific Method* (Glencoe, Ill.: The Free Press, 1931), pp. 348–356.

10. Hayek believes that in the physical sciences it is possible to specify law-like regularities to any degree of specificity desired. See "The Theory of Complex Phenomena," in *Studies in Philosophy Politics and Economics* (Chicago: The University of Chicago Press, 1967), p. 24. But, it is problematic to note that elsewhere it almost seems as if Hayek wants to argue that the natural sciences are simpler by definition. He states, "non-physical phenomena are more complex because we call physical what can be described by relatively simple formulae." *Studies*, p. 26.

11. Popper, *Conjectures*, p. 339.

12. Hayek, "Theory," p. 34.

13. Hayek, *The Counter-Revolution of Science: Studies on the Abuse of Reason* (Indianapolis: The Liberty Press, 1979), p. 42.

14. Brian Fay helped me to recognize this distinction, although the account given here is mine.

15. Karl Popper, *The Poverty of Historicism* (New York: Harper Torchbooks, 1961), p. 12.

16. This means that phenomena per se cannot be complex, but only a subject matter (phenomena as framed by a certain level of inquiry). But then complexity is *not* an absolute barrier to laws in the social sciences, because we can always change the subject matter by investigating at a different level, at which laws may be possible.

17. "… we berate the social scientist for not being able to do what even the natural scientist cannot do." May Brodbeck, "On the Philosophy of the Social Sciences" in E. C. Harwood, ed., *Reconstruction of Economics* (Great Barrington, Mass.: American Institute for Economic Research, 1955), p.47.

18. This is discussed later in this chapter.

19. In Chapter 5, I will deal with an even stronger interpretation of this view—the idea that certain descriptive categorizations are just constituitive of the subject matter of social science.

20. Michael Scriven, "A Possible Distinction Between Traditional Scientific Disciplines and the Study of Human Behavior," in *Minnesota Studies in the Philosophy of Science*, Vol. 1 (1956), p. 332.

21. Michael Scriven, "Views of Human Nature" in T. Wann, ed., *Behaviorism and Phenomenology: Contrasting Bases for Modern Psychology* (Chicago: University of Chicago Press, 1964), p. 172.

22. Scriven, "Views of Human Nature," p. 171.

23. I am not sure who first came up with this analogy, but it is a popular one in the philosophy of social science, used both by Ernest Nagel in *The Structure of Science* (New York: Harcourt, Brace and World, 1961), p. 461, and by May Brodbeck, "On the Philosophy of the Social Sciences," p. 47, where she writes, "The situation in social science … is no different from that in physics. The physicist may know all

of the principles involved yet be quite at a loss to predict, say, how many leaves will blow off a tree in the next storm. The poignant difference is, of course, that in social matters we desperately want explanation in detail, while in physical changes we are frequently indifferent."

24. I think there are examples that vindicate this approach. Cf. the example considered in Chapter 4. Also, note that it is always possible to use different descriptive terms.

25. Rollo Handy, *Methodology of the Behavioral Sciences: Problems and Controversies* (Springfield, Ill.: Charles C. Thomas, 1964), p. 112.

26. See note 35 below.

27. J. O. Wisdom, *Philosophy of Social Science, passim.*

28. Cf. note 10 above.

29. I.e., one would have to lump meteorology in with other complex phenomena. The distinction would no longer be between the subject matter of natural and social science, but between simple and complex phenomena because some natural sciences would be in the "complex" category.

30. For instance, we may be able to develop "bridge laws" that are capable of connecting two previously disparate areas of inquiry. For a discussion of this see Jaegwon Kim, "Concepts of Supervenience."

31. Barbara Wootton, *Testament for Social Science: An Essay in the Application of Scientific Method to Human Problems* (New York: W. W. Norton, 1950), p. 17.

32. This issue will be discussed in Chapter 3.

33. Michael Scriven, "Explanation and Prediction in Evolutionary Theory," *Science*, Vol. 130, No. 3374 (August 28, 1959), pp. 477–482.

34. Of course, this argument may be problematic. For the fact that the barriers are formidable means that we can't have laws, but we assume that the barriers are formidable in the first place because we cannot find laws.

35. Surely there are other examples too, e.g., in the study of "chaotic" physical systems. The example of evolutionary biology will be discussed further in Chapter 4. The issue of where to group the "fringe" sciences is a difficult one for Scriven, and he resists committing himself beyond saying that evolutionary biology has a lot in common with social science, and that meteorology suffers from some of the same problems as well. But does he feel that there is a difference in degree or in kind between these sciences and the harder physical sciences? Indeed, how is the grouping supposed to go? Either way he answers, there are problems for his view. Cf. his discussion in "Explanation and Prediction in Evolutionary Theory."

36. I plan to show that one can vindicate the possibility, and actuality, of laws in evolutionary biology, in Chapter 4. This would present a problem for Scriven's argument, if he indeed means to group evolutionary biology with social science, for if one can show that there are laws in evolutionary biology this weakens his claim against social science correspondingly.

37. That is, we cannot be sure that we have accounted for all of the influential variables, and we cannot be sure that we have excluded all of the ones that are non-influential.

38. This is perhaps a non-standard definition of a closed system. I define it here epistemologically and not metaphysically. I do this because I mean to distinguish such an epistemologically closed system from one that is epistemically (or prag-

matically) open. If one is uncomfortable with this, it can easily be fixed by noting that what I have referred to as "closed" and "pragmatically open" systems together yield the more standard metaphysical definition of closure.

39. Of course, there are also many other potential disturbing factors.

40. It is perhaps useful here to think of pragmatic openness as related to complexity.

41. It is interesting to note that the distinction between closed and pragmatically open systems is epistemological, but that between closed (and pragmatically open) versus fundamentally open systems is metaphysical. Cf. note 38 above.

42. That is, their lack of regularity is not assumed to be due to mere complexity or the amplification of effects from known variables.

43. A good example is how the economic models of J. M. Keynes provided a useful "snapshot" of the American economy in the early to mid-1900s, but the economy kept changing, partially as a result of the very application of Keynes's theories to public policy.

44. It is important to note here that to say that a system is open, though, does *not* necessarily entail that it is non-deterministic. To say that a system is an open one is making a claim about the *indefiniteness* of the influences governing it and the difficulty of shielding the system from the influence of outside variables. But there is nothing in this claim to compel a belief that the only way for this to occur is if there is a breakdown in determinism. Openness is not equal to being non-determined. For an excellent discussion of this point see Brian Fay, "General Laws and Explaining Human Behavior."

45. This is because knowledge grows over time. No matter how much we know, we still cannot close it. (This is true even if the system is determined.) This is a deeper problem than mere human ignorance. It has to do with whether our systems of understanding can ever capture truth. Cf. here Karl Popper's discussion of the growth of knowledge in *Conjectures and Refutations*. If the problem of fundamental openness is an epistemological problem, it is a deep one.

46. Hubert Dreyfus, "Why Current Studies of Human Capacities Can Never Be Scientific," in *Berkeley Cognitive Science Report*, Vol. 11 (January 1984).

47. There is a potential problem, however, due to the fact that certain areas of physics may also deal with "fundamentally open" systems. But this need not prevent the discovery of regularity. Cf. James Gleick, *Chaos: Making a New Science* (New York: Viking Press, 1987).

48. For instance, some have attempted to characterize this argument in terms of free will, human consciousness, or intentionality. Cf. Brian Fay, "Naturalism as a Philosophy of Social Science," *Philosophy of Social Science*, Vol. 14 (1984), pp. 529–542.

49. As mentioned earlier, there is a huge debate over whether prediction is equivalent to explanation, and whether nomological explanation is better than its alternatives, spawned by Hempel and Oppenheim's "Studies in the Logic of Explanation." It is sufficient here to note that many of the critics of social scientific laws have thought that there is a biconditional relationship between prediction and nomological explanation, even if some of them have remained skeptical of this (for instance, Scriven).

50. Karl Popper, *The Poverty of Historicism* (New York: Harper Torchbooks, 1961).

51. Cf. Karl Popper's, *The Open Universe* as well as "Indeterminism in Classical Physics and in Quantum Physics."

52. Popper, "Poverty," p. vi–vii.

53. Ibid., p. vii.

54. Maurice Cranston, *Freedom* (London: Longmans, 1953), p. 118. Cranston makes the argument that in order to predict a conceptual innovation one would simply be having that innovation. He anticipates Popper on this point.

55. As noted in 49 above, it is debatable precisely what the relationship is between prediction and nomological explanation. The present argument, however, seems to characterize prediction and law-like explanation as collateral effects of a common cause—closure.

56. Charles Taylor, *Review of Metaphysics*, Vol. 25, No. 1 (September 1971), pp. 3–51.

57. Indeed, the claim is that prediction is a misfounded goal of social inquiry.

58. Taylor, "Interpretation," p. 49.

59. For example, think here of voting. The act of voting is at least partially constituted by the agent's self-understanding. This example is explored in detail in Brian Fay's article "Naturalism as a Philosophy of Social Science," p. 532.

60. What is it, then, that is open? The system of human ideas. But there are always some "outside" ideas influencing our behavior. And so the system of human action is open as well.

61. Popper, *Conjectures*, pp. 336–346.

62. Ibid., p. 339.

63. Ibid., p. 339.

64. Ibid., p. 340.

65. This example is originally explored in Richard Adelstein, "Institutional Function and Evolution in the Criminal Process."

66. Alan Gewirth, "Can Men Change Laws of Social Science?" *Philosophy of Science*, Vol. 21 (1954), p. 541. It is an interesting question, however, whether mere awareness of a prediction is all that is needed to defy it. For an argument to the contrary—that human reaction to a prediction can itself be taken into account in the prediction itself—one might want to take a look at Alvin Goldman's article, "Actions, Predictions, and Books of Life," in *American Philosophical Quarterly*, Vol. 5, No. 3 (July 1968), pp. 135–151.

67. One might argue here that consciousness is that feature that cannot be accommodated. But this is to talk about the mechanism by which openness is produced and not the problem of openness itself. Surely in natural science there are examples in which we face reflexive problems, even if they are produced by different mechanisms.

68. Kincaid, "Defending Laws," pp. 6–7.

69. "Social systems ... are obviously not closed systems. ... This fact alone cannot entail [however] that social laws are impossible—unless we are prepared to grant that even physics produces no laws. Every physical system short of the entire universe is influenced by outside causes. So merely describing open systems cannot preclude laws. If it does, then the only laws of physics are those that describe the totality of the universe, an unacceptable conclusion I assume." Kincaid, "Defending Laws," p. 6.

70. I will deal with the claim that openness implies the impracticality of laws in Chapter 3.

71. On some description.

72. True, it may be that without closure we will have a problem finding social scientific laws, but this does not amount to a logical prohibition of their existence. Nothing in the claim that laws are difficult to find implies that it would be impossible to find them. It is an interesting further question whether the problems involved in facing complexity and openness render the search for laws impractical, but it is sufficient to note here that the implication that they show the impossibility of laws fails.

73. Cf. here Kincaid's discussion of whether the social sciences' use of *ceteris paribus* conditions compares favorably to their use in the natural sciences. "Confirmation, Complexity and Social Laws" address delivered at the Biennial Meeting of the Philosophy of Science Association, Chicago, Ill., October 29, 1988.

74. One is really here making closure into an epistemological condition for finding social scientific laws. Closure is not needed in order for social scientific laws to exist, but it is needed to discover them. But this is a practical problem and does not show that social scientific laws are in principle impossible.

75. We will deal with the question of whether such a point demonstrates the impracticality of social scientific laws in Chapter 3.

76. A good example here indicating the possible direction of such an approach is provided by Herbert Simon's model for predicting voter behavior, even when voters become aware of predictions made about the outcome of the election. In his article "Bandwagon and Underdog Effects of Election Predictions," *Public Opinion Quarterly*, Vol. 18 (1954), pp. 245–253, Simon provides an elegant case for the thesis that it is not in principle impossible for us to predict human social behavior. He takes on the example of "reflexive prediction," and provides a paradigm case of how one might go about finding underlying regularity, even in an "open" system.

77. I.e., it hasn't been shown that there is no regularity at all, or that if there is we could not find it. Indeed, it has been argued that to attempt to do this would be self-defeating, for if human affairs followed no regular course of development and dictated no patterns whatsoever, we would not be able to understand them at all, using any method; the nomological paradigm would not be the only casualty. One might therefore try to motivate a "pragmatic vindication" of law-like explanation in the social sciences, even in the face of the alleged openness of human systems, on the model of Salmon's vindication of induction. B. F. Skinner, indeed, has argued that if *any* method of explanation will pick up on the regularity behind human action, nomological explanation certainly will. "If a reasonable order was not discoverable, we could scarcely be effective in dealing with human affairs. The methods of science are designed to clarify these uniformities and make them explicit." B. F. Skinner quoted from David Braybrooke, *Philosophical Problems of the Social Sciences* (London: MacMillan, 1965), p. 21.

78. Richard Bernstein, *The Restructuring of Social and Political Theory* (New York: Harcourt, Brace, Jovanovich, 1976), pp. xiv–xv.

79. Bernstein, *Restructuring*, p. 42; Kincaid, "Defending Laws in the Social Sciences," p. 18.

3

Practical Objections
to Social Scientific Laws

Laws in social science, if we had them, would contain many more variables than those in physics. Yet we berate the social scientist for not being able to do what even the natural scientist cannot do. The multiplicity and complexity of factors in social phenomena impose limitations upon what we can reasonably expect to achieve. These limitations are only a practical, though perhaps practically insuperable, difficulty and we simply do the best we can.

—May Brodbeck

We have now arrived at the heart of the debate concerning the role that laws can play in the explanation of human behavior; for once we have given up on the notion that the arguments from complexity and openness demonstrate the impossibility of social scientific laws, we immediately face the question of what limitations they *do* impose on nomological inquiry. The possibility issue has been dispensed with, but we now face a very difficult *practical* issue concerning whether complexity and openness provide such formidable barriers that even if the achievement of laws is theoretically possible, it remains pragmatically unfeasible for us to discover them. Do the arguments from complexity and openness show that social scientific laws are impractical? Or can we hope to preserve a role for nomological inquiry in social science even in the face of such obstacles?

Before we launch into a consideration of such issues, it is important first to be clear about how the claims examined in the present chapter can be distinguished from those in Chapter 2. Although we will again be considering the arguments from complexity and openness, it is significant to note that here we will be examining whether these arguments imply that social scientific laws are *impractical,* rather than the stronger thesis that they are impossible. The arguments are largely the same; what is different is what they purport to imply about the status of social scientific laws.

We saw in the last chapter that no fundamental difference in *kind* between the subject matters of natural and social science (needed to establish the impossibility of social scientific laws) could be found. But we now face the more difficult issue of considering whether even a difference in *degree* could prevent the efficacy of social scientific laws, by preventing their discovery. For example, in Chapter 2 we examined the claim that the openness of human systems provided a fundamental difference in kind between the subject matters of natural and social science, and precluded the *existence* of social scientific laws. Presently, the issue examined will be whether the epistemological barriers to the closure of human systems might prevent the *discovery* of social scientific laws. The focus will be on whether an alleged difference in subject matter (in degree of complexity or openness) renders social scientific laws impractical, rather than whether a difference in kind renders them impossible.

But what is the difference between impossibility and impracticality? To say that something is impossible, is to say that it cannot obtain—that it is somehow forbidden in principle. The claim that social scientific laws are *impossible*, for instance, holds not merely that there are limitations on our ability to formulate such laws, but turns on the deeper belief that, beyond all pragmatic barriers, such laws are somehow prohibited by the nature of the subject matter of social science—and the task of social explanation itself. On this view, social phenomena are held to be the kind of things that resist all attempts at law-like systematization at any level of conceptualization; there is thought to be something about human behavior itself that cannot be captured or explained by a scientific law. That is, given the subject matter of social science, it is thought that there is certainly something incomplete—and probably something incoherent—about the task of law-like explanation of social phenomena.

To say that something is *impractical*, however, is to soften this stance somewhat. Here we might allow that social scientific laws, for example, may be possible *in principle*, but hold that they are highly unlikely due to the formidable pragmatic barriers standing in the way of their discovery and consequent availability for explanation. We may concede the point about their theoretical existence and focus instead on the real world limitations (epistemological and otherwise) preventing their formulation. It is exactly such claims that will be examined in this chapter.

In the arguments we will be considering, it will be most useful to think of the possibility-practicality distinction as follows: To claim that social scientific laws are impossible is to think that the barriers standing in the way of laws are *fundamental*, and have to do with the nature of the subject matter itself. It is to claim that there is something inherent in human phenomena (and what we want to know about it) that defies law-like codification. We have already seen in Chapter 2, however, the problems involved in making such a claim. To claim that social scientific laws are impractical, however, is to state that the barriers standing in the way of the achievement of laws are *pragmatic,* though perhaps in this world insuperable. That is, the claim is not that social scientific laws could not conceivably exist, but that, even though they may exist in principle, there are formidable obstacles that will curtail our ability to find them.[1] There are alleged to be intractable *practical* constraints on their discovery.

The argument from complexity, as articulated by Michael Scriven, and the argument from openness, as presented by Brian Fay, aim to justify just such a claim.[2] They advance the idea that there are certain limitations on our ability to discover social scientific laws, even if one concedes that there is no in principle reason to think that they cannot exist. Moreover, it is important to note that in both cases these arguments are meant to be broad enough in their focus on the general problem of complexity and openness to apply to other disciplines as well. To the extent that other fields of inquiry also face the same degree of complexity or openness that we encounter in the investigation of social phenomena, they too would be enjoined from discovering laws, and from using them in their explanations.[3] In meteorology, for instance, we note that there may be very specific laws governing the number of drops that will fall in a rainstorm, although it would be impractical to try to predict this (or to explain why that number fell). Although there is a law in principle governing this, practical circumstances conspire to prevent nomological explanation. However, it should be noted that advocates of these arguments usually claim that social phenomena are in some way unique in the degree of complexity faced, or the nature of the open systems they encounter, such that they are in a methodologically distinctive position.[4]

The above thesis is self-consciously more tempered than the earlier claims about impossibility. Here one may admit that despite the peculiarities of the subject matter of social science, it cannot be shown that social scientific laws are impossible; and yet, it is held that the degree of complexity and openness faced in social scientific inquiry is unusual and sufficient to preclude social scientific laws. It is argued that the arguments from complexity and openness render explanation by social scientific laws impractical and, given this, they advise that it is wise to look elsewhere for our explanatory models of human behavior. This new focus, where one emphasizes the practical barriers standing in the way of the formulation of social scientific laws, while conceding their theoretical existence, provides a robust argument against the nomological ideal in social science. Indeed, such arguments represent an even more challenging opposition facing the proponent of law-like social scientific explanation than those considered in Chapter 2.

It is my thesis, however, that both the argument from complexity and the argument from openness fail to demonstrate the impracticality of social scientific laws. In this chapter I will show that while complexity and openness do provide formidable practical barriers to the achievement of laws, they do not provide us with ones that are insurmountable, uniquely social scientific, or which suggest that the law-like approach to explanation in social science should be abandoned as unfruitful. That is, it will be my task to show that there are reasons to think that there are ways of ameliorating the difficulties that these potential barriers provide, while retaining the integrity of law-like explanation.[5] This task will be facilitated, in Chapter 4, by drawing a comparison with some examples from natural science, where precisely such practical barriers have been faced, and yet we have not been forced to abandon our search for laws.[6] In this chapter I will explore the contention that complexity and openness (of the degree faced in social science) renders social scientific laws impractical, and thereby counsels abandoning our search for them.

But what are the practical difficulties that complexity and openness might impose on law-like social scientific explanation? We saw in the last chapter that these factors do not render social scientific laws impossible, but here we must ask whether they might render them unfeasible. In what follows, I will examine these claims, again starting with the argument from complexity.

The Argument from Complexity

We left Michael Scriven, in the last chapter, on the horns of a dilemma. It is now time to see if we can rescue him. How?—by changing the implication of his argument. Recall that this dilemma arose because of the realization that in order to show the impossibility of social scientific laws, one needs to demonstrate a fundamental difference between the subject matters of natural and social science, based on the greater complexity of social science. Not only is this prohibitively difficult to show, however, but it seems that all Scriven has motivated is a difference in degree. But what if he were now willing to modify the implication of his argument? What if the focus were shifted so that the task is not to show that an in principle difference in complexity renders social scientific laws impossible, but that a difference in the degree of complexity of social phenomena would render the discovery of such laws impractical? If such a modification were made to Scriven's argument, would it succeed?

There is some reason to suppose that Scriven's account of complexity is robust enough to accommodate this shift in emphasis. For although he does seem to want to demonstrate that the difference between the complexity faced in natural and social science is in some way essential, he does, at times, appear to plead in the alternative.[7] Compare, for example, the following of his statements: "The reason why [social science] is in its present state is that by its very nature, it will never be in a very different state. ...

[Factors unique to the subject matter of social science make the likelihood of the achievement of laws] impracticable or, to put the matter more bluntly, impossible"[8] with,

> I am not making the absurd claim that there will be no progress [in social science], but simply the claim that simple laws will rarely be found even under the most idealized laboratory conditions. This is a claim based on the empirical evidence, not on any *a priori* necessity. If the evidence was simply that we have so far failed to discover any simple laws, then it would seem rash to claim that none will be found. I believe, however, that the evidence also suggests an explanation for the lack of such successes in terms of several factors, the most important of which [is] the multiplicity of critical variables in the *simplest* interesting cases. ... The meteorologist is in the same position; ... [but] the practical problems of [social science] are often worse than the meteorologist's.[9]

The sophisticated version of the argument from complexity, as articulated by Scriven, can easily accommodate a shift in emphasis away from the claim that the difference in kind in subject matter (due to complexity) between natural and social science shows that social scientific laws are impossible, and instead may focus on the claim that the difference in the degree of complexity faced in the two fields renders the discovery of social scientific laws *impractical*. Indeed, Scriven seems to believe that upon either view, complexity is sufficient to recommend against the search for social scientific laws, and, whether the argument from complexity shows that social scientific laws are impossible or impractical, it matters little for the desired outcome: Laws will not be forthcoming and thus cannot be used in the explanation of human behavior. But having said this, and realizing that the argument from complexity failed to motivate the claim that social scientific laws are impossible, it is important to examine in detail Scriven's contention that social scientific laws are impractical.

That Scriven believes that the argument from complexity shows at least that social scientific laws are *impractical* is beyond dispute. Scriven states:

> The basic generalizations [in social science] are more complex [than those in natural science]. ... [Consequently the] practical problems of prediction, or explanation, *at any level* ... are more likely to be *insoluble* in the study of human behavior. ... There are too many cases where the problems that we wish to solve are demonstrably dependent for their solution upon information about, or control of, variables we cannot get at or cannot control because of the practical circumstances.[10]

His primary thesis, then, is that there are insurmountable practical barriers standing in the way of social scientific laws, due to the "relatively greater complexity of the *simplest phenomena we are concerned to account for* in a behavioral theory."[11] So despite the fact that the difference cited may merely be practical, Scriven believes that it is enough to preclude the use of social scientific laws for the explanation of human behavior.

What is his argument for this claim? It is essentially the same as that examined in the last chapter. The cornerstone of Scriven's argument for the impracticality of social scientific laws is that in the social sciences we are dealing with a subject matter that is many orders of magnitude more complex than that faced in the natural sciences. Why is this?—because of the complexity encountered at the level at which we wish to investigate human affairs. We just are interested in conducting social inquiry and seeking social scientific explanation at a level at which the phenomena are complex. Consequently, he contends, the social scientist faces problems of explanation that are far more difficult than those faced in the natural sciences.[12]

Recall here Scriven's admission that the social sciences are derivatively complex. That is, that they are complex because in social science we are left with all of the hardest problems to solve. Due to long commonsense reflection, and poaching by other disciplines, all of the "easy" regularities have been skimmed off, and it would be trivial to try to generate social scientific laws only about banalities.[13] So it is unfortunately the case that in social science we must therefore engage the phenomena at a level at which any interesting regularities will not be forthcoming, because of the greater number of critical variables that determine their interaction—and the difficulty of expressing them—at this higher level of description. Consequently, in social science we are forced by default into studying the phenomena at a level of description where laws will prove to be elusive.[14]

Scriven has thus admitted that the complexity of social phenomena is due to their level of engagement. But *given* this level (because it is at such a level that we wish to have social phenomena explained) practical difficulties will prevent us from formulating social scientific laws.[15] We will have difficulty in measuring the effect of any experimental changes, performing any controlled or repetitive experiments at all, determining the interaction between the critical influential variables, and even in knowing what or how many critical variables there are in the first place. By dealing with a larger number of critical influential variables we confront a complexity that generates practical problems that stand in the way of the discovery of social scientific laws.

In natural science, however, Scriven contends we are fortunate that we encounter relatively simple phenomena, and that we engage them at a level that does not preclude the nomological expression of basic relationships. Scriven attempts to illustrate this schism with an example drawn from chemistry. He writes:

Dalton was faced with a large number of precise laws of chemical combination, and had precise data about the substances which thus interacted. Suppose that he had observed only the results of experiments with highly stable, highly heterogeneous mixtures labeled perhaps A, B, or C. His results would be inexplicable in terms of any simple theory. It is this situation which faces the student of behavior—and for him there can be no reduction of the macroscopic data to simple invariable regularities, whose existence could perhaps be explained by reference to a theory of the micro-structure. Why not? Because the fundamental experimental element is the human being, or his responses, enormously complex in structure and function and reared in an enormously complex environment. There can be no *practical* sense in which this element can be reduced to simpler ones.[16]

Scriven hereby hopes to show that there is a sense in which we are bound to engage social and natural phenomena at different levels of description, and that this inevitably produces complexity and practical problems in finding laws for the social sciences. In sum, his aim is to show that the derivative complexity of social scientific investigation presents us with practical obstacles that may well forbid our discovery of social scientific laws.

Thus, Scriven's earlier argument about the complexity of the subject matter of social science has now been refined, and its implications for the social sciences can be tempered. He need not deny the in principle possibility or existence of social scientific laws, the truth of determinism, or even that there indeed seem to be regularities behind human behavior.[17] However, what he does deny—indeed, what he must deny if his claim is to go through—is that we can subsume any of these regularities under a "simple" system of laws that can be used for the explanation of human behavior. Scriven's aim, therefore, is to show that social scientific laws are impractical due to the ill effects of the complexity that faces their formulation at the level at which we demand social scientific inquiry and explanation. As we noted in the last chapter: at a level at which laws would be practical, the phenomena are described so simply that any laws would not be explanatory, and at a level at which the phenomena are engaged in such a way that laws would be explanatory, the practical barriers brought about by complexity would forbid their achievement. Thus, Scriven guards against the evil of truism by embracing the specter of complexity. He rules in favor of preserving social phenomena at the level at which we find them interesting at the expense of foregoing social scientific laws.

In sum, as was the case in the last chapter, Scriven hopes to present us with an argument that preempts the ideal of nomological explanation in social science. The implication this time is more measured, but the outcome (that we will not be able to obtain social scientific laws nor use them for the explanation of human behavior), he hopes, will be the same. Even after admitting the possible theoretical existence of social scientific laws, we can see how little Scriven's goal has changed. He still hopes to preempt the explanatory power of social laws, but this time because of the practical problems generated by complexity. Scriven still concludes that social scientific laws are not going to be useful for the explanation of human behavior.

But is this version of the argument from complexity any more successful than the last one? Does the argument from complexity succeed in showing that social scientific laws are impractical? No. While the argument from complexity does, perhaps, point out genuine practical difficulties for the achievement of social scientific laws, it does not succeed in demonstrating that these difficulties are insuperable. There are problems internal to the argument itself as well as reason to believe that the practical problems generated by complexity are not fatal to the goal of nomological explanation.

Despite the subtlety of Scriven's revitalized account of the argument from complexity, he falls prey to one overarching and recurring error. He confuses the thesis that there can be no laws of social phenomena at one level of description, with the thesis that there can be no social scientific laws at all (using any other descriptions). Why does he do this? Because he believes that there is only one level of description of social phenomena that is legitimate, and that does not inevitably lead to truism.

Of course, Scriven is right to guard against truism. He correctly recognizes that it is just not adequate to come up with trivial laws, based on some truistic redescription of social phenomena into unfamiliar categories, at some superficial level, as if, in concert with the underdeterminist thesis that there are an infinite number of ways of connecting the same data, any regularity would do. Scriven is right to believe that wholesale redescription of social phenomena may lead to truism, and possibly may lead to a degeneration of social scientific laws into mere naive correlation. Moreover, Scriven also seems right to point out that we just seem interested in social phenomena *at* a particular level of description, where it is unfortunately the case that complexity may be present.

But where Scriven fails is in pushing the implications of these two theses too far—for he seems to believe that *any* redescriptions will *inevitably* lead to truism, an assumption which, if true, would preempt almost all of natural scientific, as well as social scientific, practice. Scriven has not allowed for the idea that redescriptions may be useful in the search for social scientific laws *without* leading to truism; he has failed to recognize that our interest in having social phenomena explained at a certain level does not preempt nontruistic inquiry at other levels of description.[18]

Here Scriven has confused the worthy goal of explaining human phenomena at a level at which we find them puzzling with the spurious goal of engaging them only with a particularly narrow set of theories, descriptions, and vocabulary sanctioned by our intuitions. He feels as if once we have chosen the level of our interest, we also have determined all of the natural kinds governing that level as well. But he has not realized that even *at* one level of interest there are many possible descriptions, categorizations, theories, distinctions, and possible vocabularies—some of which are more amenable to nomological inquiry than others. Thus, Scriven is not allowing the categorization of social phenomena to evolve along with our theories about them and has insisted that if they are to be explained at all, they must be captured in terms of a vocabulary and theoretical framework that we have antecedently deemed legitimate—as if we have already discovered all of the proper natural kinds governing social phenomena, and the job of science is merely to find the connections between them. But science, either natural or social, does not work this way; even *at* one level of description there is more than one way of proceeding.

In criticizing Scriven's account, it is important to realize that even in natural science we could not produce law-like explanations under the conditions he imposes on social science. For one level of interest does *not* necessarily afford only a single descriptive vocabulary or set of natural kinds, and redescription does *not* necessarily lead to engagement at a truistic level. In natural science we allow our theories and descriptions (and categorization into kinds) to evolve in response to our search for regularity. We assume that laws exist and formulate our theories in an attempt to uncover them. Consequently, we may find ourselves investigating natural scientific phenomena in terms that are, at first glance, far removed from the terms of our original query. But this does not necessarily mean that our inquiry is now truistic!

What is required for scientific explanation is that the theories and laws reflected in our inquiry *link up with* the real world questions that we ask about natural phenomena. There must be a legitimate theoretical relationship between the explanations that we give in terms of "wavelength" and "spectrum" and the everyday questions we ask about "light" and "color." But scientific inquiry does not require that this relationship be so close that we are bound only by one set of descriptive terms and distinctions, despite the fact that the everyday inquiry that generated our investigation in the first place, perhaps, proceeded only under very narrow terms.

Science grows by allowing our theories and categorizations of the familiar to expand, as we look for the regularities underlying them, and to link up with our commonsense questions in novel and illuminating ways. But we must learn that this linkage does not proceed by refusing to allow science to develop its own theoretical framework, make its own distinctions, or even redirect the focus of our inquiry. So we must realize that it would be improper to handicap social scientific inquiry by insisting that there be only one proper mode of categorization of social phenomena, and that should we fail to find law-like connections between these referents, then there is no role for laws in the explanation of human behavior. Scriven may be right that we demand explanation of human behavior that links up with the phenomena at a level at which we are interested in having them explained, but he is wrong to think that this means that social inquiry can be carried out only in terms of the particular vocabulary that exists at that level. We cannot expect social science to succeed under a burden that would surely crush the natural processes of scientific explanation in any field of inquiry.

Of course this response brings up a raft of complex issues: Why suppose that any redescriptions will be legitimate? Wouldn't this just be to change the subject matter? Would we still be doing social science? These issues will be dealt with more fully when I consider arguments about the alleged irrelevance of social scientific laws, in Chapter 5. In Chapter 4, however, I will offer a more immediately compelling account of the legitimacy of redescription by considering an analogy with how it is used in natural science, along with an example of its potential in the social sciences. At present I will limit discussion to showing that Scriven's account suffers from its "descriptivist" bias—the idea that one level of description is just constitutive of the subject matter of social science and that any explanations must therefore be given in terms of it—and that its failure to take account of redescription weighs against its credibility, leaving until later a more complete defense of why I think that redescription is credible.[19]

At one point in his article, Scriven comes close to seeing the problems engendered by his "descriptivism." He tells us that Dalton couldn't find laws if he were in the same position—with respect to the level of description of the phenomena—that social science is in. But even here Scriven misses the point of his own example. The point that one should take away from this is not that there is an essential difference in the levels at which we must conduct social and natural scientific inquiry due to a difference in the level at which we describe them. Rather, the point is that not even in natural science could we hope to find laws if we were biased by adherence to one specific vocabulary and a commitment to carry out investigation only in terms of it. We could not have gotten very far in discovering the laws governing combustion, for instance, if we had been required to use only the vocabulary and theoretical terms of Becher's theory of "phlogiston." We don't think in terms of "negative weight" much these days, but we can try to explain the phenomena it was meant to account for by redescribing them in terms of the theoretical framework that has evolved since then. Similarly, we have given up "final causes," "animal spirits," and even "absolute rest" in favor of new theories and taxonomies that more adequately capture the phenomena we desire to have explained. Just imagine our dilemma if we insisted, though, that the job of science were only to find the connections between certain natural kinds that we believed, a priori, to be legitimate. Under such circumstances it would not be surprising if we failed to find laws throughout natural science.[20]

Thus, perhaps Scriven is right about the deleterious effect of long commonsense reflection on our ability to find social scientific laws, but for the wrong reason. It's not because common sense skims off all of the "easy" regularities (at least this is not the full extent of the problem). Rather, the problem is that the existence of such homilies, and their expression in commonsense terms, lulls us into thinking that any legitimate social inquiry must mirror this level of engagement and must be bound by using the method, vocabulary, and distinctions already familiar to us in informal inquiry.[21] But in doing this we are unjustly limiting the tools available to social science. We are insisting that social science be carried out in terms of natural kinds and distinctions that are already familiar to us because anything else, we fear, would be truistic. But, I argue, to redescribe phenomena does not necessarily have to lead to truism. To believe so is to confuse the goal of having social phenomena *explained* at the level at which we find them interesting with the dubious goal of having them *investigated* only in terms of the natural kinds and descriptions that have previously framed our interest in them.

So it seems that all Scriven has shown is that if we pick one particular level of description (and don't allow the theoretical vocabulary or categories to evolve in response to our inquiry), we will have trouble finding laws. But this *is not* to show that there cannot be social scientific laws that are explanatory; it is only to show that there can be no laws (perhaps) connecting social phenomena *as described in a particular way*.[22] But this, I think, would not be surprising. Thus, if Scriven succeeds he does so only in a narrow sense. He has made it a trivial truth that we cannot have laws in social science, only because by "social science" he means inquiry at a level of description of social phenomena that is so narrow that it all but preempts any meaningful search for laws at all.[23] What he has shown is that we, perhaps, cannot have laws connecting "beliefs" and "desires," or "alienation" and "anomie"(which is itself controversial), but certainly this is something less than purporting to have shown that there cannot be any social scientific laws. It does not show that we cannot explain these terms, and indeed hope to do so in terms of a law-like relationship, by allowing for nontruistic redescriptions and recategorization of the phenomena they are meant to capture. Our concern with the *phenomena* of social science at the level at which we wish to have them explained should not prejudge the issue of how we might best go about trying to explain them.

The goal of social inquiry, and of natural science, should be to explain the phenomena in terms of a theoretical vocabulary large enough to uncover the underlying relationships between them, while still linking up with our questions about them expressed at a more common level. But such a vocabulary evolves only in response to the search for regularity, and since inquiry proceeds at many different levels itself, it cannot be anticipated by the level of our initial interest. Consequently, it is unfair to handicap social scientific inquiry by insisting that it explain social phenomena only in terms internal to one particular vocabulary or theory and then pronounce the nomological goal a failure when it cannot succeed on these terms. Law-like explanation—science itself—works by trying to show that a given set of phenomena are really connected in terms of some larger pattern. And the mechanism that drives this is a willingness to let science develop its own categories, kinds, and descriptions, as long as they are embedded in a theory and have as their goal explanation of the phenomena that we were originally interested in. But by prejudging the issue of the kinds and categories legitimate in social inquiry, Scriven has prematurely closed the question of laws in social science. However, if we are interested in the larger issue of whether—upon a nontruistic redescription of social phenomena that may initially seem to be complex—we may yet discover social scientific laws, the question is far from closed.

In the next chapter, I will have more to say about the perceived analogy between the situation facing natural and social scientific inquiry and the implications this may have for the search for social scientific laws. In this vein, I will consider an example drawn from natural scientific practice in order to show that complexity need not serve as an insurmountable barrier to the achievement of laws, and to gain a more realistic picture of how science works. I will proceed from there to develop further the positive arguments in favor of redescription and to consider not only how it works in natural science, but also how it may work in social science. At the moment, however, I would like to turn to the argument from openness, as articulated by Brian Fay, for this argument too suffers from some of the same problems and confusions as does the argument from complexity in its attempt to demonstrate the impracticality of social scientific laws.

The Argument from Openness

We saw at the end of Chapter 2 that there were problems with the claim that the openness of human systems implies the impossibility of social scientific laws. We also saw, however, that perhaps openness does provide certain pragmatic barriers to their discovery. In this section, I will examine the nature of these alleged barriers and the argument for the claim that the openness of human systems implies the impracticality (even if not the impossibility) of social scientific laws.

Although it is clear that Popper and Taylor desire to show something more than the mere unfeasibility of laws of human behavior (hoping instead to prove their conceptual impossibility), their failure to show this does not warrant dismissal of the argument from openness as an important one for the question of social scientific laws. Indeed, one philosopher, Brian Fay, has sought to develop the Popper-Taylor line of argument as a *pragmatic* point against social scientific laws, primarily in his "General Laws and Explaining Human Behavior,"[24] in which he revitalizes the Popper-Taylor thesis that the unique subject matter of social science provides insuperable barriers to the achievement of social scientific laws. But, Fay immediately strips off the claim that openness could show anything like *impossibility*, and focuses instead on the claim that it provides enormous *practical* barriers that prevent law-like systematization in the social realm. Fay's claim, then, is not that social scientific laws cannot exist, but that, given the practical obstacles standing in the way of their formulation, we will be unable to find them. Thus, he ultimately hopes to show that social scientific laws cannot be used in the explanation of human behavior because at the level at which we desire to have human action explained, practical problems will prevent us from discovering them.[25]

What are the obstacles that allegedly show social scientific laws to be impractical? Exactly those we faced in the last chapter, which were not enough to show that social scientific laws were impossible, but which may yet be enough to prevent their discovery. Problems like insulating a system from outside influence, defining exactly what the influential variables are in a given case, and determining the nature of the interaction between the variables—these are all practical problems that are potentially fatal to the nomological ideal in social science, not because they present any *in principle* barrier to the achievement of laws, but instead because, as is so often the case even in natural science, the devil is in the details. The unique practical problems encountered when one confronts a constantly changing subject matter will present barriers to the achievement of laws which are so formidable that they all but preempt their usefulness as a mode of social scientific explanation.

What is Fay's argument? In his article, Fay makes a very sophisticated argument concerning the role of "causal generalizations" (of which laws are one type) in explaining human action. His general thesis is that while there is a role for a genuinely theoretical science of human behavior, it is highly unlikely that this science will be able to refine the causal regularities behind human action into covering laws. Fay thinks that this is the case because of certain practical barriers that stand in the way of the formulation of social scientific laws (due to the openness of human systems), but which do not prevent alternative explanatory forms using other types of causal generalizations.[26] In support of his view, he makes two central claims.

First, Fay attempts to clear the air of what he argues are spurious reasons for thinking that we will not have causal generalizations in social science, and specifically social scientific laws. Here he aims to defend the "nomological thesis" against those critics who would hold that laws could not be explanatory, or that, even if they were, the fact that we do not have any undermines their usefulness as a mode of social scientific explanation. Fay here draws a clever distinction, which enables him to preserve the "nomological thesis" despite the absence of any putative laws in social science. He points out that:

> [The nomological thesis] does not consist of the claim that for every particular causal explanation there is ready at hand a general law under which it can be subsumed, indeed, the thesis does *not* entail even that it be known what form the relevant general law would take if it were statable. All that the nomological thesis asserts is that there is *a* general law under which the events invoked in a causal explanation fall.[27]

Thus, by pointing out that a proponent of the nomological thesis need only believe that there *is a* law that would cover the phenomena, he withdraws the threat that the absence of present laws provides.[28] And, in this, we note an important departure from Hayek, Popper, Taylor, and even passages in Scriven, for Fay hereby admits the in principle existence of social scientific laws—he agrees that they cannot be shown to be impossible—although we will see later that he nevertheless does believe that such laws will never be *available* for explanation.

From here, Fay goes on to recount an advanced account of law-like explanation, in which he develops the case for the idea that events we wish to link causally, by means of a covering law, must sometimes be redescribed in order for the law to emerge. Fay writes,

> Indeed, it is normally the case that scientists have had to redescribe events which they believed (correctly) to be causally related in order to be able to formulate the general laws which govern them. Thus, for example, it was necessary to redescribe the event type originally described as "the production of warmth" as "the increase in molecular motion" in order to generate the causal laws governing heat.[29]

Fay then concedes an important point, which we earlier found crucial in our analysis of the argument from complexity: he admits that "phenomena as such are never explained, but only phenomena as described in some way."[30] He hereby recognizes the important role that our *level of description* plays in the search for scientific laws and their role in explanation. When coupled with what Fay then calls a "relatively obvious point"—that there are a potentially infinite number of possible descriptions of the same phenomena—he then derives the desired conclusion, which is that,

> one can easily see how events that are described in one set of terms, and related to one another by means of these terms, may well be redescribed in

conceptually quite dissimilar terms from those employed in the original descriptions, and, as a result, only then be able to be seen as part of a generally recurring pattern of events.[31]

From this point on, Fay recounts the balance of his defense of the nomological thesis. He successfully debunks the "doctrine of superficial generalization," which holds that if one claims that there is a causal relationship between two events, then one must expect to find the law expressing this relationship at the level of description at which we originally described the events.[32] Fay deftly dismisses the threat this allegedly poses against the nomological thesis by pointing out that:

> this sort of objection is rooted in the mistaken assumption that the nomological thesis consists of the claim that the laws which a particular explanation instantiates will be formulated in the same sorts of terms as those to be found in the descriptions in the particular case. In fact, however, the nomological thesis only asserts that there must be a covering law in order for a singular causal statement to be true; and it is quite in keeping with this that the actual laws that do cover these instances will be formulated in terms other than those found in the particular explanation.[33]

In sum, Fay has now done several important things in defense of the nomological thesis: (1) he has pointed out that laws can play an important role in explanation, (2) he has drawn a crucial distinction between asserting that there *is a* law versus the claim that we *have a* law ready at hand, (3) he has suggested that the phenomena as such are never explained, but only the phenomena as described in a certain way, (4) he has provided reason for thinking that, through redescription of the phenomena, we may be able to find a law at another level, (5) he has dismissed the false claim that a law can only be given at the level at which we have framed the original events to be subsumed, and (6) he has defended the idea that, in light of the above considerations, the absence of social scientific laws provides no reason to think that the nomological thesis is false.[34]

But we now arrive at the second central claim behind Fay's analysis. Up to this point, one might think that Fay is in total agreement with the position that I defend in this book. Indeed, up to nearly the end of section 2 of his article, this seems true. At the very end of section 2, however, Fay foreshadows his deep commitment to the bankruptcy of nomological explanation in the social sciences. Here he borrows a distinction from Davidson and argues that if he can show that the causal generalizations of the social sciences are "heteronomic" (as opposed to "homonomic"), he will have isolated a "deep difference" between the natural and social sciences.[35]

He then leaves off his defense of the nomological thesis with the enigmatic statement that, "it is certainly possible for someone to be a proponent of the nomological thesis and at the same time believe that the general laws under which ... singular causal explanations are subsumable will not be formulated in the same terms as those found in the causal explanations [one] presently gives." [36] But why is this an enigma? After all, doesn't Fay state that laws could be formulated in terms different than those used to describe the original events to be related? Yes, but although he does not flag it here, the statement above indicates the direction of Fay's departure from a full defense of social scientific laws—for the issue for him is *not* whether we can *have* laws, by using suitable redescriptions, but whether these laws are at all *explanatory*. So we see that Fay *does* believe in the nomological thesis, and he also believes even that, through redescription, we will be able to find laws at other levels. But he *also* believes (although he does not tell us this explicitly) that for a social scientific law to be explanatory *it would indeed have to be formulated* at the level of description at which we have originally framed those events we wish to have explained. Despite his earlier disapproval of the "doctrine of superficial generalization," it would appear that he himself embraces some qualified version of it.[37] Thus, along with Scriven, despite his argument that laws may be present at other levels of description, he nevertheless believes that redescription of social phenomena will not lead to laws that are *explanatory*.[38]

From this point on, Fay embarks on an attempt to characterize this alleged distinction between the role that laws can play in the explanation of social and natural scientific phenomena, based on the likelihood that at the level at which we would be able to produce social scientific laws, they would not be explanatory, but at a level at which they would be explanatory, practical barriers will prevent their formulation.[39]

In section 3 of his article, Fay begins his argument for the claim that there are insurmountable practical barriers, provided by the subject matter of social science (and our level of engagement with it), which preclude our formulation of social scientific laws at the level at which we would find them explanatory. In short, much as Scriven's updated version of the argument from complexity purports to show that there are intractable practical barriers at the level at which we engage social phenomena, Fay attempts to show that, "there is ... good reason to believe that ... laws ... will not be forthcoming at the level of discourse that social scientists have used to describe and explain actions."[40] Moreover, in concert with Scriven's updated account, Fay's focus too is on the *impracticality* of formulating social scientific laws rather than on attempting to show their impossibility.

Thus, Fay here attempts to defend the importance of causal generalizations in social scientific explanation but gives up on social scientific laws. He tells us that,

> In the social sciences there are genuine causal explanations rooted in the genuine causal generalizations about how certain kinds of people think and act in

certain sorts of circumstances; but these generalizations are *not* genuine laws, nor is it at all probable that they ever will be purified into general laws properly so called.[41]

The balance of his argument, devoted to defending the claim that social scientific laws are impractical, is examined below.

Fay roots his argument for the impracticality of social scientific laws in the claim that human systems are open and the implications that he thinks follow from this. At its core, his argument bases the impracticality of social scientific laws on the epistemological problems that arise from predicting human thought and action. The claim here is that, since thought affects action, we would need to be able to predict human thought in order to be able to predict human action. He then argues, independently, that the system of human ideas is part of an open system and cannot be captured in predictions. But given the important influence that these thoughts have over our behavior, this similarly renders human action as part of an open system as well, and thus makes it an unlikely candidate for prediction. Such openness to influence by outside variables is evidence of a subject matter that is constantly changing and thereby would preempt the stability and regularity that is needed to formulate social scientific laws. Thus, because of the openness of human systems, the formulation of social scientific laws is thought to be impractical.

As was noted at the beginning of this section, Fay's argument here has much in common with Popper and Taylor's, which was examined in Chapter 2. But, as is now apparent, Fay desires to show not the impossibility of social scientific laws, but instead their impracticality. Yet this, he feels, is enough to preempt the goal of nomological social scientific explanation. He thereby roots the impracticality of social scientific laws in the problems derived from predicting human thought; he uses Popper and Taylor's *argument* in support of the *implications* that Scriven, in the last section, failed to demonstrate. All of the wrinkles of such an ambitious hybrid argument are difficult to follow but deserve closer inspection. One may schematize Fay's argument for his claim as follows:

1. Human self-understanding at least partially constitutes the subject matter of social science (which is social phenomena).

2. But, these self-understandings are *constantly changing* as a result of human self-consciousness (reflection, conceptual innovation) and interaction.

3. Popper and Cranston have argued that it is logically impossible to predict human conceptual innovation.

4. And although the logical argument here extends only to a fairly limited class of human thought, it does highlight the enormous *practical* problems involved in trying to predict the future course of human thought.

5. Popper points out that prediction requires a closed system.

6. But *human* systems, due to the dynamic character of human thought, are not closed. The changes in human systems wrought by the influence of human thought are practically innumerable.

7. So these kinds of practical problems (generated by openness) effectively rule out the prediction of human thought.

8. Human thought influences human action.

9. So to the extent that we cannot predict human thought, we will not be able to predict human action.

10. In sum, prediction requires stability and regularity, but in social science we have constant change and openness.

11. Therefore, for practical reasons (due to the openness of human thought) we cannot predict human action.

12. *Suppressed premise:* (Prediction and nomological explanation are logically equivalent … that is, both require the same degree of stability and regularity, and if there is not enough for one, there will not be enough for the other).

13. There is not enough regularity and stability for us to formulate social scientific laws.

14. Therefore, we cannot rely on social scientific laws for the explanation of human action.

Fay hereby has completed his quest to show that the practical problems generated by the openness of human systems present barriers that will preempt our ability to formulate social scientific laws (at the level at which we would find them explanatory). In the rest of his article (section 4), he then presents an alternative mode of causal generalization, which he believes to be explanatorily superior to social scientific laws. This alternative, however, will not be explored in the present chapter, so that we may instead examine more closely his arguments against social scientific laws.[42]

Has Fay succeeded in showing that the argument from openness renders social scientific laws impractical? I argue he has not. Although, in many ways, Fay's argument against laws in social science is the most developed one yet examined in this book (in that he borrows the best from Scriven, Popper, and Taylor, and thereby attempts to avoid most of the criticisms leveled at their accounts), it is also the most disappointing—for, after reading section 2 of his article, one would not expect him to be open to the very same criticism that he there provides against critics of the nomological thesis—and which were the very same ones that, in the last section, thwarted Scriven's revised account of the argument from complexity. Namely, Fay seems to have missed the point of his own defense of the nomological thesis and, like Scriven, falls into the trap of "descriptivism."

As indicated earlier, I believe that Fay's account of law-like scientific explanation is subtle, interesting, and largely correct. The role of levels of description in determining our ability to explain nomologically, the way that redescription often leads to such laws and the idea that a law connecting two events need not be formulated in the terms used to describe the original events, seems correctly to recount what goes on in scientific explanation and, in large measure, mirrors the criticisms raised against Scriven's underdeveloped account of explanation examined in the previous section of this chapter.

But what is baffling about Fay's subsequent argument is that he goes on to develop the idea that, in contrast to natural science, we cannot have *social* scientific laws that are *explanatory,* because we cannot have them at a level at which we have previously defined social scientific phenomena. He seems here to be in grave contradiction, however, with his previous contention that laws will probably emerge only *after* we break away from one narrow level of engagement, in favor of redescription. In large part the practical problems that Fay alludes to for social scientific laws are problems only at *one particular level of description.* He himself admits that there seem to be regularities behind human action, and that these may, at some levels, exist in the form of a law; but he denies that these can be formulated at a level at which we would find them explanatory. But why believe that there are no other levels of description at which we can engage social phenomena that we would find interesting or explanatory? The obvious question now facing Fay is why he does not allow a role for the redescription of *social* events, in order to better find the laws that he believes exist? And, if such laws exist, why would they not be explanatory? In short, why is Fay so catholic in his account of how redescription affords us possible laws connecting social phenomena, but so parochial in his belief that no such law would explain what we want to know about social events? Why does he link social scientific inquiry to one particularly narrow level of description of social phenomena and insist that this is the only level that is legitimately suitable for the explanation of human behavior?

In his defense, perhaps one might point out here that it is just the case that Fay's reading of what would be explanatory in social science is quite narrow. Perhaps, like Scriven, he believes that law-like social scientific explanation would have to proceed at the level at which we use terms like "belief," "desire," "intention," and "meaning"—that these are simply the terms that capture what we find interesting about the phenomena. And his point may therefore be that, at this level of description—using these terms— we cannot overcome the practical barriers standing in the way of social scientific laws.

But why would one want to limit social scientific inquiry to such a narrow avenue of discourse? What possible explanatory goal can we hope to serve by reserving the term "social science" only for social inquiry at such a particularly narrow level of description, using such a limited theoretical vocabulary and set of natural kinds? To do so would be to abandon as not social scientific much of what we legitimately recognize to be good social science.[43] And if the adequacy of redescriptions to serve as the basis for potential explanations is not open to social science, why spend so much time suggesting that this is the only way that social scientific laws will emerge?

In the natural sciences, Fay seems to believe that redescription and inquiry at other levels is legitimate in search of the laws that will help us to explain natural phenomena. The point one takes away from his defense of the nomological thesis, in section 2 of his article, is that in natural scientific investigation we need to be flexible in our descriptions of the phenomena under investigation if we aim to explain them using scientific laws. But why does he not allow this same flexibility in *social* scientific inquiry? What is there that is so special about social phenomena that we feel that it can only be explained at the level at which we have heretofore examined it? And, most troubling of all, why when one recognizes the danger of "descriptivism" in formulating good explanations in the natural sciences would one be so cavalier in embracing it in the social sciences?

Yet, if this narrow reading of his argument correctly depicts Fay's thesis, then it would not be surprising if he succeeds in demonstrating what he hopes.[44] The demonstration that there are practical barriers to the achievement of social scientific laws would become trivial—because what we would then mean by "social science" so severely limits the possible range of scientific discourse that we would have all but admitted the impracticality of social scientific laws in the very definition of the terms.[45] It would be as if, as 14th-century physiologists, we insisted that the proper natural kinds defining physiological phenomena consisted of terms like "black bile," "yellow bile," and "balance," and, since we could not find any general laws connecting such terms (although it is interesting that the medievals perhaps did, by naive correlation), there could not be any laws of medicine or physiology that we would find explanatory. The practical barriers from such a viewpoint may well seem insurmountable. But perhaps we have used the wrong natural kinds—one here wants to object—and may yet seek explanation of the phenomena at another level at which laws are more feasible.[46]

Either way, it seems that there are problems for Fay's account: his point about social scientific laws seems to be either trivial or wrong. If he thinks that there is something about social phenomena itself that preempts legitimate attempts at redescription or inquiry at other levels, he is wrong. He may not be willing to call it "social science," but the sociobiologists, psychohistorians, and even social psychologists may legitimately push the limits of our definitions, for they have shown that there are interesting questions that can be asked about human social behavior at other levels, at which we may legitimately seek explanation.[47] But if Fay means instead that there cannot be any laws connecting "intentions," "beliefs," and "desires," then his point runs the risk of being trivial. For surely the long-standing debate over the status of social scientific laws purports to be about something more than that which could be solved by a redefinition of our terms! When one attempts to rule out as impractical the hope of explanation by social scientific laws, it is assumed that one means more by the term "social science" than one particularly narrow level of description of social phenomena.[48] Social science should be understood, as is natural science, to be broad enough to encompass a wide range of alternative theories and taxonomies. In short, it serves no methodological or explanatory purpose, and does not advance the debate, to stand on such a narrow definition of terms.

Thus, even if one concedes that (1) thought influences action, and (2) there are practical problems in predicting human thoughts and action, why would these practical difficulties at *one* level of description preempt the discovery of law-like regularities, that would be potentially explanatory, at any others? Fay's definition of "social science" seems to be too narrow for us to worry much about his assertion that there are no social scientific laws due to the openness of human systems.[49] Perhaps openness, just as complexity, is not quite so troubling an obstacle at another level of description. As in natural science, the social scientist may find that when given the flexibility to develop alternative categorizations and vocabularies for examining the phenomena under consideration, the search for laws proceeds more smoothly.[50] For to believe that truly explanatory laws could exist only at one privileged level of description is a position too narrow for the natural, or the social, scientist; so even if one did find, perhaps, that there were no laws at a given level of description, this would not settle the methodological debate about laws in social science.

Finally, there is a troubling equivocation at the very core of Fay's argument from open systems itself. In his account of why the openness of human systems provides insurmountable practical barriers to social scientific laws, Fay moves back and forth between the issue of prediction and explanation, treating them as though they are exactly the same. But are they perfectly extensionally equivalent? If not, what is the relationship between them? Why think that the practical problems of predicting human thought (or action) in any way impacts on the role of laws in the explanation of human behavior?

Fay does present an answer to this last question. For his account attempts to root the impracticality of social scientific laws squarely in the deep epistemological problems facing the *prediction* of human thought (see steps (3) and (4) of my outline of Fay's argument earlier in this chapter). Yet the connection seems spurious. In step (12) we see that Fay believes that the connection between explanation and prediction is close (and probably biconditional). But if prediction and explanation *are* structurally equivalent, why introduce all of the points about prediction at all, when the subject of the argument is explanation? If the same barrier—a constantly changing, and perhaps open, subject matter—stands in the way of explanation as well as prediction, then why spend so much time considering the difficulties of prediction? In short, if the relationship between explanation and prediction is biconditional, then all of the material on prediction seems redundant. But if they are not structurally equivalent, then what is the role of prediction vis à vis explanation?

When faced with this dilemma, Fay chooses the first horn. He supports Hempel's view that there is symmetry between prediction and explanation, and in the conditions necessary and sufficient for their presence.[51] But even if one accepts this "logical" equivalence, within the context of his argument it is a curious admission.

In a much overlooked article, Michael Scriven himself has explored the question of the relationship between explanation and prediction. In "Explanation and Prediction in Evolutionary Theory,"[52] Scriven points out that even if one believes there is a *logical* equivalence between explanation and prediction, there is an obvious *practical* difference between the two that cannot be overlooked. Specifically, Scriven points out that the practical problems involved in predicting a given piece of human behavior is often many orders of magnitude more complex than the problems faced in explaining, nomologically, the same event. The number of possible variables, and the interaction between them, Scriven argues, relentlessly biases explanation as the easier practical task.[53]

But in light of this it seems curious that in the middle of an argument that purports to be concerned with the *practical* barriers provided by the openness of human systems in using laws to *explain* human behavior, Fay would spend so much of his effort demonstrating the problems we have in *predicting* it and would choose to emphasize the *logical* equivalence between prediction and explanation. By dealing with prediction throughout the main part of his argument, Fay has probably overestimated the practical barriers standing in the way of law-like social scientific explanation. But the practical barriers facing nomological social explanation are *precisely* the issue at hand. The fact is that only very rarely does one need to be able to predict anything about human behavior in order to be able to attempt to explain it nomologically.[54] True, there are practical problems involved in trying to arrive at laws for even the most general regularities behind human action, and I do not mean to trivialize these. But by focusing so intently on the problem of prediction, Fay has equivocated on a point central to his argument and, in light of Scriven's thesis about the practical disanalogy between explanation and prediction, we are left with a lingering doubt about their substitutability. Indeed, if his argument from openness succeeds in showing that there are intractable practical problems involved in the law-like explanation of human behavior, Fay owes it to us to provide such an argument free from consideration of the problems involved with prediction, since even if one grants for the sake of charity the logical equivalence of prediction and explanation, it is the *practical* difference between them that is clearly at issue. If Fay's argument stands, it should stand independent of the question of prediction. I have provided reason, however, for thinking that it does not stand at all.

Conclusion

In conclusion, we should see that there surely are enormous practical difficulties involved in formulating social scientific laws, and it is also probably true that at least partially these are due to the complexity and openness of human systems, at certain levels of description, which Scriven and Fay have emphasized. But the interesting question we are now left with is whether there is reason to think that these practical problems are unlike those faced by other fields of scientific inquiry—whether they are so formidable, and the tools we might use against them so weak, that we will be unable to ameliorate them in our quest for social scientific laws. Fay and Scriven have put their fingers on two important aspects of the possible source of this impracticality—but as we have seen they fail to demonstrate that we have no useful way to combat them (i.e., through redescription of the phenomena), and we must conclude therefore that their pessimism about the practicality of social scientific laws is unfounded.

But where do we turn next, in the hope of providing more positive reasons for supposing that social scientific laws are not impractical? Both Scriven and Fay's versions of the arguments from complexity and openness fail to demonstrate the impracticality of social scientific laws (indeed they both fail for similar reasons) because each underestimates the tools available to social science and the similarities between the tasks facing social and natural science. Indeed, it is appropriate to note here that *all* of the arguments encountered so far (Hayek, Scriven, Popper, Taylor, and Fay), in their attempt to show that social scientific laws were either impossible or impractical because of the complexity or openness of their subject matter, have suffered from the same misguided commitment to "descriptivism." The difficulties presented by such factors are not unique to the social sciences, and are largely derivative from the kinds of descriptions that we allow to form the basis of our explanatory accounts, and not from the phenomena themselves. Thus, the attempt to draw a clean break between natural and social science on the basis of the complexity or openness of the subject matter in social science seems spurious. However, it is nonetheless important to point out that even the failure of these arguments does not warrant our dismissal of complexity and openness as potentially important barriers to social scientific laws. So where do we go from here?

Recall here Scriven's early thesis that the *practicality* of social scientific laws is an *empirical* issue and is not based on any a priori necessity.[55] So far, however, we have engaged only in the conceptual decomposition of alternative *accounts* of the arguments for complexity and openness and have yet to provide positive reasons for thinking that complexity and openness are not likely themselves to present insurmountable practical barriers in the actual pursuit of social scientific laws. In order to defend social scientific laws against the charge of impracticality, we must do two things: First, we must show that the arguments purporting to demonstrate that (due to the intractability of the subject matter of social science) social scientific laws are impractical, fail; this task has now been completed. But the second task, to show that we have reason to suppose that in actual social scientific practice we will be able to deal effectively with such barriers as complexity and openness, and therefore that we are justified in our optimism about the status of social scientific laws, has yet to be accomplished. Thus, our next task should be *empirical* and must involve the search for a counterexample to the thesis that complexity and openness, of the degree faced in social science, renders social scientific laws impractical.[56]

It is now time to turn to the more constructive task of showing that there is additional reason, beyond the failure of intractability arguments, for our confidence in laws and their potential role in the explanation of human behavior. This will be accomplished by considering an analogy with the practice of natural science.

In facing this task, recall the earlier implication of both Fay and Scriven's choice to focus upon intractability arguments in the first place, in their attempt to demonstrate the impracticality of social scientific laws—that if it is the complexity and openness of the subject matter of social science that makes the pursuit of laws impractical, then it must also be the case that any other field of inquiry that faces the same degree of complexity or openness in its own subject matter will be similarly impeded from the use of law-like explanation.[57] But this means that we may, in our search for a counterexample, legitimately explore other fields parallel to social science in the alleged intractability of their subject matter, in order to examine what the status of law-like explanation is in those fields. That is, we should search for an analogy drawn from the natural sciences, so that we may better understand how it is that complexity and openness are supposed to prevent laws and see how the social sciences might hope to ameliorate these problems in their goal of preserving the nomological ideal.[58] If it is the intractability of the subject matter of social science that influences the methodology used and the mode of explanation best suited to that field of inquiry, then we may hope that by establishing continuity between the barriers faced in the social and natural sciences, and by looking at how such problems are handled in natural sciences, we may learn more about how to deal with such problems when offering nomological explanations in the social sciences.

Thus, we may now begin to compare the situation facing social science with that faced in those natural sciences that confront similar degrees of complexity and openness in their subject matter. In the next chapter, I will explore an extended example drawn from a field that also faces enormous practical problems in overcoming the barriers generated by complexity and openness, and where the debate over the status of law-like explanation is more fully developed—evolutionary biology.

Notes

1. Later, in Chapter 5, I will examine whether even if laws are available, we would find them to be explanatory.

2. Note that I am here using Scriven's version of the argument from complexity again, this time to see whether it implies the impracticality of social scientific laws, instead of their impossibility. I do this because Scriven himself equivocates on which of these two outcomes he aims to show.

3. Scriven, for instance, has claimed that complexity may prevent laws in evolutionary biology too. Cf. note 57 of the present chapter.

4. We have already seen though, just how hard it is to cash out what this difference is supposed to be. See Chapter 2.

5. Does this amount only to a priori vindication? I don't think so, since to show that the law-like approach is unfruitful one would need to show that there is reason to think there are no analogies between the situation faced in social science and any other fields of inquiry, that there are no available tools we might use to ameliorate these difficulties in social science, and that there is good reason to think that social science therefore cannot deal with these barriers in a scientific way. To rebut these claims, as I hope to do in this and the following chapter, would seem to amount to more than a priori vindication.

6. Note that although the barriers themselves may be the same (e.g., complexity, open systems, problem of experimentation), they may well be generated by different mechanisms. For instance, in evolutionary biology and much of social science we face the problem of reflexively open systems, although one would not want to claim that the openness in biology is caused by a reflectively self-conscious subject matter that is taking predictions about its own behavior into account. Nonetheless, despite the difference in mechanism, the problem is largely the same.

I will be drawing an analogy between the social and natural sciences in the hope that by examining how the natural sciences deal with such problems as complexity, we can better learn how we might deal with them in social science. Recall here the idea that if the arguments from complexity and openness work, they would apply to fields beyond the social sciences—to the degree that they suffer from the same barriers. Thus, if we can isolate an example in another field of inquiry, which faces and surmounts either complexity or openness, it raises the status of our belief that the same thing might be done in social science.

7. Scriven probably does this because either way it comes out that there will be no laws available for social scientific explanation, and it matters little to him whether this is because they are impossible or impractical. Cf. here Hayek, "The practical limits determined by the impossibility of ascertaining all the relevant data lie so far inside the logical limits that the latter have little relevance to what in fact we can do." Citation at note 12, Chapter 2 of the present book.

8. Michael Scriven, "Views of Human Nature" in T. Wann, ed., *Behaviorism and Phenomenology: Contrasting Bases for Modern Psychology* (Chicago: University of Chicago Press, 1964), pp. 166 and 171.

9. Michael Scriven, "A Possible Distinction Between Traditional Scientific Disciplines and the Study of Human Behavior," *Minnesota Studies in the Philosophy of Science*, Vol. 1 (1956), pp. 335–337.

10. Scriven, "Possible Distinction," p. 332 and Scriven, "Views," p. 171.

11. Scriven, "Possible Distinction," p. 332.

12. Scriven, "Possible Distinction," p. 334. One might simplify the dialectic of Scriven's argument here as follows: The level of our interest in the phenomena leads to complexity, which leads to practical problems in discovering regularity, which means that we cannot discover any laws.

13. I contend that this claim is somewhat *ad hoc*. He calls trivial those attempted laws that deal with the leftover phenomena and "easy" those laws that have already been established. Yet it may not have always seemed so to the practitioners. Recall here a similar claim by Hayek, "non-physical phenomena are more complex because we call physical what can be described by relatively simple formulae," citation at note 10, Chapter 2, of the present book. The ad hocness of Hayek's contention is more overt, but the implication of Scriven's view—that we have already discovered all and only easy regularities—makes one suspicious.

14. See Chapter 2 for further explanation of this claim.

15. His argument here is that our *level of interest* in the phenomena generates the practical problems. If we were interested in this same level in astronomy, for instance, maybe we would be unable to discover laws there too, even if they did in fact exist. Scriven writes, "If it were the case that the problems of predicting astronomical positions involved predicting the behavior of the planets to within a micron or an inch, astronomy would be in its infancy." "Views," p. 172.

16. Scriven, "Possible Distinction," pp. 337–338.

17. At pages 331–332 of "Possible Distinction," Scriven discusses this.

18. That is, one might say that there are two different kinds of redescription: one that is truistic (because it is based on naive correlation), and one that is grounded in a scientific theory (and therefore is not truistic). Perhaps there is no easy way to demarcate between these two in principle (just as philosophers of science have had a hard time providing a logical distinction between a naive correlation and a law), but in practice we may recognize a genuine distinction between truistic and non-truistic redescription and should be wary of lumping them together.

19. I discuss the value of redescription in Chapter 4. The term "descriptivism" was arrived at in conversation with Brian Fay, although I am now unsure who

came up with it. It is meant to cover those critics of nomological social science who believe that one is not doing legitimate social science unless inquiry proceeds at a particular privileged level of description and that explanations are given in terms of it.

20. At some level Scriven seems to see this. He correctly points out that the issue in the Dalton case is one of the level at which we are interested in investigating the phenomena and offering an explanation of it. But he *couldn't* also believe that *if* it were the case that we were interested in a very precise level of inquiry in the Dalton case—or any other in natural science—we could not allow redescription in the interest of discovering regularities. Or could he mean this? If he does, it is a naive view of scientific practice. If not, then why is the situation thought to be so different in social science?

21. Of course, there is also prior *social science* as well. I do not mean to imply that all inquiry prior to this has been commonsense. Still, it is interesting to note that even the terms of social scientific theory—witness "delusion," "resistance," and "retentive"—have a way of working themselves into our common vocabulary.

22. This point, perhaps, can also be made against Donald Davidson. In arguing against "social laws" one gets the sense that Davidson means that there cannot be any laws connecting social phenomena as described by a particular vocabulary, using terms like "belief" and "desire." But even if this can be shown (which is itself controversial), it is something less than showing that there are no laws that can explain human behavior (even if Davidson would not find them acceptable).

23. Again, we see a possible *ad hoc* component to Scriven's argument; one might interpret him as saying that there are no laws of social science, defined as that set of phenomena complex enough that there cannot be any laws about it.

24. Appears as Chapter 5 in Daniel R. Sabia, Jr. and Jerald Wallulis, eds., *Changing Social Science* (Albany, N.Y.: SUNY Press, 1983).

25. As promised, in Chapter 5 I will examine whether, even if such laws are available, we would find them explanatory.

26. Such as those in critical theory.

27. Fay, "General Laws," p. 111.

28. In a similar way, Hempel's early introduction of the notion of "explanation sketches," as part of his defense of the covering law model against the charge that it was false because we could not point to full and comprehensive covering laws already existing, performs a related function.

29. Fay, "General Laws," p. 111.

30. Ibid., p. 111.

31. Ibid., pp. 111–112. Fay borrows much of his analysis here from Arthur Danto's chapter, "The Problem of General Laws" in his *Analytical Philosophy of History* (Cambridge: Cambridge University Press, 1965). Indeed, one might think that Fay has borrowed too much, for he makes the same mistake in thinking about redescription as does Danto.

Danto, in the preface to *Narration and Knowledge* (New York: Columbia University Press, 1985), p. xii, argues that there are many alternative redescriptions of one and the same event, and that not all of these will be adequate as the basis for scientific explanation. He goes on from this to conclude that since the descriptions useful to science are unlikely to be the same as those useful for narrative explanations

history is an autonomous subject. But herein he misses the pluralism of explanatory stances that lies beneath his reasoning by assuming that the historian would
never be interested in discovering laws of human behavior. But instead why not
believe the opposite view, which his reasoning would also support—namely, that
it is justifiable to have descriptions of human action that support a science of human behavior as long as they do not purport to undercut the legitimacy of alternative descriptions that would underwrite narrative explanations. The parochialism
of Danto's view about what sort of explanations are legitimate in history could
usefully be replaced by a commitment to the pluralism of explanatory stances in
history, which is also supported by redescription. Thus, he could save narrative
explanation without making the stronger claim that nomological explanation in
history is irrelevant. Cf. my argument on this point in Chapter 5.

32. Recently, Jaegwon Kim has made a related claim about the singularity of
explanations despite divergent levels of description and inquiry in his "Mechanism, Purpose, and Explanatory Exclusion," in J. Tomberlin, ed., *Philosophical Perspectives*, Vol. 3 (Atascadero, Calif.: Ridgeview, 1989), pp. 77–108.

33. Fay, "General Laws," p. 113.

34. What Fay *hasn't* done, though, is tell us that he thinks that the laws connecting the redescribed phenomena will be *explanatory*. Indeed, this is something he
will ultimately deny.

35. "Homonomic generalizations are those whose positive instances give us
reason to believe that the form and vocabulary of the finished law will be of the
same type as the generalizations themselves; heteronomic generalizations are those
which lead us to believe that the precise law at work can only be stated by switch-
ing to a different vocabulary altogether." Fay, "General Laws," pp. 114–115.

36. Fay, "General Laws," p. 114.

37. One may question here whether Fay has violated his own defense against
the charge of the "doctrine of superficial generalization." That is, he seems to hold
a derivative of the doctrine itself: he may not believe that for a law to *exist* it must
be statable in the terms used to described the original component events, but he
does seem to think that for a law to be *explanatory* it must be expressed at one particular level of description. Therefore, he rules out the possibility of redescription
as an aid in discovering *explanatory* laws (in social science), even though he is not
prepared to rule it out as a guide to discovering *any* laws.

38. In Chapter 5 I will deal directly with the issue of whether redescription
"changes the subject matter" of social science—of whether laws are explanatorily
irrelevant because they are not explaining the same thing once redescription takes
place.

39. In this, his view has a certain similarity to Scriven's.

40. Fay, "General Laws," p. 115. Again we see how Fay's claim here is David-
sonian.

41. Ibid., p. 115.

42. In his essay, Fay discusses the alternative of critical social science.

43. Later, in Chapter 5, I will examine in more depth the fundamental argument
that lies behind such a claim—which is common to "descriptivist" arguments like
those of Scriven and Fay—when I look at arguments concerning the alleged "irrel-

evance" of laws to the explanation of human behavior. There I will consider the motivation for these claims and will explore the reasons for their failure.

44. But the claim could still fail. It may yet be possible that there are laws even at the level of description depicted by Fay's narrow reading of "social science." However, I do concede that if the claim is that his argument purports to show the impracticality of social scientific laws at this level, it is more likely that he will be able to show this easier claim than the broader claim that social scientific laws are impractical at *any* level of investigation. Still, even though my aim is to defend the broader claim, it is important to note that there still may be flaws within Fay's argument that there are no laws *at* any particular level of description either.

45. This is not to say that Fay's view is a tautology or that its aim at truth is solely analytic. Fay does not seek to make it true by definition that social scientific laws are impractical; he intends it to be an empirical discovery. In this, I think he is correct. However, it is still important to point out that his claim is quite narrow and does serve to "define away" one of the most interesting questions in social science, which is whether there can be explanatory social scientific laws based on redescriptions of social phenomena.

46. A Kuhnian might object, though, that when we have changed the description of the phenomena, we have changed the phenomena itself. It is important to realize, however, that this objection would similarly undercut the role of redescription in helping us to find laws in natural science as well. Cf. here Thomas Kuhn's discussion of the problem of "incommensurability" in *The Structure of Scientific Revolutions* (Chicago: University of Chicago Press, 1962).

47. This point seems true even if it turns out that there are no laws (or no explanatory laws) turned up by present inquiry. My point is that these areas are legitimate ones for future study, and we should not be so anxious to prejudge the question of where our "explanations" of social phenomena may ultimately come from.

48. To say that there are "no laws of social science" *sounds* as if one is making a claim that there are no regularities behind human behavior, or that there are deep problems involved in formulating or discovering these laws at any level of investigation, and not simply that "there are barriers to formulating laws of social science at one particular level of description, because it is this level at which we must conduct all social scientific inquiry."

49. Although one could certainly worry about the very same kinds of barriers to laws *at* a given level of description as we would be concerned to worry about at *any* level. As pointed out earlier, this could very well mean that since even the narrow arguments about laws at a given level of description mean to be empirical claims, it could be false, and the arguments for it must attempt to address the objections I have brought up against "intractability" claims throughout this book.

50. Although it is true that there will still be barriers, just as there are in natural science. The issue, however, is whether these barriers can be dealt with in a scientific way. Cf. Harold Kincaid, "Defending Laws in the Social Sciences," *Philosophy of the Social Sciences*, Vol. 20, No. 1 (March 1990), pp. 56–83.

51. In some of his later work, Hempel himself reconsiders the issue of the structural symmetry between explanation and prediction. In his essay, "Aspects of Sci-

entific Explanation," in *Aspects of Scientific Explanation and Other Essays* (New York: The Free Press, 1965) Hempel reaffirms his belief that every adequate explanation may serve as the basis for a potential prediction, but he also reviews arguments that suggest it may not also be true that every prediction may serve as a potential explanation. Although he presents reasons for thinking that even this thesis may ultimately be upheld, he leaves it an open question. Fay, however, would seem to be adhering to Hempel's earlier statement on this issue, where he holds that, "the logical structure of a scientific prediction is the same as that of a scientific explanation. ... The customary distinction between explanation and prediction rests mainly on a pragmatic difference between the two." Carl Hempel, "The Function of General Laws in History," *Aspects of Scientific Explanation* (New York: The Free Press, 1965), p. 234.

52. Michael Scriven, "Explanation and Prediction in Evolutionary Theory," *Science*, Vol. 130, No. 3374 (August 28, 1959), pp. 477–482.

53. Although it is clear, even in this article, that Scriven does *not* support lawlike explanation either.

54. Certainly this is true in natural science as well. Prediction is often used to *test* a theory, but it is not often the case that one must rely on precise predictions in offering the explanation of the phenomena the theory itself was meant to cover.

55. See text accompanying note 9 of the present chapter.

56. Later, in Chapter 5, I will consider arguments that go beyond the availability of laws and question their relevance and explanatory status.

57. It is interesting to note that Scriven has also argued that complexity serves as a barrier to laws in evolutionary biology, cf. his "Explanation and Prediction in Evolutionary Theory," *Science*, Vol. 130, No. 3374, (August 28, 1959), pp. 477–482; and his "Explanation in the Biological Sciences," *Journal of the History of Biology*, Vol. 2 (1969), pp. 187–198. Even if the mechanisms that *generate* complexity in biology are different than those in social science, Scriven has argued that it is the complexity itself that is the barrier to laws. Of course, this means that if one could show that there were laws, for instance, in evolutionary theory, despite the presence of complexity, this would correspondingly weaken Scriven's claim that complexity is such a formidable barrier to laws in social science. For just such an argument, see Mary Williams' defense of the status of laws in evolutionary biology described in Chapter 4 of this book.

58. But why do this?—because in other areas of natural scientific inquiry these very same problems (i.e., complexity, openness of systems) are also faced. It is my hope that an analogy will be instructive for the situation faced in social science when it confronts these same problems.

4

The Role of Laws in
Scientific Understanding:
The Case of Evolutionary Biology

I think the most important lesson to be learned is that our understanding of the structure of a science is likely to be seriously obscured by the failure to properly identify the referents of the laws. ... The extent to which this has obscured the structure of laws, predictions, and explanations ... in evolutionary theory for more than one hundred years after the basic theory was understood (at an intuitive level) is astonishing. My feeling is that the same will be true in the social sciences.

          —Mary Williams

Having completed analysis of the conceptual arguments that purport to show laws are impractical—and finding them wanting—it nonetheless falls to us now to establish that even in the face of such objections, we have good reason to think that there can be social scientific laws. I will now proceed with the positive task of demonstrating this by constructing an analogy with the practice of natural science.

Drawing from evolutionary biology we find a useful counterexample to the thesis that barriers like complexity and openness are sufficient to prevent laws. In doing so it is important to explore the role of redescription in aiding scientific inquiry to find laws despite practical barriers. For comparison, I will suggest an example from social science that may serve as a candidate for nomologicality, and which suggests a useful analogy between the practice of natural and social scientific explanation, as well as a role for redescription in the latter. I do not present this example in the hope of vindicating all of the components of my previous argument by providing a full-fledged law of social science, but merely to give the reader purchase on what I mean by "redescription," and its potential importance in social scientific explanation.

In addition to exploring these examples, and attempting to establish an empirical analogy between natural and social science, in this chapter I will try to clarify my account of redescription and its role in the search for laws, begun in Chapter 3. In Chapter 5, I will then examine some of the major objections to the use of redescription in social science.

The Status of Laws in Evolutionary Biology

David Hull tells us that "the existence of 'evolutionary laws' is one of the most confused issues in the philosophy of biology."[1] And yet it is better developed than the same debate in the philosophy of social science! Indeed, there are interesting parallels between the debates about laws in evolutionary biology and in the social sciences. One might even think that each discipline had "reinvented the wheel," in its consideration of issues common to the debate about the existence and formulation of laws. In both cases we find concern with problems in defining the proper level of analysis in our search for laws, problems surrounding the issues of reduction and autonomy, and consideration of identical alternatives to law-like explanation.[2] But perhaps the most important similarity occurs in their respective discussions of the barriers to nomological inquiry due to an alleged intractability of their subject matters.

In evolutionary biology, for instance, we find general agreement that the main barriers facing the formulation of evolutionary laws are the complexity of the subject matter, openness of biological systems, uniqueness of biological phenomena, singularity, historicism, and so on.[3] Likewise, in the philosophy of biology, just as in the philosophy of social science, despite this general agreement about what the barriers *are,* we find a heated debate over what the *implications* of these barriers are for the status of nomological explanation. Can we have laws in evolutionary biology? Do the barriers listed above render such laws impractical? It is hoped that an examination of these issues will give us insight into the same questions raised by the philosophy of social science.

There are, of course, several controversial examples of laws in evolutionary biology, drawn from empirical generalizations about the process of evolution by natural selection and based on evidence culled from the paleontological record. Before considering such examples, it is important first to try to frame any alleged laws of evolution in the proper theoretical setting. Darwin's theory of evolution by natural selection has three main tenets:[4]

1. There is a struggle for survival, due to the overabundance of progeny.
2. Spontaneous mutations occur, some of which prove beneficial to the organism in this struggle, and some of which do not.
3. Genetic characteristics are heritable across generations.

Thus, the idea behind evolution by natural selection is that, given the selective pressures of the environment, certain organisms having characteristics that put them at a relative advantage in this struggle for survival will be selected for, and will be more likely to live longer and to produce more progeny bearing their genetic characteristics. Conversely, those that are poorly adapted to their environment will be more likely to die out, leading to the more rapid extinction of their characteristics. The theory of evolution by natural selection, therefore, attempts to explain the remarkable "fit" we observe between organisms and their environments, without resorting to hypotheses about "design."

Now, within the evidence drawn from the paleontological record (which has corroborated this theory) biologists have noticed several *patterns* to the process of evolution by natural selection, reflected in structural similarities and differences across phylogenetic sequences. Many of these patterns have been entrenched into so-called "laws" of evolution. Some of the best examples are:

- Dollo's Law: A structure (i.e., a complex part of an organism or the entire organism itself) can never undergo complete reversal, so that it perfectly attains a previous ancestral state. Secondary convergences can always be recognized morphologically by preservation of some trace of an intermediate stage.
- Cope's "Law": Unspecialized species tend to avoid extinction longer.
- Cope's "Rule": Body size tends to increase during the evolution of a phylogenetic sequence.
- Williston's Law: In species with redundant parts, the number of these parts will decrease as evolution occurs, and the remaining parts will become more specialized.
- Dacque's Law: Cotemporaneous species in the same environment tend to change in analogous ways.
- Bergmann's Law: In cold regions, warm-blooded animals are physically larger than the races of the same species in warmer regions.
- Allen's Law: In cold regions, the geographical races of mammals have relatively shorter feet, ears, and tails than the same races in warmer regions.

And indeed there are many more examples. In his *Biophilosophy*, Bernhard Rensch lists an even hundred.[5] But of course, there is controversy over whether *any* of these regularities reflect genuine laws, or whether they are mere empirical generalizations. The use of terms like "tend to" and the presence of numerous exceptions (although some, like Dollo's Law and others listed by Rensch, arguably have none), have led some to deny that they are laws at all.[6]

It has been claimed, by Stephen J. Gould and Ernst Mayr, for instance, that such "laws" fail to achieve true law-like status precisely because they *are* fraught with exceptions, reflect "tendencies" rather than "necessities," and are merely "descriptive" rather than "explanatory." Indeed, it has been claimed by these two thinkers that the attempt to codify such regularities in nomological form ignores an important "historetic" quality present in evolutionary phenomena and thus perverts the meaning of biological explanation all together. Thus, many have been tempted to maintain that such generalizations are merely "rules," and do not live up to the criteria required for true law-like status.[7]

In this section I hope to vindicate the idea that such correlations are (or could be) genuine laws, through consideration of one specific example—Dollo's Law. In our search for a counterexample to the claim that the subject matter may present difficulties that render nomological inquiry impractical, Dollo's Law seems to be the best candidate for true nomological status. Indeed, both supporters and critics of evolutionary laws agree that Dollo's Law is the best candidate for nomologicality:[8] it has mountains of empirical confirmation, virtually no exceptions, is theory based, and seems to be attempting to be genuinely explanatory.[9] Yet even this example has been criticized as failing to achieve law-like status and, moreover, Gould has argued that Dollo's Law provides us with the grounds for rejecting the nomological approach to explanation in evolutionary biology all together. We shall now turn to the examination of such claims.

On the face of it, Dollo's Law looks fairly straightforward and uncontroversial. Simply put, Dollo claims that due to the complexity of the dialogue between the environment and an organism during the evolution of a phylogenetic sequence, it is overwhelmingly unlikely that ancestral structures will be perfectly recoverable; convergent secondary forms will always be morphologically (structurally) distinguishable through the preservation of some trace of an intermediate stage. That is, *complete* structural reversal of *complex* forms is impossible. Dollo himself put it this way: "An organism never returns exactly to a former state, even if it finds itself placed in conditions of existence identical to those in which it has previously lived. But by virtue of the indestructibility of the past ... it always keeps some trace of the intermediate stage through which it has passed."[10] The lungfish, for example, has both gills and lungs, despite the fact that the gills are thought to be vestigial.

In his article, "Dollo on Dollo's Law," Stephen J. Gould provides us with an excellent exegesis of Dollo's account of irreversibility.[11] He points out that although there are at least two distinct readings of the scope of Dollo's Law (one claiming that an *entire organism* can never return to a former state, and the other that a *complex part* of an organism can never do so), the unifying theme behind both of these interpretations is the notion of *complexity*.[12] As Gould puts it: "Precise reversal does not occur because this would require that the organism retrace, exactly and in the same order, an extremely large number of steps.[13] But given the overwhelming number of independent steps involved in such a backwards journey, we can rule it out as statistically impossible. Probabilistically, the chances of such an event are so slight that we can rule it out all together.

Thus, Gould has identified a significant theme behind Dollo's account of irreversibility; for Dollo has rooted his law of irreversibility in the idea that the complexity of the process of evolution by natural selection rules out the chance of complete structural reversal as a "circumstance so complex that we cannot imagine that it has ever occurred."[14] Indeed, Gould seems right that the underlying notion behind Dollo's claim (that reversibility is statistically impossible) is that of complexity.

In this we find evidence of philosophical genius in Dollo (if indeed the "complexity" interpretation of his notion of irreversibility is correct), and a subtlety that Gould has underemphasized. For what better way to forestall the criticism that we cannot have laws in the face of a complex subject matter, than to root the very claim to nomologicality itself in the complexity of the phenomena! Dollo has performed a cunning reversal on the critics of laws in evolutionary biology by pointing out a way in which we *can* indeed have laws governing complex phenomena—indeed, complexity is *crucial* to his law. Far from being a barrier to nomologicality, Dollo's Law may illustrate an example where complexity is absolutely essential to the very claim of nomologicality itself. Thus, criticism of Dollo's Law on the grounds of its complexity, at least, seems reflexively refuted once one presumes to be able to define what it is for a subject matter to be "complex" in the first place.

Yet Gould does *not* buy into the idea that Dollo's Law has achieved true law-like status. Indeed, his account seems more like an attempt to rescue the importance of the notion of irreversibility from being thrown out in the attempt to refute *all* claims to have found evolutionary laws—Gould wants to preserve irreversibility as an important idea in evolutionary biology, even while stripping it of the nomological framework in which Dollo had cast it. Moreover, somewhat ironically, Gould goes on to hope that Dollo's Law will provide us with the very means by which we may "reject … an approach to phylogeny based on a search for such historical laws."[15] Such an ambitious task, however, has required Gould to be absolutely meticulous in dispensing with spurious reasons for criticizing Dollo's Law, and in anticipation of his own criticism, he clears the field of several misconceptions about Dollo's Law.

First, Gould points out that Dollo did *not* mean to rule out irreversibility for *all* evolutionary events.[16] *Functional* reversal, for instance, he allowed. But Dollo also argued that functional reversal was never accompanied by complete structural reversal. Even in those instances where functional reversal occurred, Dollo held that convergent forms could be morphologically distinguished.

Moreover, Dollo also did not intend to rule out "simple" structural reversals nor those that were incomplete. As Gould points out, Dollo's claim was that *complete* structural reversal of *complex* forms was impossible. And yet numerous atavisms have continued to be cited as alleged evidence against Dollo's Law. Such examples have focused, however, on reversals that are either simple or incomplete, and thus they do not count against the proper interpretation of Dollo's Law. A favorite technique used by Dollo to make this point was the use of alleged counterexamples to support his theory. For instance, one might point out that the whale returned to water, and developed certain structural atavisms concurrent with this. But, the reversal was not complete since the whale failed to re-evolve gills. Thus, Dollo could count this, along with virtually thousands of other such examples derived from the paleontological record, as confirmation of his insight about irreversibility. Dollo's Law has proven robust in its ability to accommodate such alleged counterexamples, all of which relied on reversals that were either simple, incomplete, or functional. The central theme behind Dollo's Law—that complete structural reversal of complex forms is impossible—remains intact.

Yet it is the very robustness of Dollo's Law that has led Gould to claim that Dollo's insight on irreversibility is not a genuine law and furthermore provides grounds for thinking that there can be no laws *at all* in evolutionary biology. It has been claimed both that there could not be any laws in evolutionary biology, and, more specifically, that the failure of this one (best) case—Dollo's Law—reveals why.

I won't rehearse again my reasons for thinking that one cannot demonstrate the a priori impossibility of laws in a domain due to peculiarities in its subject matter; we can be confident that this component of Gould's argument fails before we have even examined it. I have argued earlier in this book that one cannot show on a priori grounds that there *cannot be* laws in a discipline merely because of barriers provided by its subject matter. One just cannot show that evolutionary laws are *impossible* on such grounds, any more than one could in the social sciences.[17] Thus, no matter how powerful Gould thinks his argument to be, it cannot achieve the result he ultimately desires.

However, it is worthwhile here to examine in more detail the *specific* claim that Dollo's Law *in particular* fails to achieve law-like status, for if we can show that it does *not* fail, then we have found the counterexample we have been looking for and may gain confidence that there may yet be laws in the face of *practical* barriers—such as complexity and openness—provided by the subject matter. The possibility claim certainly fails, but what about practicality?

Just what is Gould's argument for criticizing Dollo's claim that his insight on irreversibility is a genuine law? To begin with, Gould concedes that Dollo's Law is indeed distinct from other alleged laws in evolutionary biology in that it is not merely descriptive but instead purports to be explanatory. Moreover, he admits that it has no uncontroversial exceptions to it. As noted before, Gould admits the robustness of Dollo's Law, but rather than finding this to be evidence in favor of its claim to nomologicality, he instead uses it to attack the claim that irreversibility constitutes a law.

The central idea behind Gould's attack on the nomological status of Dollo's Law is Dollo's alleged equivocation on the definition of "complexity." Recall here Gould's earlier contention that the notion of complexity was the key to understanding Dollo's Law. But an ambiguity in the very definition of "complexity" itself, Gould claims, insulates Dollo's Law from criticism, and thus empties it of empirical content. In Popper's terminology, Gould would seem to be arguing that Dollo's account is "unfalsifiable," since "any reversion can be excluded from its domain by claiming either that the structures involved were not sufficiently complex or that the genetic basis for an elaborate morphological change was simple."[18] At base, the criticism is that Dollo can interpret "complexity" relentlessly in his favor, in the face of each alleged counterexample, and thus can insulate his "law" from refutation. This, Gould contends, undercuts its legitimacy as a "law" of evolution.

But Gould goes on from here to raise a phoenix from the ashes—for he claims that Dollo's "principle" of irreversibility represents an important insight into the uniqueness of all "historical" phenomena, derived as it is from the idea that it is overwhelmingly improbable that two events could occur exactly in the same way twice. Gould plausibly contends that we cannot have laws about essentially unique or historical phenomena and then goes on to hold that irreversibility itself therefore provides the basis for rejecting the search for laws in those disciplines that deal with such "unique" and "historical" events.

Dollo's Law, Gould argues, is thereby "not an adjunct of evolutionary theory. It is a statement, framed in terms of animals and their evolution, of the nature of history; or, put another way, it is an affirmation of the historical nature of evolutionary events."[19] Gould goes on to explain that:

> since irreversibility is an acknowledgement of the historical nature of evolutionary events and since that very nature precludes the formulation of laws for these events, 'Dollo's Law' is a particularized statement of our reasons for rejecting the approach to evolutionary biology that led to the laws of Cope and Williston. ... [T]he search for ... laws is outmoded because we have now recognized the significance of irreversibility in Dollo's sense.[20]

Gould thereby appeals to the very notion of irreversibility as his basis for rejecting the search for any laws in evolutionary biology, and so while he thinks that Dollo has made an important discovery, he accuses him of having misunderstood its significance. Instead of supporting a law, Gould feels that irreversibility corroborates our rejection of laws in all cases where our subject matter is essentially "unique."

Philosophically, however, it is hard to imagine a weaker argument. Gould's account of the way in which the "historicist" nature of evolutionary events, or the "uniqueness" of biological phenomena, would prove to be a barrier to the search for laws is radically underdeveloped and ignores the numerous successes of natural science in the face of such barriers. Here one suspects that Gould is in company with Hayek, Mayr, and other unsophisticated critics of laws who feel that all one needs to do is merely mention such notions as "uniqueness," "singularity," or "historicism," and one will immediately understand why laws are impossible. I have shown in Chapter 2, however, just how difficult it is to offer a rigorous argument for such a thesis. And since we concluded that it cannot be shown a priori that laws are impossible, one must find this account to be fatally flawed. As I have pointed out earlier, one just cannot make such sweeping generalizations about the *possibility* of laws, even in the face of a seemingly intractable subject matter; the possibility of laws is just not a matter that can be settled on conceptual grounds. So we immediately recognize two fundamental problems with Gould's account: (1) his task of showing that laws in evolutionary biology are *impossible,* because of the nature of the subject matter, can never be realized, and (2) he has not even provided us with an argument for why he thinks this in the first place. Indeed, it seems that Gould has only been successful in eloquently capturing a prejudice for which some argument should now be forthcoming.

To be charitable, however, we might now best proceed by following the same strategy that we did when considering critics of laws in social science—that is, we should interpret Gould's claim not as one against the *possibility* of evolutionary laws but as one against their *practicality* and, in particular, against the practicality of Dollo's Law. Upon this reading, we are able to piece together the parts of an argument that might stand behind Gould's prejudice. Indeed, his claim about the chilling effect that "uniqueness" and "historicism" have on the search for laws reminds one of the argument examined in Chapter 3 given by Scriven.[21]

Recall here that Scriven's account was based on the idea that, at the level at which we are interested in having human phenomena explained to us, there are barriers preventing the formulation of laws. Gould's claim, in concert with Scriven's, can be most rigorously interpreted as a claim that it is *impractical* to expect that we will be able to produce laws at a level at which we are interested in having the phenomena explained, because *at this level* barriers like "uniqueness," "complexity," "singularity," and "historicism" stand in the way of our formulation of them.[22] The phenomena present barriers at the level at which we would like to have them explained, and at a level at which the barriers are not present we would not find any regularities to be explanatory. So one might best interpret Gould's point about the "unique" and "historicist" nature of biological phenomena as a claim that it would be *impractical* to try to discover laws that are meaningfully explanatory, because at this level uniqueness and historicism simply are barriers to the formulation of laws.

Now against this account one might be tempted, as we were against Scriven, to point out that *all* phenomena are unique at some level of description—even in physics. So in order to find laws, mustn't we redescribe the phenomena at other levels at which laws are more forthcoming? Here Gould would probably make the expected reply (in concert with Scriven) that while we surely could find regularities at other levels of description, we *just are interested* in having them explained at a level of description at which barriers like uniqueness are a problem. And, at this level, the phenomena we are dealing with are so complex that it is practically impossible for us to derive the laws that may underlie them. Thus, upon this interpretation of his argument, Gould may even concede that there are certain "nomothetic undertones" that lie behind biological phenomena (just as Scriven admitted there may be laws at truistic levels of description), but what he would then have to deny is that these regularities were capable of being expressed at a level of description at which we would find them to be explanatory.[23] Put another way, because of practical difficulties presented by the complexity of the subject matter at this level of description, resulting in the essential uniqueness of the phenomena at this level of inquiry, we are just not going to be able to formulate laws.[24] As with Scriven, the claim is that the complexity of the subject matter defeats our formulation of laws.

However, when we unpack this view, we must find this implicit reliance on the notion of "complexity" to be problematic. Although he does not mention it explicitly in his article, Gould has since conceded that his appeal to uniqueness and historicism boils down to a claim that biological phenomena, at the level at which we desire to have them explained, are too complex for us to formulate laws about them.[25] He admits that his earlier appeal to uniqueness and historicism is closely linked to the practical problems generated by the complexity of the subject matter at this level of description.

But how can it be that Dollo's claim to nomologicality failed because he could not offer a consistent account of complexity, and yet Gould's criticism of Dollo's Law itself depends on the very existence of such a consistent account of this notion? If a consistent and unambiguous definition of complexity can be offered for Gould, then one must also suppose that it is available to support Dollo's law of irreversibility; but if one *cannot* provide a consistent account of complexity, then Gould's account must go down with Dollo's. Thus, Gould's argument against the nomological status of Dollo's Law is reflexively refuted; if Gould's argument succeeds, then so must Dollo's (so Gould's fails), but if Dollo's fails, then so must Gould's (so Dollo's succeeds).[26]

Perhaps Gould might yet offer a better way to explain his view that uniqueness and historicism prevent evolutionary laws, but until this happens we should note that the radically underdeveloped account he offers in his article does not even *provide* an argument against evolutionary laws, but only identifies a prejudice against them, and that the most charitable interpretation of what the argument behind this prejudice might be relies squarely on a notion that Gould himself earlier repudiated. Thus, (1) Gould has not shown that Dollo's Law fails to achieve law-like status, and (2) even if he *had* done so, this would provide no grounds for inferring that there could be no other laws in evolutionary biology.

But have we, then, found a genuine counterexample to the claim that complexity and openness provide barriers that undermine the practicality of laws? What about the other constraints on nomologicality—such as being exceptionless, non-contingent, and not merely descriptive—stressed by Gould, Mayr, and other critics of evolutionary laws? Does Dollo's Law fulfill all of these criteria? Could any purported law of evolutionary biology fulfill them?[27]

No, but it is now time to realize that neither could anything else throughout the practice of natural science! For the criteria themselves reflect a naive and overly idealized view of the practice of natural science—and the role laws play in scientific explanation—and have probably led one to overestimate the robustness of laws in the rest of natural science. Indeed, if such conditions needed to be met before we could have genuine laws, there would be few laws even in physics.[28] This realization raises several questions:

1. Is there a sharp line between description and explanation? Gould tells us that there is (even though he allows that Dollo's Law is unique in that it is genuinely attempting to be explanatory). But perhaps this is unfair to all of the other purported laws of evolutionary biology. Whether a law is explanatory, one might argue, has to do with whether it is embedded in a scientific theory, and is consistent with other scientific results outside of the theory itself. But what is there in this that is at odds with description? Certainly Bergmann's Law, as well as Allen's Law, rooted as they are in the idea that heat conservation by warm-blooded animals living in cold regions will increase the survival value of the organism, are both descriptive and explanatory. Indeed, the fact that as an animal increases in physical size, its volume increases at a proportionally faster rate than its surface

area (yet it is only on its surface that the animal loses heat) goes far towards *explaining* the theoretical basis for the law itself. Similarly, one might offer further accounts of how purported "laws" of evolution by natural selection root descriptive facts about the process of evolution in theories that are consistent with the theoretical basis for evolution.

2. Why think that a law must be exceptionless? This sets the standard far too high for nomologicality—indeed, it sets it so high that most of what we recognize to be good scientific practice outside of evolutionary biology could not meet it either. One might argue that any good scientific theory that is falsifiable possesses anomalies. But rather than counting this as a fact against nomologicality, one must recognize that the existence of exceptions is part and parcel of doing good science and may indeed suggest fruitful areas of further research.[29]

Of course, the issue of when we have too many anomalies (exceptions)—and this begins to count against the scientific value of a theory—is itself an important one within the corpus of science. The point here, however, is that it is a *scientific* matter, and not an a priori matter, when the number or character of exceptions to a purported law begin to erode our confidence in it and suggest that we should abandon it. Even the most important laws in science have their exceptions. The simple claim that the existence of even one or two exceptions, no matter what they are, preempt a claim to nomologicality is terribly naive.[30] Again, by this standard we could expect no laws even in physics.[31]

3. How can one tell that a correlation is accidental, or genuinely reflects a nomological relationship, outside of the strength of the correlation itself? We have no special insight into the nature of necessity in science outside of empirical observation. We simply cannot always tell in advance (witness Bode's Law in astronomy) which regularities are mere empirical generalizations, and which reflect true nomological relationships, until we gain more empirical information.[32] But even before Nelson Goodman it was recognized as naive to suppose that we could demarcate sharply between accidental and law-like correlations on such a consistent a priori basis.[33]

So we here begin to see that although it is indeed true that none of the laws of evolutionary biology (including Dollo's Law) can pass the criteria set out by the critics of nomologicality, this does *not* demonstrate that there cannot be laws in evolutionary biology. It is important to realize that rather than there being something wrong with the laws, there instead may be something wrong with the criteria themselves—for they seem rooted in a naive and idealized picture of natural scientific practice that was inherited from an outdated conception of scientific laws, which it is doubtful natural science has ever fulfilled. Indeed, over the last three decades, the philosophy of science has gone far towards demonstrating that even the best explanations in natural science could not meet such rigorous criteria. And yet, for good reason, we are reluctant to condemn them as unscientific.

I think the best solution to this dilemma is to realize that it would be rash to claim that we have no laws in physics, chemistry, or biology simply because most of the actual practice of these disciplines cannot live up to the methodological standards required for nomologicality, as spelled out by one particular view within the philosophy of science. If Kepler's Laws fall short in universality, and Boyle's Law begins to have exceptions at high temperatures, so much the worse for these criteria of nomologicality. We recognize such results as good science and are reluctant to withhold the title of "laws" merely because they do not meet an arbitrarily defined a priori standard. Of course we *do* need standards by which we may evaluate nomologicality and demarcate between good and bad scientific practice, but the issue is one of where these standards come from.

Even before Goodman, philosophers of science were busy reevaluating the adequacy of our previous standards for science and nomologicality— realizing that it is probably impossible to set forth a sharply defined a priori criterion, involving the repudiation of non-necessary connections, exceptions, or the use of *ceteris paribus* conditions. Our standards instead, it has been realized, must be derived from the corpus of good scientific practice. But this does not necessarily lead us, as some have feared, down the road to arbitrariness. We may still legitimately recognize some scientific results as genuine, and some as spurious—some generalizations as law-like, and some as naive correlations. But the criteria for determining this must be derived not from an a priori standard, but instead from the body of well-recognized scientific practice to date. It is important to note that, in the philosophy of science, the criteria often come after the science, as we seek to find logical justification for the practices of science. So any attempt to legislate on philosophical grounds what will count as legitimate science (or laws) is constantly open to amendment by the continually evolving standards of nomologicality as defined by scientific practice itself. It is the job of the philosophy of science, therefore, to derive the standards of nomologicality based on what is recognized in practice to be the body of genuine scientific laws. When legitimate science does not meet our criteria, however, we must reevaluate the criteria. The final arbiter of what counts as a law is the extent to which the purported law lives up to the standards for nomologicality derived from good scientific practice, which is the source of the nonarbitrary standards we use to judge other laws. But when the standard is defined in such a way that most of what we antecedently recognize to be good science cannot pass it, we have no other choice than to change the standard.

What is the upshot of all this for the status of laws in evolutionary biology? It would seem to show that we would be foolish to try to draw a sharp line and motivate a claim that there are laws in chemistry and physics but not in evolutionary biology; for some of the problems that were alleged to count against evolutionary laws—such as the presence of exceptions, lack of necessary connection, and so on—also would count against laws almost anywhere else in natural science as well. This, I have argued, would be too high a price to pay for the preservation of our standards. But where does this leave us? We are left to show that the actual practice of evolutionary biology is continuous with good scientific practice in the rest of natural science. We need to show that we have good reason to believe that evolutionary biology can deal with the barriers to nomologicality in a way that is consistent with those techniques employed throughout the rest of natural science.[34]

First, it is important to come to grips with the implications of our thesis that science does not work as the idealized picture provided by the critics of evolutionary laws would have us think. As suggested above, that standard was derived from an outdated picture of scientific practice that, when compared to actual scientific practice, we have reason to doubt. Recall here the criticism leveled against Scriven's account of how complexity allegedly rendered social scientific laws impractical, detailed in Chapter 3. We saw that we may have been deluded, by examination of only a few salient examples, into thinking that science is only robust enough to handle a subject matter that is simple, repetitive, and set within a closed system. Of course, certain areas of physics *do* deal with simpler phenomena than we sometimes face in economics or sociology and also may deal with closed systems. There certainly are easily identifiable cases throughout natural science where we deal with phenomena that are simple and repeatable and that are embedded within a stable system of influences. But this should not lead us to overlook those cases in which science has also conquered complexity, openness, and uniqueness.

Certainly we cannot perform controlled experiments in astronomy or geology, nor can we deny an important "historetic" component to such inquiry—and yet we have found laws there. Similarly, certain areas of meteorology or sub-atomic physics deal with systems that are equally as complex as those in social science or evolutionary biology, facing the full range of "practical" barriers generated by the complexity of the phenomena at high levels of description, and yet, even in those cases where laws are most difficult to formulate, we do not give up on the nomological ideal when structuring our explanations. Finally, the new field of "chaos" continues to give us new insight into how we may search for regularity in nature even in the face of a non-linear and complex subject matter.

It is often the case, however, that such instances have been obscured and have been thought of as "special cases" to the more paradigmatic enterprise of science. Indeed, the most salient examples of the success of scientific explanation are usually drawn from cases in which the phenomena are examined at a level simple enough that the laws discovered tap some intuitive understanding we may already have had about the phenomena themselves. The most often cited cases of the success of science—the prediction of a new planet, the time of an eclipse, or the movement of the tides—all deal with phenomena at a level at which we are already used to thinking about them and merely provides the missing link, properly embedded in a theory of course, which connects them. But the important point is that the theory seldom changes our idea of what the phenomena *are*. To a large extent the "natural kinds" that serve as the referents of the laws in these cases match the natural kinds we already use to think about the phenomena in question.[35] The theory may change, but our taxonomy does not.

To say that these instances—even though spectacular—are not *representative* of the corpus of science, is not to discount the ingenuity of those like Kepler and Newton, who discovered them. Indeed, Kuhn has emphasized the magnitude of the genius required to find even those laws that, once found, cause one to think, "I should have thought of that myself." My point here instead is that when we think of scientific laws, and the role that they play in explanation, we are usually drawn to the "big" cases of scientific achievement, which are often embedded in those fields in which the explanations offered link up directly with the phenomena at a level of description that we find familiar. That is, we are not usually dealing with "theoretical" entities, and the phenomena are usually described at a level at which they are simple enough, at least in a rough intuitive sense, so that we can understand the nature of the nomological connection without rebuilding our conceptual apparatus. The natural kinds in these cases, though they may be embedded within a theory that explains them, are not usually *perceptually* or *conceptually* derivative. That is, we usually depend on science in these instances to connect the variables we have antecedently sanctioned, and not necessarily to tell us what the important variables are that need to be connected. Sometimes, of course, this does happen. But according to Scriven's "commonsense" view of scientific methodology, we usually rely on science to explain the phenomena we are puzzled about by seeking a nomological explanation between the natural kinds at a level of description at which we are used to thinking about them.[36]

But this is a misleading picture of how science works and gives rise to false expectations about the role that laws would have to play in the explanation of scientific phenomena. Indeed it tempts us to overlook the very foundation of the success of natural science in its search for laws—which is flexibility in developing new theories and descriptions of familiar phenomena—and instead to attribute that success to features (like simplicity) that merely *facilitate* the search for credible theories. It persuades us to underestimate the extent to which science can deal *precisely* with those cases in which we *cannot* find simple and straightforward relationships between an antecedently given set of variables, but rather require that the scientist reinterpret the phenomena in order to tell us what they are. We are thus encouraged by this view both to underestimate science and to expect too much of it. It is important, however, to realize that science has a role not only in those cases in which we are dealing with simple, repeatable, "human sized" phenomena. Although these cases may be the most salient, they are not what science is most basically about.

Mary Williams, in a brilliant article entitled "Similarities and Differences Between Evolutionary Theory and the Theories of Physics,"[37] has pointed out that we are often misled into thinking that we cannot have laws—and that science will not be able to succeed—in those cases in which we are dealing with phenomena unlike those studied by "big" physics. She points out that there indeed *are* laws underlying the relationships between phenomena expressed at a level of description at which complexity, for instance, inhibits our formulation of them (in physics and elsewhere). However, we just do not realize this in most cases because the nomological relationship is obscured by the "size" of the theories used to examine them. So we are led into the false belief that practical barriers generated by the subject matter, for instance, prevent the formulation of laws. But what does she mean by the "size" of a theory? The notion is a subtle one.

Williams uses the notion of "human-sized" and "non-human-sized" theories to make the point that there are some theories in science that deal with the phenomena at a level of description at which we are not used to thinking of them. This is meant to be a point about the nature of our perception (or conception) of the phenomena and strives to give us insight into the intuitions that we may make about scientific phenomena. In short, her point is this: There are some scientific theories that deal with phenomena at a level of description at which we are used to thinking about them and where we find it easy to understand the nature of the variables being discussed. The "natural kinds" we encounter perceptually are matched up with those used by the scientific theory in such cases. However, Williams notes, there are also other cases in which we are unable to identify the referents of any purported laws (i.e., the primitive terms) because they are so heavily embedded within a theory that defines the very nature of the phenomena itself. An example of the former might be the planets moving around the sun or balls rolling down an inclined plane.[38] An example of the latter might be "charm" or "color" in quantum theory, or even "species" in evolutionary biology. Moreover, it is important to realize that, as Williams points out, "[such a distinction is] clearly not independent of background conditions and theories."[39] The planetary model of the atom, for instance, though not an object of direct perception, is nevertheless "human-sized" since it is intuitively familiar to us *conceptually*, and thus may not obscure the nomological referents. That is, whether a theory is "human-sized" does not have to do with the actual physical size of the referents, nor even with their perceptual status, but instead with the extent to which we find them intuitively familiar enough to conceive of them without the aid of a scientific theory. Williams defines this notion as follows: "I will hereinafter refer to phenomena which our ordinary intuition regards as individuals or individual events as 'human-sized'; their physical size may differ by many orders of magnitude, but if the untrained intuition sees them as a whole, in a single gestalt, their size, psychologically, is 'human-sized.'"[40] Thus, Williams has attempted to draw a distinction between different kinds of scientific theories.[41]

But what use is this distinction? Williams uses it to explain why it is that in some cases we may fail to recognize an underlying nomological relationship even if there are no fundamental—or even practically insuperable—barriers to their discovery. The reason is that we often mistakenly assume that there is no role for nomological explanation in those cases in which the entities or processes to be explained do not deal with phenomena that are "human-sized." Why? Precisely because we have the wrong picture of science. We have been led to suppose that we can only have laws that connect those referents we are used to dealing with, and mistakenly suppose that there is no nomological relationship that could be legitimately explanatory outside of this. If the nomological referents are not "human-sized," she argues, we often jump to the conclusion that they are beyond our ability to comprehend—that barriers like complexity and openness would render their discovery either impossible or impractical. Indeed, such is the case, she argues, in evolutionary biology.[42]

Of course this criticism is precisely in concert with the one we offered in Chapter 3 against Scriven's view that derivative complexity prevents social scientific laws on the grounds of the impracticality of their formulation, at a level of description at which we would find a law to be explanatory. Recall here Scriven's view that we sometimes do legitimately seek explanation at a level at which the phenomena are complex. And at this level complexity would seem to forbid our formulation of *nomological* explanations. In Williams' terminology, Scriven is saying that we cannot have nomological explanations connecting "non-human-sized" natural kinds.[43] But why not?

In our earlier criticism of Scriven, we suggested that it is illicit to think that social science can only succeed in finding nomological relationships by connecting those referents antecedently deemed legitimate—a view we called "descriptivism." But we are now in a position to understand why this view is mistaken, and how it came about. First, it is based on a misunderstanding of natural science (caused by looking only at a narrow selection of salient examples) that seduces one into thinking natural science succeeds in its search for laws only because it connects "human-sized" phenomena. This erroneous view, in turn, leads directly to the "descriptivist" error—that laws in social science (or evolutionary biology) can be found only if they connect phenomena as described in terms that we find legitimate. Thus, when this task fails we are encouraged to believe that social science and evolutionary biology, in contrast to physical science, cannot produce laws. However, this is simply wrong precisely because the picture of how natural science works is also wrong. For with Williams, we now understand that science may also succeed in formulating laws by redefining what the entities are that characterize the underlying causal relationships in the phenomena we would like to have explained. So it turns out that we may be able to find laws even when the phenomena are complex at the level at which we are used to conceiving of them because it is *not* required that science proceed only by using these descriptive terms, at this level of complexity. Science does not work in the way that Scriven and other critics of laws have thought.

Indeed, as Williams points out, we often practice science precisely by *redescribing* the phenomena in terms that may *not* be familiar to us, or similar to those in which we frame our original proto-scientific questions about scientific phenomena. We often seek explanations by connecting newly defined "theoretical" entities—new natural kinds—that may be nothing more than redescriptions of the phenomena we observe in everyday life conceived of in a new way. Yet we do permit science to cut nature at different perceptual "joints" than we do in our everyday experience. We do so because we recognize that science *is* robust enough to deal with complex and unstable phenomena and indeed is capable of formulating law-like explanations about them, despite practical barriers generated by the subject matter as described at any given level of inquiry. As Williams explains, we use scientific theories to codify these redescriptions in an attempt to capture the underlying relationships that may elude us at the surface level. We allow our scientific investigation to evolve a new vocabulary and taxonomy, perhaps unfamiliar to common sense, in order to redefine perceptually familiar phenomena in novel ways and to codify these redescriptions in sometimes highly derivative theories *precisely because* we understand science to be about something different than that which the critics of laws have thought it to be. Indeed, redescription is not just tolerated, it is required for the growth of science.

Scriven is right, of course, that we must guard against truism and must not engage in wholesale redescription simply for the sake of discovering new correlations—this would defeat the very purpose of explanation. But as pointed out in Chapter 3, redescription does *not* inevitably lead to truism, and we may yet hope that we can find law-like connections even at a level at which the phenomena, on our commonsense understanding of them, appear to be complex.

In science the search for laws is primary. When faced with the dilemma of choosing between a descriptive vocabulary that seems sacred (but is not producing laws) and the challenge of producing a new categorization of nature that may yet reveal law-like connections, science has relentlessly (although sometimes over great periods of time) chosen the latter course. In natural science it has been recognized that redescription—even when it means giving up a favored level of inquiry—is valuable for its potential in revealing more basic insights into the regularity that stands behind surface diversity. In the history of chemistry, to pick up on an earlier example, we see that this is true. For instance, in the transition from theories about "phlogiston" to those concerning "oxygen" (in the explanation of the phenomenon of combustion) one quickly recognizes the role of redescription. If one had insisted, in the face of growing anomalies, that "phlogiston" adequately captured a true "natural kind" and gave up on law-like explanation, it is easy to see the poverty of the explanations that might have resulted. The "descriptivists" are wrong to suppose that explanation can only be given at a single level of description, and given only a single categorization of nature. The correlation between our scientific explanations and our commonsense questions must not be thought to require identity between the level of our questions and explanations.[44]

Indeed, we have no real reason to expect that there will be laws at all given any particular mode of description. Why should we? The job of science is not necessarily to find law-like relationships between familiar referents—it is often to redefine the phenomena in such a way that we come up with new referents all together, and thus may arrive at a law-like connection that gives us new insight into what the phenomena most basically *are*. Thus, the task of nomological explanation is framed by trying to link our theory-based understanding of the phenomena as redescribed in the perhaps highly derivative vocabulary of science to the more commonsense view of what the phenomena are.

To think otherwise is to have an unnecessarily impoverished view of scientific explanation; for we use theory to redefine our understanding of what we take to be the natural kinds at stake, and then to discover the relationship between them. We aim to show how the observations of common sense are an implication of, and thus can be explained by, underlying nomological regularities. The development of new theories, therefore, is crucial for the success of science.

In some cases, like the orbit of the planets, the perceptual shift required to bring our commonsense understanding in line with the underlying scientific theory may seem slight. In others, however, as Williams has noted, the shift may be so radical as to obscure the very nature or possibility of laws themselves. Thus, through redescription, the evolution of a new vocabulary (employing perhaps novel natural kinds), and the role of theory in defining the phenomena itself, we may hope to discover laws even where a seemingly "intractable" subject matter has obscured them. Of course, even with these tools we cannot hope to find laws in *all* cases—at least not right away. The nature of the subject matter sometimes guarantees that complexity or openness will obscure an underlying nomological relationship. My point here has been that even if this process must in some cases be slow and imperfect, our tools in the face of complexity and openness are not quite so blunt as Scriven, Fay, and the other critics of laws have supposed. The subject matter in some individual instances may compel us to proceed slowly, but it should not lead us to abandon the nomological ideal as a valuable source of scientific understanding.

Thus, we see that upon a more sophisticated understanding of the practice of science, we may yet hope to find laws in evolutionary biology. For once we have abandoned the spurious criteria, which were based on an overly idealized picture of scientific practice, we can see that many of the results of evolutionary biology fit well within the boundaries of nomological scientific inquiry and are continuous with the standards followed in other scientific investigation. Indeed, Williams herself has done outstanding work in demonstrating this by dispelling the myths that have surrounded the debate about the status of laws in evolutionary biology. A large portion of her work has been to show that the theory of evolution by natural selection is axiomatizable and indeed yields certain qualified predictions.[45] She has vindicated both the possibility and the practicality of laws in evolutionary biology. Moreover, she has shown that this success has been achieved through redescription.

One might take the debate about the proper definition of the terms "species," "race," and "clan" in evolutionary biology as evidence for precisely this type of concern with finding the best level of description at which to capture the regularities behind the process of natural selection. Williams has pointed out that in order to find a law, one must first correctly identify the "primitive terms" in which the law is to be stated and that—absent such precise definition—we will find no laws. The central question in the "species are individuals" debate in evolutionary biology, for instance, is what level of description of the phenomena affords law-like explanation. If, as had been thought, evolutionary laws (or predictions) would have to be given in terms of individual organisms, law-like explanations would continue to elude us. But it has been forcefully argued by Williams and others that if we are prepared to redefine our referents and think of "species" as themselves individuals, laws begin to crop up.[46]

In her identification and defense of laws in evolutionary biology, Williams has argued that even if laws are available they must be expressed in terms of the proper referents and suitably embedded in the correct theory, before we can recognize a law and deem it to be explanatory. Unwillingness to redefine our concepts, however, will surely prove to be a barrier to the discovery of laws. Thus, the search for the best "primitive terms," through the process of redescription and theory development, is central to the search for laws in evolutionary biology.

Thus, we may now see that certain empirical regularities drawn from the process of evolution by natural selection—such as Dollo's Law—that are firmly embedded within a scientific theory, are well confirmed, and are consistent with other scientific results about the process of natural selection, can be defended as law-like. Moreover, Dollo's claim about irreversibility seems to be a consequence of larger regularities at work in the process of evolution and is supported by further results derived from microbiology and the underlying genetic basis for evolution by natural selection. In short, Dollo's Law seems to fulfill the standards required for nomologicality drawn from a more realistic picture of scientific practice.

Thus, we now have a counterexample to the thesis that there cannot be laws in evolutionary biology because of the barriers provided by its subject matter. And based on the new criteria outlined above, we may also realize that if Dollo's Law can pass, so too may the regularities cited by Cope, Williston, Bergmann, and Allen. Of course, it is still a matter of individual empirical judgement about each case, based on its own merits, whether it is a legitimate law of evolutionary biology. If no rigid demarcation could be drawn using the old criteria, we would be foolish to try to do so with our new standards. But what I hope to have shown is that we have no reason to suppose, outside of those standards derived from the actual practice of science itself, that *no* regularity in evolutionary biology could qualify for nomological status (even though certainly not all of them will succeed). To have shown that it is a matter of individual empirical judgement, on a case by case basis, and that one cannot sweep away as spurious *all* purported laws in evolutionary biology as impractical, is certainly progress towards a more sophisticated understanding of nomologicality. I conclude that the standards by which we must judge the nomological status of purported laws in evolutionary biology are continuous with those used throughout the rest of science.

But what may we learn from this about the status of laws in social science? Plenty, for many of the claims against laws in the social sciences, we shall see, are based on an equally idealized view of scientific practice as those which purported to count against laws in evolutionary biology. I have shown in this section that there can be laws in evolutionary biology, and I have produced a counterexample to the thesis that there could not be. Through this, we have seen the failure of the claim that complexity and openness provide barriers which render the search for laws impractical, and have attempted to develop more realistic standards for judging nomologicality. In the next section, I will examine what may be learned from this for the debate about the status of laws in social science.

Lessons for the Social Sciences

In this section I will show that there is an analogy between the situation just examined in evolutionary biology and that of social science—for in both cases the rejection of the claim to nomologicality (made by appeals to complexity and openness) was rooted in adherence to an overly idealized view of the role of laws in natural science. To see that this is the case in the philosophy of social science, recall here the views of such critics of laws as Scriven, Fay, Taylor, and Hayek about such topics as the problems that would be faced in natural science if it were to examine its phenomena at a level of description at which practical barriers were present: Hayek writes that "in … the physical sciences … it will in principle always be possible to specify … predictions to any degree desired."[47] Taylor explains that this is because "the data of natural science admit of measurement to virtually any degree of exactitude.[48] And although Scriven correctly realizes that "people think of physics in a monolithic way if they are outside it,"[49] he goes on to speculate that, "One might say that the essence of the success of the natural sciences is the possibility of finding simple laws referring to ideal cases that are or can be realized in empirical cases to an indefinitely high degree of approximation."[50] Fay reveals little more insight into the nature of laws in the explanation of natural scientific phenomena when he writes:

> I hope to demonstrate that there is a good reason to believe that the laws which underlie [social science] will not be forthcoming at the level of discourse that social scientists use to describe and explain actions. … I want to show that the generalizations they employ possess features which make them … incapable of being *indefinitely refined.*[51]

As if indefinite refinement were somehow a precondition for nomologicality and could be realized in natural science either!

Surely such views reflect a naive understanding of the constraints facing the formulation of laws in a good deal of natural science and thus lead critics to overestimate the difficulties facing social scientific laws when they face these same barriers. Certainly physics *cannot* refine the phenomena to any degree desired—it faces the practical barriers of complexity and openness at high levels of description just as surely as does any theory in evolutionary biology or social science.[52] But the critics of social scientific laws cited above have been lulled into thinking that the level of description chosen does not hinder our ability to find natural scientific laws (thus requiring no use of redescriptions), probably because they are unfamiliar with the interesting scientific results derived from the search for laws outside of the more salient picture of physics painted by Ptolemy, Kepler, and Newton.

Consequently, when we *do* find in social science that at certain levels of description the practical barriers seem formidable, we are too quick to think that this is somehow distinct from the situation we face in natural science, and that we must give up on the search for laws. But certainly, this is a naive picture of physics, subscribed to by those who are so certain that we cannot have laws in social science that they have not realized that the very same criteria they use to critique laws in social science are also present and can be dealt with throughout the rest of science.

Indeed, those who tend to criticize the possibility or practicality of laws in social science, strangely enough, seem to accept a quite outdated analysis of laws in the natural sciences, which the last three decades of research in the philosophy of science has led us to doubt. But certainly, to insist on these standards would serve no useful explanatory purpose. Fortunately, we do not need to meet such criteria to show that we can formulate laws in the face of such practical barriers. We do not need to show that social science deals with a subject matter that is simple or closed in order to vindicate the legitimacy of our search for laws to explain human behavior. All that we need to show is that we have good reason to expect that social science will be able to deal with the barriers of complexity and openness in a scientific fashion—that the tools available to it are continuous with those employed throughout the rest of science and that there is no in principle reason to think that we cannot handle these difficulties as well as they are handled in natural science.[53]

By examining those barriers faced in the search for laws in evolutionary biology, as well as the tools of redescription and the development of new natural kinds and theories, I have laid the groundwork for a methodological analogy between natural and social science. For the alleged barriers to laws in evolutionary biology were precisely the same as those that purport to defeat the search for laws in social science. By finding Dollo's Law to be a counterexample to the thesis that complexity and openness, of the magnitude faced in social science, render the search for laws impractical, we may now be more confident that despite such barriers, it is open to social science to use some of the same techniques—such as redescription—in an attempt to overcome them. We have increased the credibility of the nomological ideal in social science by way of analogy with evolutionary biology.

It is now important, however, to provide reason for thinking that something like redescription can be similarly useful in the search for laws in actual social science. Below, I will outline some examples that may move us towards a demonstration of this. It is important to note at the outset, however, that I do this not because I think that the examples provided represent full-fledged laws of social science, or by themselves vindicate the thesis that I have been defending throughout this book. Rather, I offer them in order to give the reader purchase on what I mean by redescription. I hope to clarify and illuminate the concept of redescription, and its potential role in social scientific explanation, by providing examples that present *candidates* for social scientific laws.

Of course, there are those who have objected that redescription would not be legitimate in the social sciences. They have argued that any redescription would just be to change the subject matter of social science, given the fact that certain descriptive terms in our social vocabulary just seem to be constituitive of the subject matter of social science. Indeed, some have gone so far as to claim that unless we are aiming at explanations that can be given in terms of a privileged social vocabulary, we are just not doing "social science."

This argument is often made in defense of the idea that in social science we are concerned solely with phenomena under intentional descriptions and that at this level of interest, we are just going to be talking about things in terms of the "beliefs" and "desires" of the agent. Insofar as we could redescribe such phenomena in alien terms, and perhaps come up with regularities based on new categorizations, we would not find them to be explanatory concerning what we desire to know about our social behavior. However, if we resolve to stick to our original vocabulary, it has been found, there appear to be no law-like regularities that are expressible in these terms. The literature in social science is full of inconsistencies in the regularity of human beliefs and desires, as they relate to action, in a way that would seem to undercut the regularity needed to establish laws.

I nevertheless propose to defend a role for redescription in the search for social scientific laws. I will examine some particular cases from legitimate social scientific inquiry that seem to bear out the use of redescription as well as the search for laws. That is, I will look at examples where we seem to be doing good social science—where, by the above definition, we are concerned with overtly intentional behavior—and yet only upon redescription of talk about "beliefs" and "desires" do we begin to be able to explain the regularities manifested in our social behavior.

Moreover, it is also important to realize that in the actual practice of social science, we are often interested in going beyond what is "intentional" in order to uncover the causal genesis of some of our beliefs and desires and to frame the external circumstances that provide their context. We are not *only* interested, as social scientists, in the way in which our ideas affect our action, but are also often interested in the way in which those ideas have been shaped by the external constraints that have led to their development. Explanations given only in terms of the intentions of the agent would seem to be terribly impoverished when compared to the actual domain of social scientific research and would only be moving at the periphery of the larger network of causal forces we know to be at work and that are required for a more complete explanation.

Some of the best illustrations of these points can be seen in the literature on "cognitive dissonance," drawn from social psychology. "Cognitive dissonance" is the concept that in our cognitive processes we strive for harmony, as we try to make sense of the world. Thus, when we encounter pieces of information that are "dissonant," we attempt to reduce the cognitive tension this produces by trying to bring the beliefs into harmony, usually by altering one of them. For instance, suppose I am buying a car and have a choice between two different models. Model A has a sun roof and a radio, and Model B has neither. These are the only differences in the two vehicles. I choose Model A. Now suppose that the sun roof causes no end of problems for me—it leaks, lets in a cold draft, and so on. I may begin to think that I should have chosen Model B, only to find out that it is too late to make a trade. I thus face dissonance between my belief that I am a person who makes intelligent and well-informed decisions and the knowledge that I obviously chose a vehicle with flaws. Perhaps I will resolve this dissonance by overvaluing the radio that I also got with Model A. I may tell myself, "well, it's worth all of these other problems with the sun roof, because I like music so much." I begin to play the radio constantly, turning it way up every time it begins to rain, convincing myself that I made the right choice. The dissonance is thus resolved in the least threatening way; I retain my confidence in myself by believing that the flaws in Model A are more than outweighed by the radio.

The model of cognitive dissonance is a good one for our purpose because it deals with intentional and freely chosen action that is nonetheless highly regular. Moreover, it is often the case that dissonance reduction takes place at a level of awareness at which straightforward talk about the "beliefs" and "desires" of the agent are not going to go very far towards explaining the regularity behind the phenomena. Verbal reports from the subject about his or her beliefs and desires can certainly be given, but in the experimental literature on this subject one quickly sees that explanations that hope to cut to the deepest level of what is causing the behavior must be given in terms that may not make much sense to the actor, or which he or she may even be at pains to deny. Such circumstances, I will argue, present a role for redescription and suggest the value of nomological models in the explanation of human behavior.

Some of the best examples of the explanatory value of alternative levels of description can be found in the literature on subjects' lack of awareness of causal mental processes. In one study (Nisbett and Wilson, 1977), several experiments were conducted to assess subjects' awareness of the causal factors behind their behavior. I will report two of the experiments here.[54]

In one experiment, subjects were asked to memorize a list of word pairs, some of which had been previously found to elicit specific target responses with high frequency. For instance, the word pair "ocean-moon" was found to elicit the response "Tide" more frequently than in control groups when subjects were asked to name a detergent. After the experiment, subjects were asked to report on why they had chosen "Tide" as a detergent. Various responses were given, most of which included vivid and salient factors such as "I just saw the box," "it's the kind my mother uses," and so on. When specifically asked about the possible effect of the word pairs and told of the statistically significant increase in the response "Tide" given by other subjects after the word prime, two-thirds of the subjects denied their potential causal role in priming their own target response.

In another experiment, subjects were presented with four identical pair of nylon stockings under the guise of a consumer preference survey and were asked to identify which one was of the highest quality, and why they had chosen it. A marked "position effect" preference was noted for the right-most object, which was chosen by a margin of almost four to one. When asked about the reasons why they had chosen this one, subjects reported various factors influencing their decision but never mentioned the position of the item in the array. When asked afterwards whether this could have affected their preference, subjects uniformly denied it and in some cases became hostile.

These experiments were taken to indicate a lack of awareness by subjects of some of the important causal factors influencing their behavior and their nonrepresentation in conscious cognitive processes. When subjects were asked to report on why they had acted as they did, the "beliefs" and "desires" they reported had little to do with the actual choices they made. Much better explanations could be given in terms of the causal role of the word primes and position effect.

In a third study (Brock and Grant, 1963), we see one of the most elegant demonstrations of the explanatory value of redescriptions in the literature on cognitive dissonance.[55] In this study, subjects were hypnotized and, after post-hypnotic assurance that they would forget all suggestions given under hypnosis, they were awoken and fed. Half the subjects were given very spicy and thirst inducing crackers, and the other half were given bland and low thirst inducing crackers. The subjects were again placed under hypnosis. Subjects in the experimental group were told that upon awakening they would experience a feeling of water bloatedness, while control subjects were told that they would feel tired. Upon awakening the subjects were offered water. It was hypothesized that bloatedness juxtaposed to high thirst would create more dissonance than bloatedness juxtaposed to low thirst. Further, it was hypothesized that high thirst would lead to greater water consumption in the control group, but that in the experimental group these results would probably be reversed. These were in fact the results attained. The subjects who experienced greater dissonance consumed less water despite the fact that the suggestion of water bloatedness had been unconsciously implanted, and they were in fact very thirsty. Dissonance reduction thus took place at a level of awareness unavailable to subjects; indeed, in a survey they were found to be unable to account for their surprisingly low consumption of water based on actual causal factors.

This study provides an interesting example of the role of redescription in the explanation of human behavior. In the survey, subjects who reported their beliefs and desires said nothing about the dissonance between their feeling of water bloatedness and high thirst. Perhaps they reported that they "were not very thirsty" or that they "just didn't feel like drinking any water," but we can clearly see how inquiry at this level does not capture the genuinely causal role of the posthypnotic suggestion.[56] Thus, in this case we are dealing with important causal factors that lie behind highly regular human behavior, about which subjects have limited access and thus cannot include in their verbal report. Clearly, the explanation given by the experimenters is not in the form of a fully developed law; yet it is a good candidate for nomological explanation in that it reveals the regularity in the causal factors behind the behavior as well as their inaccessibility to other levels of inquiry.

But does it demonstrate a role for redescription? I think it clearly does. Causal explanation of the low consumption of water by the very thirsty subjects is achieved only by redescribing their belief that they were "not very thirsty" with something more like, "subjects experienced cognitive dissonance between the posthypnotic suggestion that they were bloated juxtaposed to high thirst, resolved by not wanting to drink much water." Of course, we are still talking here about the mental states of the agents and even at some level about what they believed and desired—we are still dealing with freely chosen and intentional behavior. Yet it now seems clear that if one wants a better explanation of the regularity manifested in their behavior, one will have to redescribe the beliefs and desires of the subjects in terms they may not understand or have access to. Straightforward talk about the beliefs and desires of the subjects will not do—we must redescribe the behavior in terms of the theoretical model of cognitive dissonance in order to move towards a better causal explanation. Such redescription, I argue, presents us with a role for nomological explanation.[57]

Moreover, as stated earlier, it is also important to realize that in the actual practice of social science, we are often interested in going beyond explanations that are given only in terms of "intentions," even when we are dealing with intentional human action. For instance, suppose that a sociologist is interested in the phenomenon of juvenile delinquency.[58] It would certainly behoove him or her to talk with the juvenile delinquents in order to find out what they believe and desire and even to reinterpret their statements in terms that make clear the "considered" intentions behind their actions.[59] But clearly, even this would be incomplete, for one is also interested in the external circumstances that led them to have the intentions they did. To insist that, as social scientists, we are only interested in inquiry concerning intentional action—understood as the beliefs and desires of the agent—is to miss much that would be important in explaining the phenomenon of juvenile delinquency. A more complete account would include an examination of their home life, whether they are in school, whether they tended to come from single parent families, or even what they eat. Absent this, one will probably fail to come up with an adequate explanation in any terms. In short, to claim that in social science we are only interested in "intentional" human behavior and seek explanation only in terms of those intentions, is to miss the important contribution of many valuable perspectives within legitimate social scientific inquiry, such as those of psychohistory, Marxism, William McNeill's attempt to explain world history through the passage of disease in *Plagues and Peoples*, sociobiology, and countless others. Such concern with "external" circumstances, I would argue, suggest a potential role for laws.

My point here is that the intentional perspective on human events is certainly important, but it does not alone provide a complete picture of human action, nor is it exhaustive of the subject matter of good social science. It is just not adequate to say that we are "not doing social science" if we are inclined, at times, to try to redescribe human action in terms that may not make much sense to the agent in order to come up with better explanations. Redescription, therefore, can be useful throughout social science in just the same way that it has been helpful in the natural sciences. The revivifying effect it can have on social inquiry, as we try to explain events in new ways by developing new theories and alternative vocabularies, should not be discounted or underestimated a priori.

As I have said, the examples just elaborated are not meant to be complete accounts of social scientific laws, nor do I intend to say that they can single-handedly exonerate the nomological model of explanation in social science. Instead, I have offered them in order to suggest the potential role that redescriptions may have in advancing our explanatory accounts of human action, and in developing new theories, by showing that there is already some good social science making use of it. Surely, one might point out here that it would be ideal to have in hand some already complete and uncontroversial examples of social scientific laws. But it is illegitimate to require that this be necessary in order to defend the status of social scientific laws. Indeed, my point in this chapter has been to show that we are laboring under the wrong conception of nomologicality and the conditions under which the search for laws could thrive in social science. We have been held back in the development of the theoretical framework, categorizations, and vocabulary that would be necessary in order to produce laws. In this book, I aim to clear the path of spurious reasons for thinking that we cannot have laws in social science so that the important empirical work necessary to find them can move forward. But it is too much to expect such an enterprise to anticipate the future development of social science, or itself to produce laws, when my point has been to vindicate the search for the better theories and categorizations that would be necessary to produce laws.

Of course, there have been recent instances of pathbreaking work in the philosophy of social science, which have attempted to identify and defend good candidates for nomologicality drawn from current social scientific research.[60] Surely, it would be too strong to argue that in over two hundred years of formal social science, if laws are both possible and practical, we have yet to stumble upon one genuine social scientific law. My point, however, is that such cases will continue to be isolated and controversial—no matter how clever—until we wholeheartedly embrace the nomological ideal in social science on a par with the natural sciences, and, most importantly, begin the task of redescription and the development of new categorizations, which will lead us to the kind of theories that are needed to produce and test social scientific laws.

Indeed, if Mary Williams is right, we just won't be able to *recognize* any straightforward laws in social science—even where they exist—until we have better theories in place and are more flexible about the value of redescription. Even where laws (and redescriptions) are possible, Williams points out, we can be handicapped by employment of the wrong natural kinds, or by refusal to consider alternative explanatory models or theories; descriptivism will continue to take its toll. By analogy with the discovery of laws in evolutionary biology, we should understand that the discovery of laws (absent the correct theories and the willingness to look for them) is no easy affair. But it is not impossible either.

In the end, of course, it is an empirical question whether social science will be able to handle the barriers of complexity and openness in the same way, and as successfully, as they have been handled in the natural sciences. But my point here has only been the modest one that in light of the analogy with evolutionary biology, we have good reason to be optimistic about the prospect of finding laws in social science. We have at least, in evolutionary biology, a prescriptive model for what needs to be done in social science in order to discover laws: we must be willing to use redescription in order to find the "primitive terms" needed to express laws and must allow for the theory development required for them to be explanatory. Perhaps there is more continuity in the tasks facing natural and social science than one might have initially thought. And if one throws out the unrealistic picture of natural scientific practice that motivated the idealized set of requirements for the formulation of social scientific laws, we may begin to see certain similarities in the practical barriers facing natural and social science. Thus, methodological continuity in dealing with them would appear to be more reasonable.

On this subject, Mary Williams has written:

> I think the most important lesson to be learned is that our understanding of the structure of a science is likely to be seriously obscured by the failure to properly identify the referents of the laws (i.e., the relevant variables—or, in more formal language, the primitive terms). The extent to which this has obscured the structure of laws, predictions, and explanations, etc., in evolutionary theory for more than 100 years after the basic theory was understood (at an intuitive level) is astonishing. My feeling is that the same will be true in the social sciences (although the lesson learned from the experience with evolutionary theory should shorten the time needed to recognize the relevant variables). I suspect that it will not be possible to recognize them until social science has had its Darwin—I just don't think you can recognize such highly theoretical entities until the theory is available; Newtonian entities are visible in everyday experience, and can be recognized without a strong theory, but entities which are not literally visible are probably not recognizable until they are embedded in a theory.[61]

Although she is skeptical about the extent to which it will be recognized, Williams here concurs in the belief that there is an underlying continuity between the natural and social sciences. And even if it does not turn out to be the kind of continuity hoped for by the positivists, in their desire for a unified science (brought about by making the social sciences more rigorous through use of an objective language), it may yet be that this continuity has important methodological implications for the role that laws can play in the social sciences and perhaps even for our understanding of the role of laws in natural science as well.

For it now seems clear that perhaps even natural science does not work in accordance with the idealized criteria set out by the critics of social scientific laws. Indeed, philosophers like Nancy Cartwright have gone far towards showing that even physics, perhaps, does not work as we thought it did and have sought to redefine the way that we think about nomologicality. Cartwright, in her important book *How the Laws of Physics Lie*,[62] argues that the theoretical laws of physics are not likely to be true; we use them in explanation, of course, but this does *not* increase the likelihood that they are true. Indeed, she argues that to the extent that they are good explanations of the phenomena, they are likely to be false! Her underlying anti-realism motivates the claim that we must separate explanatory merit from evidence for truth. The laws of physics are not what we thought they were. And even if one does not accept her specific views about the nature of laws in physics, one may yet appreciate the importance of the "gestalt switch" she has performed on our understanding of laws. For in her own way, Cartwright has revealed a new way to establish continuity between natural and social science. For we may now legitimately attempt to establish continuity between natural and social scientific methodology not just by trying to make social science more rigorous—in search of the impossibly high standards set out by the logical positivists—but instead by showing that upon a more realistic picture of natural science, it is more like social science than we initially might have thought.[63] And yet despite this, we continue to recognize a legitimate role for law-like explanation in natural science.

Of course, one possible conclusion from this analysis could be to say that there just aren't laws anywhere in science, natural or social, because one just means by "laws" some very stringent entity. The idea here would be that after someone like Cartwright has "debunked" physics (although she would almost certainly disapprove of this interpretation of her work), we may now see that the standards of explanation in natural science are just as wanting as those in any other kind of explanation.[64] But it is fruitless, I claim, to argue endlessly over whether or not even science is "science"—whether even natural science can make good use of laws. For if this view is taken seriously, it would require a radical revision of our conception of scientific explanation. Of course, one could argue that such a radical revision is precisely what is needed, but there are legitimate fears that such an enterprise would turn into exactly the kind of Pyrrhic victory that we sought to avoid earlier.

And for the purpose of my argument in this book, even the possibility of such a radical revision would be allowable. All that I require is that if we undertake such a revision, we recognize the continuity between the methodological position of natural and social science with respect to laws and put them in the same boat.[65] Indeed, all that I need to show here is that *whatever* natural science does in its quest for explanation (even if we are not willing to call it a search for laws), there is good reason to believe that social science can do it too.[66]

I *do* believe that there are independent arguments that can adequately establish laws as sufficient for scientific explanation, and that natural science actually uses them.[67] However, it is beyond the scope of my present argument to offer them, and I will abstain from further consideration of this issue, being satisfied here to have shown that there is continuity in the subject matter and methodology of explanation in natural and social science, no matter how it is understood.

The lesson to be derived from this is not to despair about whether we can have laws even in natural science, but instead to find in the continuity between natural and social science renewed grounds for optimism about the possibility and practicality of finding laws in social science, despite the barriers of complexity and openness. Indeed, there are practical barriers to the achievement of laws brought about by such factors in the social sciences, just as in the natural sciences. But the extent to which these impinge on our abilities to find laws probably does *not*, contrary to earlier critical views, split neatly along disciplinary lines, nor does it suggest that we have no adequate tools with which to deal with them.

It is a matter of individual empirical judgement, on a case by case basis, to determine those instances in which the barriers have, so far, proven to be so great as to exclude laws, and to suggest that alternative modes of explanation should be pursued in the interim. But the extent to which these factors prove to be barriers at all is subject to constant erosion in the face of future scientific advancement. Thus, even if one may not hope to eliminate them entirely (as we have not in natural science), I hope to have shown that it would be rash to give up on the nomological *ideal* as a useful structure for the explanation of social scientific phenomena.

Thus, we have found reason to be optimistic about the future role of laws in the explanation of human behavior in light of (1) the failure of the conceptual arguments against laws to show that they are impossible or impractical, and (2) the strength of the analogy with the methodological situation faced in natural science. But have we, then, settled the case about the status of laws in social science, by showing that they are available? What about questions concerning their desirability?

In the next chapter, I will examine those arguments that have claimed that no such analogy between natural and social science is appropriate because we want to have something different explained *about* human behavior than we do about natural phenomena, which laws could not give us. Such arguments include yet further objections to the use of redescription and will therefore require closer inspection of their applicability to social science. Having just finished our consideration of the claim that social scientific laws are impossible or impractical, we will turn next to the claim that they are irrelevant.

Notes

1. David Hull, *Philosophy of Biological Science* (Englewood Cliffs, N.J.: Prentice-Hall, 1974), p. 76.

2. For instance, one alternative to law-like explanation is that of "narrative" explanation, explored by William Dray in his *Laws and Explanation in History* (Oxford: Oxford University Press, 1957).

3. For instance, complexity is cited as a barrier to laws in Michael Ruse, *The Philosophy of Biology* (London: Hutchinson University Library, 1973); Bernhard Rensch, *Biophilosophy*, C.A.M. Sym, trans. (New York: Columbia University Press, 1971); Alexander Rosenberg, *The Structure of Biological Science* (Cambridge: Cambridge University Press, 1985); and Eli Minkoff, *Evolutionary Biology* (Reading, Mass.: Addison-Wesley, 1983). Openness is mentioned in Hull, *Philosophy of Biological Science*, and Bernhard Rensch, *Biophilosophy*. It is interesting to note that both propo-

nents and opponents of laws in evolutionary biology tend to agree that these are the main barriers to laws. Further, note that these factors are the very same ones that were alleged to have prevented laws in social science, discussed in Chapter 1 of this book.

4. Some have argued that these tenets themselves qualify as laws of evolutionary biology, including Rensch, *Biophilosophy* and Mary Williams, "Deducing the Consequences of Evolution: A Mathematical Model," in *Journal of Theoretical Biology*, Vol. 29 (1970), pp. 343–385; but they seem more like fundamental axioms or principles that serve as the foundation for the theory itself. Still, whichever way the debate goes, there are yet better examples of laws in evolutionary biology than these.

5. Rensch, *Biophilosophy*, pp. 132–139.

6. Cf. Rensch, *Biophilosophy*. Rensch feels that the presence of any exceptions enjoins law-like status, and yet he waffles a bit about this later in the same work. Clearly, though, other writers, like Ernst Mayr, feel that the presence of any exceptions unequivocally reduces a purported "law" to a "rule." See Ernst Mayr, *The Growth of Biological Thought* (Cambridge: The Belknap Press of Harvard University Press, 1982), p. 37. For a counterbalance, however, one might want to look at Harold Kincaid, "Defending Laws in the Social Sciences," *Philosophy of the Social Sciences*, Vol. 20, No. 1 (March 1990), pp. 56–83, in which he argues that the use of *ceteris paribus* conditions in the social sciences (which are necessary because of the presence of certain exceptions and "tendencies") do not exclude nomologicality. Indeed, *ceteris paribus* conditions are used throughout physics. Kincaid argues vigorously that no firm line can be drawn between "tendencies" and "laws" merely on the basis of the presence of exceptions.

7. E.g., Scriven, Mayr, Gould, Smart, and Rensch.

8. Hull, *Biological Science*, p. 82; Ruse, *Philosophy of Biology*, p. 61; Stephen J. Gould, "Dollo on Dollo's Law: Irreversibility and the Status of Evolutionary Laws," *Journal of the History of Biology*, Vol. 3, No. 2 (Fall, 1970), pp. 189–212, *passim*.

9. Gould, "Dollo," pp. 207–208.

10. Ibid., p. 16.

11. Much of the exposition of Dollo's Law explored in the next few pages is based on Gould's presentation of these issues in his article.

12. Gould, "Dollo," p. 198.

13. Ibid., p. 198.

14. The quotation is from Dollo, cited in Gould, "Dollo," p. 199.

15. Gould, "Dollo," p. 190.

16. Ibid., p. 196.

17. Rosenberg issues a stinging reply to those like Mayr, who think that one can demonstrate the impossibility of laws in evolutionary biology while remaining committed to a causal picture of explanation in his book, *The Structure of Biological Science* (Cambridge: Cambridge University Press, 1985), pp. 124–125.

18. Gould, "Dollo," p. 208. Gould addresses the issue of falsifiability in a footnote, where he writes, "[Dollo's Law] is a testable statement only if 'good faith' is maintained in interpreting the qualifying term 'complex.' This term gives the statement an 'open texture' that allows an unscrupulous supporter to exclude any event from its domain by claiming that the event was not sufficiently complex. ... With a

reasonable limit upon the term 'complex,' Dollo's statement is testable; if 'complex' is used to exclude any possible counterinstance, the statement becomes unfalsifiable." Ibid., p. 197. Popper's account of falsifiability is explored in his *Conjectures and Refutations* (New York: Harper Torchbooks, 1965).

19. Gould, "Dollo," p. 208.

20. Ibid., p. 209.

21. Also, it should remind us that there is no such thing as an "essentially unique" subject matter. Phenomena are unique only "as described."

22. Gould has recently, in conversation, agreed that this is an accurate interpretation of his view. Personal communication, December 1, 1989.

23. Gould, "Dollo," p. 209. It is interesting to note that this claim sounds very close to Brian Fay's as well, detailed in Chapter 3.

24. Gould has recently characterized his argument in this way. See note 22 above.

25. Personal communication, December 1, 1989.

26. I intend this strategy to be modeled on the technique of "reflexivity," used both in Gödel's incompleteness theorem and Church's thesis on undecidability.

27. Of course, as we saw in Chapter 1, it is an ongoing controversy precisely what the adequate conditions for nomologicality are. What is at issue here is whether one could reasonably expect any purported laws in evolutionary biology to pass those criteria set out as necessary by the critics of evolutionary laws—e.g., not having any exceptions, being explanatory rather than descriptive, and capturing non-contingent regularities.

28. This point is often made by Harold Kincaid.

29. Cf. Thomas Kuhn, *The Structure of Scientific Revolutions* (Chicago: The University of Chicago Press, 1962).

30. This condition is often cited by Ernst Mayr, Stephen Gould, and, surprisingly (since he supports the existence of biological laws), Bernhard Rensch. The issue, however, is whether biology can deal with its exceptions in a scientific way.

31. Cf. note 28, above.

32. Indeed, at no point can we know with certainty when we have a true nomological relationship. Of course, when an empirical regularity is embedded within a theory, it should decrease the chance that it is *ad hoc*. And no matter how strong a correlation is, without a suitable theory we cannot honestly contend that we have explained it. But even the presence of a strong empirical correlation that is embedded within a theory cannot *guarantee* that we do not have another "Bode's Law." Strong empirical correlation and the presence of a theory seem necessary but not sufficient for nomologicality. And whether a nomological relationship is genuine often cannot be decided by comparison to rigid a priori criteria.

33. Perhaps one might think that the claim Gould is making here against laws in evolutionary biology is similar to the one that is sometimes made against the second law of thermodynamics. Namely, that it only shows why certain outcomes are *likely*, and not why they are *necessary*. But why think that one needs such necessity? Why can't high probability be seen as explanatory, or even as amounting to the foundation for a law-like explanation? Why set the standard for nomologicality so high as to require necessity? Thus, one might take comfort in the fact that the existence of laws in evolutionary biology may be no worse off than the situation in

thermodynamics or even chaos theory. It is not quite so uncontroversial as Gould might think that laws require necessity. Cf. Peter Railton, "A Deductive-Nomological Model of Probabilistic Explanation," *Philosophy of Science,* Vol. 45 (1978), pp. 206–226.

34. This strategy has been successfully employed by Harold Kincaid in his "Defending Laws in the Social Sciences." See note 6 above.

35. Now, of course the evolution of science may compel us to change some of our conceptions of nature. But my point is that this process, in simple cases of science, is often *accommodating* our intuitive conceptions, rather than forcing us to embrace totally new natural kinds. For an opposite point of view on this subject, see Kuhn's work on "incommensurability" in *The Structure of Scientific Revolutions,* where he argues that to change one's conception at all is to change the natural kind.

36. This misunderstanding of natural science (based on looking only at salient cases) is what leads to the mistaken view of the conditions governing nomologicality in social science. It is what leads directly to the "descriptivist's" error—that it is all right to think that laws are only found between those terms we antecedently understand. But this is not how science works. Science just sometimes does use redescription.

37. *PSA 1980,* Volume 2 (East Lansing, Mich.: Philosophy of Science Association, 1980), pp. 385–396.

38. Ibid., p. 389.

39. Ibid., p. 389–390.

40. Mary Williams, "Falsifiable Predictions of Evolutionary Theory," in *Philosophy of Science*, Vol. 40, pp. 518–537. See p. 533.

41. Williams points out, however, that she does not mean this to be a dichotomy; she believes that the distinction represents two different poles on a continuum. Williams, "Similarities," p. 390.

42. Williams herself deplores this tendency and has written several landmark articles in which she tries to uphold the nomological status of certain regularities in evolutionary biology. Two of the best are "Falsifiable Predictions of Evolutionary Theory," and "Deducing the Consequences of Evolution: A Mathematical Model." Citations in note 40 and 3 above, respectively.

43. There is perhaps an interesting relationship between Williams' distinction between "human-sized" and "non-human-sized" theories, and Scriven's distinction between "simple" and "complex" phenomena; are human-sized referents conceptually "simpler," and do those that we find conceptually "complex" end up being "non-human-sized"?

44. There must, however, be a legitimate theoretical linkage between our scientific explanations and the phenomena we were initially puzzled about, hopefully by showing that there is an underlying regularity that eluded us given our initial conceptualization.

45. See references cited in note 42 above.

46. Mary Williams, "Species Are Individuals: Theoretical Foundations for the Claim," *Philosophy of Science,* Vol. 52 (1985), pp. 578–590; and "Is Biology a Different Type of Science?" in Sumner, Slater, and Wilson, eds., *Pragmatism and Purpose: Essays Presented to Thomas A. Goudge* (Toronto: University of Toronto Press, 1981).

47. F. A. Hayek, "Theory of Complex Phenomena," in *Studies in Philosophy, Politics, and Economics* (Chicago: The University of Chicago Press, 1967).

48. Charles Taylor, "Interpretation and the Sciences of Man," *Review of Metaphysics*, Vol. 25, No. 1 (September 1971), p. 49.

49. Michael Scriven, "Views of Human Nature," in T. W. Wann, ed., *Behaviorism and Phenomenology: Contrasting Bases for Modern Psychology* (Chicago: The University of Chicago Press, 1964), p. 177.

50. Michael Scriven, "A Possible Distinction Between Traditional Scientific Disciplines and the Study of Human Behavior," in *Minnesota Studies in the Philosophy of Science*, Vol. 1 (Minneapolis: University of Minnesota Press, 1956), p. 338.

51. Brian Fay, "General Laws and Explaining Human Behavior," in Sabia and Wallulis, eds., *Changing Social Science* (Albany, NY: SUNY Press, 1983), p. 115. Emphasis added.

52. Of course, the issue is *at what level* we *want* explanation, and whether there are barriers there. Yet the misunderstanding of natural science is still instructive. Surely there are cases where we have laws in physics at low levels of description. But the critics cited above seem to think that the level of description in physics just does not matter.

53. This has been forcefully argued by Kincaid in his "Defending Laws in the Social Sciences."

54. R. Nisbett and T. Wilson, "Telling More Than We Can Know: Verbal Reports on Mental Processes," *Psychological Review,* Vol. 84 (1977), pp. 231–259.

55. T. Brock and L. Grant, "Dissonance, Awareness, and Motivation," *Journal of Abnormal and Social Psychology,* Vol. 67, No. 1 (1963), pp. 53–60. Also see T. Brock, "Dissonance Without Awareness," in R. Abelson, ed., *Theories of Cognitive Consistency: A Sourcebook* (Chicago: Rand McNally, 1968), pp. 408–416.

56. This is not to deny the potentially causal role of thought. But the interesting question in these experiments is what caused the subjects to have the thoughts that they did. That is, if one is looking for a scientific explanation of the regularity in their behavior, one cannot just be concerned with the level at which one is talking about the beliefs and desires of the subject. One must also wonder how they were formulated. Some of the experiments, indeed, show that the beliefs and desires of the subject were manipulated by the experimental design. So, for a full explanation of their behavior, one must get behind their thoughts so that we may try to understand what caused them.

Similarly, one can say that even though we are dealing in these instances with intentional human actions, this does not mean that we must only be concerned with them under intentional descriptions. Why did the subject have the intentions that he or she did? What caused him or her to feel as he or she did? These are important factors in understanding the behavior and present a role for law-like explanation.

57. The question may now legitimately arise, however, of just how radical our revision of social scientific inquiry must be in order to produce these laws. At times in this book it may seem as if one must abandon all reference to our current theoretical vocabulary in order to find social scientific laws. This is not the case. I take the import of the examples I have just explored to be not that we must immediately

replace all talk of "belief" and "desire," but that we indeed must be willing to change our conceptions about them in the search for better explanations of human behavior. This may ultimately lead us to drop certain descriptive terms that cease to be useful, but I do not pretend to know in advance which ones these will be. All I have tried to show here is that if we do *not* allow for the evolution of our theories and descriptive terms, we may well fail to discover not only laws, but also explanations that are worthwhile on any other terms as well. An integral part of scientific explanation is to push the limits of the descriptive terms and theories that we currently employ. This process, however, must be gradual and continuous and would not sanction the immediate replacement of all of our current vocabulary. Thus, even within the vocabulary of "belief" and "desire"—as the examples explored here have shown—there is much work that can be done to further the search for social scientific laws.

58. I owe this example to Peter Railton.

59. That is, one wouldn't necessarily need to take the verbal reports at face value in order still to be concerned with intentional explanations.

60. Harold Kincaid, "Confirmation, Complexity, and Social Laws," *PSA 1988*, Vol. 2 (East Lansing, Mich.: Philosophy of Science Association, 1988), pp. 299–307.

61. Mary Williams, personal communication, October 17, 1989.

62. Nancy Cartwright, *How the Laws of Physics Lie* (Oxford: Oxford University Press, 1983).

63. Of course, there is still going to be "bad" social science, just as there is bad natural science, but the point is that it's not *all* bad. It is important to realize that the new criterion of comparing actual social scientific practice to the standards set by the practice of natural science does not allow *all* current social scientific research to be deemed "scientific." The quest is not to show that *all* social science is "scientific," but to show that *not all* of it is *un*scientific.

64. Cf. Paul Feyerabend, *Against Method* (London: Verso, 1978).

65. Even if it leaks.

66. I owe this point to Harold Kincaid.

67. A good review of these arguments is provided in Lee Brown's dissertation, "The Sufficiency of Nomological Subsumption for the Explanation of Events" (Ph.D. dissertation, The University of Michigan, 1986).

5

A Question of Relevance

In thus penetrating to the inside of events and detecting the thought which they express, the historian is doing something which the scientist need not and cannot do. ... The historian need not and cannot (without ceasing to be an historian) emulate the scientist in searching for the causes or laws of events. ... For history, the object to be discovered is not the mere event, but the thought expressed in it.

—R. G. Collingwood

In Chapters 2 and 3, we examined some of the problems facing the attempt to formulate laws in the social sciences, generated by claims about the alleged intractability of the subject matter of social science, which purported to show that laws were either impossible or impractical. In Chapter 4, we explored an analogy between the methods of natural and social science, based on the thesis that there is underlying continuity between some of the practical problems facing the formulation of laws in both disciplines. Through this, I have provided grounds for optimism about the prospects for social scientific laws, despite problems like complexity and openness.

But is the analogy close enough to warrant this conclusion? Are the cases examined "relevantly similar" in their consideration of the barriers provided by the subject matter of each discipline? Aren't there special problems provided by the study of social systems that have no echo in natural systems, and which would, even at this late juncture, stand in the way of our formulation of social scientific laws? Would we even find laws relevant to the phenomena we are concerned with having explained in social inquiry?

It is now time to change gears a little. So far in this book we have been considering arguments that allege to show the unavailability of laws to the explanation of human behavior, given certain features of its subject matter. But there is another dimension to the debate that we have yet to consider—whether laws are *relevant* to what we want explained *about* human behavior. Even after one has shown (as I have in Chapters 2–4) that complexity and openness do not demonstrate social scientific laws to be impossible or impractical (nor that the problems they generate are unique to social science), there are several lingering objections to the use of nomological explanation in the social sciences. Even if available, would laws be desirable? And if not desirable, what should we pursue instead?

Some have claimed that no analogy works between the natural and social sciences, given the fact that in social science we want to have something different explained *about* human action than we do about natural phenomena, due to basic differences in how we conceive of the subject matter. This claim is based on the idea that in social science we are dealing with essentially meaningful behavior, which is reflective of the thoughts and intentions of the agent who is expressing them. Thus, it is argued that in doing social science, we desire an explanatory account that is sensitive to the phenomena as conceived at this level of interest, and that we should give up on the search for laws. Others, however, have concluded from this not that laws are irrelevant, but merely that they are not forthcoming at the level of engagement at which we conduct social science and ought to be pursued at other levels of inquiry. Despite their disagreement on the issue of relevance, however, both sides agree on one thing—that it is fruitless to pursue law-like explanation within the domain of social science.

In the face of this, however, different "prescriptions" have been offered for what ought to be done in social scientific inquiry. And such views split precisely on the question of relevance. Thus, it is here appropriate to consider a new distinction, which cuts across the availability versus unavailability one we have already considered. Namely, in considering normative theories about how one ought to conduct the study of human behavior, we must now examine the distinction between those views that uphold the relevance of the nomological explanation of human action versus those that contend such laws are irrelevant. When set alongside earlier commitments regarding the availability of laws, we may formulate a two-by-two matrix of possible positions, which will frame the debate in the next two chapters:

	Laws relevant to the explanation of human behavior	Laws *irrelevant* to the explanation of human behavior
Laws possibly available to social scientific inquiry	Naturalism	Interpretivism (II)
Laws *not* available to social scientific inquiry	Physicalism	Interpretivism (I)

In brief, in this chapter we will consider the alternative views that: (A) laws are irrelevant to the explanation of human behavior, whether they are available or not, and (B) laws are relevant to the explanation of human action but are just not available at the level of "social scientific" inquiry. Such views, it is important to note, are implicitly prescriptive—they offer alternative ideas about what ought to be done in social science, based on their differing commitments concerning the availability and relevance of laws to social scientific explanation. Since we have already examined the question of availability in previous chapters, we will now explore these positions by considering their alternative commitments about the *relevance* of laws to the explanation of human behavior.

The Argument from Irrelevance

Beginning with the argument from irrelevance, we face squarely what is perhaps the most far-reaching (and, I will argue, the most misguided) criticism of the status of nomological explanation in the social sciences.[1] The claim that laws would be *irrelevant* to our explanatory task in the social sciences seems distinct from any other so far examined in this book. For the argument here does *not* seem to be based on the idea that the subject matter provides barriers preventing us from *discovering* laws. Instead, the point is that even if we could find laws, they might still fail to be explanatory because they would not capture what we are most basically interested in knowing about human affairs. I hope to show, however, that this claim is only superficially distinct from those already examined and is indeed deeply rooted in a commitment to "descriptivism," which we have already evaluated in Chapter 3.

Initially, it is interesting to note that at base the argument from irrelevance is still one about the *subject matter* of social science.[2] Despite the fact that we are now talking about whether laws could capture what we want explained about human behavior, and not whether it is possible to have them, the claim is still fundamentally rooted in views about the proper subject matter of social science. Indeed, we are still talking about things like the relationship between human thought and action, and other factors allegedly unique to the subject matter of social science. In this, the argument from irrelevance has kinship with those views already examined in this book, concerning the alleged intractability of the subject matter of social science.

Instead of now holding that such factors render social scientific laws impossible or impractical, however, the point is that in light of what we take the subject matter of social science to be, social scientific laws are *irrelevant* to what we desire to have explained about it. Although still a claim about the subject matter of social science, the theme now argued for is that because of what human action is, the search for laws is not an appropriate mode of investigation.

Of course, such a claim is fundamentally rooted in how we have chosen to define our subject matter. Namely, as we have seen, some have taken the subject matter of social science to be human action *as described* by a particularly narrow vocabulary, using only those "natural kinds" that are a priori sanctioned by our intuitions.[3] And not surprisingly, given such parameters they have failed to find any laws connecting the theoretical terms as defined at this level, and so have concluded that laws are explanatorily irrelevant.

The fundamental argument behind such a view is what I have called "descriptivism."[4] It is the view that there is only one proper level of description of human phenomena that can count as a legitimate focus for our social scientific inquiry. It is founded on a belief that the phenomena of human behavior, as captured by certain descriptive terms, are *constitutive* of the subject matter of social science, and that any attempt at redescription into other categorizations is just to change the subject matter, so that one is no longer doing "social science." For instance, one might claim that the proper subject matter of social science is human thoughts, intentions, and self-understandings, as captured by vocabulary concerning our "beliefs" and "desires."[5] Furthermore, it is often maintained that at this level of description, we are only interested in knowing about such things as the "meaning" and "purpose" of human actions, which laws could not explain. Thus, even if we could find laws that related the terms as described at this level, it is argued, they would not do justice to the nature of our interests.

This serves then as the foundation for the claim that a social science that systematically relied on changing the subject matter in order to find laws would just be *irrelevant* to what we want to know about human behavior. For on this view, what we want to know about is something laws are just not equipped to give us. Consequently, one comes to reject as irrelevant all attempts to search for social scientific laws.

Now, there are two versions of the descriptivist's argument for irrelevance.[6] One is that laws are both irrelevant and impossible. The other is that laws are simply irrelevant (and that their possibility is moot).[7] The first claim attempts to draw a theoretical connection between the ideas of irrelevance and impossibility. The notion here is that laws are irrelevant *precisely because* they are impossible to have at the only level at which we would be interested in having them, and that they are irrelevant (even if possible) at all other levels of description. This claim is firmly rooted in a commitment to descriptivism, seen through the thesis that we may only legitimately seek to explain social phenomena at a single level of description. Schematically, the argument might look like this:

1. There is one correct level of description of human behavior at which we desire social scientific explanation.

2. No laws can be given at this level.

3. Explanations given at other levels of description (whether nomological or not) are irrelevant to what we want to have explained in social science.

4. Therefore, social scientific laws are irrelevant to the explanatory task in social science because they are impossible at the only level of description at which social scientific explanation is relevant.

Thus, we see that this version of the argument from irrelevance has its roots in earlier claims made about the impossibility of social scientific laws—but in a special sense. The claim here made about the relevance of social scientific laws to the explanatory task faced in the investigation of human behavior is *based* on the view that laws are indeed incapable of explaining the phenomena at the only level of description at which such explanations would be legitimate. That is, given the way that we have conceived of the subject matter of social science, laws are both impossible and irrelevant. Thus, we can see how this version of the relevance argument is rooted in prior commitments to the impossibility of laws, as well as other views about how to define the proper subject matter of social inquiry (through a commitment to "descriptivism").[8] In short, the argument comes down to this: It is just not possible to have laws about the things we want to have explained about human behavior, given our interests, and the way that we have defined the phenomena—this is why laws are irrelevant. Indeed, we often find those who make irrelevance claims about the status of laws in social science offering them in concert with various "impossibility" arguments similar to those already examined in Chapter 2 of this book.[9]

But in light of previous arguments made in Chapter 2, concerning the failure of such impossibility arguments against social scientific laws, we may now be tempted to dismiss all such irrelevance claims, given their implicit reliance on dubious notions about impossibility. Such a move, however, would be rash. For the very core of the relevance claim stands independent of any such claims about impossibility ar d can be preserved in an alternative reading of the argument from irrelevance. A less problematic rendering of the claim about the irrelevance of social scientific laws is that any dispute over whether laws are available at any given level of description is immaterial, since they are simply moot in illuminating what we want to know about human action.

This second version of the argument from irrelevance strips off commitments to any specific claims about the impossibility of social scientific laws and instead chooses to focus on the central idea that laws, at any level, are uninteresting. This view holds that terms like "meaning" and "purpose" simply cannot be analyzed in nomological terms, and insofar as we want to know about them, laws will not be able to help us. So it is not a matter, really, of laws being *unavailable* at the level of description at which we would want them, but that laws are *uninformative* at *any* level of description of social phenomena. Given what we want to know about social interaction (i.e., the meaning of the action to the individual who performed it) their availability is moot. Laws, on this view, just cannot capture what we want to know when engaging in social inquiry. Schematically, this second version might look something like this:

1. There is one correct level of description of human behavior at which we desire social scientific explanation.

2'. Laws would not capture what we want to have explained here; even if they could be given, they would be irrelevant.

3. Explanations given at other levels of description (whether nomological or not) are irrelevant to what we want to have explained in social science.

4'. Therefore, social scientific laws are irrelevant because (a) even if they could be given at the level we desired, they would not be explanatory, and (b) explanation at other levels is uninformative. So, laws are irrelevant irrespective of their possibility.

The implications of the commitment to descriptivism here are therefore even more far-reaching than in the first reading—for one is not merely holding that we want social scientific explanations that can be given at a particular level of description (using a particular vocabulary), but that *at* this level of description, there is only one type of inquiry that will answer what it is we are interested in having explained about human behavior (which laws cannot capture). That is, one is here defending not merely the idea that the subject matter of social science is constituted by a particular level of description, but that social science itself is characterized by a single mode of inquiry—one that is essentially non-nomological.

It is important here to point out, however, that despite such fine-grained distinctions between different readings of the argument from irrelevance, in light of the *current* unavailability of laws at any level of description, most would hardly bother to differentiate between the two. Indeed, for our purposes the crucial thing to notice is what both readings hold in common—the idea that due to our explanatory interests in conducting social inquiry, laws are thought to be irrelevant; in light of this, adjudicating their availability is extracurricular.

The most developed form of the argument that holds laws to be irrelevant to what we want explained about human behavior is made by the "interpretivists," who are sometimes called "hermeneuticists." Using a descriptivist blueprint for their assault on nomological social science, the interpretivists argue that the proper subject of study in the investigation of human affairs is human motives, intentions, beliefs, and desires, and that what we want to know about these is the *meaning* that lies behind them. In short, the proper focus of social inquiry is held to be *human thought*.[10]

But according to the interpretivist, we are not even interested in thought itself merely in order to discern the network of causes leading up to human action. Instead, we start from the premise that humans are self-interpreting beings with self-understandings of their actions. The job of social science—conceived of as an interpretive enterprise—is thereby a process of trying to understand the nature of these thoughts and self-understandings, in order to see the action from the actor's point of view. We want to understand how the action fits into the context of the agent's beliefs, desires, and goals in order to discover the purpose of the action—and the meaning that lies behind it—relative to the intentions of the individual who performed it. In short, we want to "rethink the thoughts" of the rational individual in order to achieve a kind of "empathetic understanding" of the action, which is not available through nomological investigation. We seek to put the action in context, given the actor's worldview.[11]

And, it is argued, no nomological inquiry—no search for the causal patterns that may have led up to the action—can do justice to this purposeful character of human action, since it cannot tell us about the meaning of the action to the individual who performed it. Instead, it is claimed, in social science we are trying to do something the natural scientist need not and cannot do—we are trying to *interpret the meaning* that lies behind intentional human action by uncovering the thoughts and self-interpretations that lie behind it.[12] Given the way that we have conceived of the phenomena, and what we want to know about it, we seek to understand human action through a process of interpretation, which is totally distinct from the kind of understanding sought in natural science. When we want explanation in natural science, we are seeking a causal account—we want to know how the event came about. On the other hand, when we want an explanation in social science, it is claimed, we want to know what the action meant to the individual. This, however, is something that laws make no attempt to capture. In the context of social inquiry, it is argued, laws are an answer to a question that was never put. The goals of inquiry just seem to be different: the discovery of causes versus the elucidation of meaning. Thus, given what we want to know in social science, laws are thought to be not merely impossible, but in some sense incoherent.

Charles Taylor, one of the most distinguished advocates of this point of view, has held that there is, therefore, a radical break in the methodology appropriate to the explanation of human action from that we use in natural science. Based on a conception of human behavior as essentially "meaningful," and our interest in having this meaning illuminated by our inquiry, nomological investigation is thought to systematically ignore precisely those aspects of human action that we are most interested in having explained. Given our interest in meaning, Taylor argues, interpretive social science is more appropriate to our task.

In his important essay "Interpretation and the Sciences of Man," Taylor outlines what is at stake.[13] He writes:

> Interpretation, in the sense relevant to hermeneutics, is an attempt to make clear, to make sense of an object of study. This object must, therefore, be a text or a text-analogue, which in some way is confused, incomplete, cloudy, seemingly contradictory—in one way or another, unclear. The interpretation aims to bring to light an underlying coherence or sense.[14]

Thus, Taylor recounts his belief that the type of understanding sought in social science is more akin to the task of interpreting a text or a film, where we are perhaps only peripherally interested in the causes that have led up to it and are instead more concerned with what the text or film means. At times, of course, we may be interested in the genesis of an action (as we are sometimes interested in a text's evolution through successive drafts, or what scenes were left on the cutting room floor) insofar as it illuminates the context in which the action was performed and therefore its meaning. But our primary focus in the explanation of human action, Taylor argues, is uncovering the meaning that lies behind it. Rabinow and Sullivan, in the introduction to their landmark anthology on interpretive social science, put it this way: "the aim [of interpretation] is not to uncover universals or laws but rather to explicate context and world."[15] Transcending questions about the availability of laws, the interpretivist holds that they are simply inappropriate.

It is easy to see how such a view may be properly characterized as a claim about the "irrelevance" of laws to social scientific inquiry, for fundamentally the claim is that at the level of description at which we are interested in having human action explained, laws would not be able to tell us what we want to know. Even if available, laws would be moot—for we are not interested in the objective fact of why certain thoughts and beliefs caused the agent to act in the way that he or she did, but are instead interested in understanding the meaning of the action from the actor's own point of view, given his or her thoughts and beliefs.[16] We want to understand why the action was seen by the actor as appropriate, given the circumstances in which it was performed. And such understanding, it is held, can be achieved only by interpretation.

By now it should be clear that the interpretive view relies on an underlying commitment to "descriptivism." For the central claim behind the idea that laws would be irrelevant to the task of explanation in social science is that there is only one level of description at which we would find any social scientific account to be explanatory; and, at this level, we want something explained about human behavior—the meaning of human action—that laws cannot offer. Nomological social science, then, is seen as irrelevant, given the way that we have conceived of the subject matter of social science and the nature of our explanatory interests. The level of description at which we talk about "purpose" and "meaning" is just taken to be constitutive of the subject matter of social science. Thus, there is no room for nomological explanation. Surely this is the very heart of the descriptivist's argument for irrelevance.

Yet it is unfortunately the case that, at times, interpretivists have flirted with claims about impossibility. Sadly, many advocates of the interpretive point of view have thought it necessary to offer independent arguments for the impossibility of social scientific laws—at the level at which we desire social scientific explanation—in order to bolster their claims of irrelevance. It is almost as if they find the case against laws to be so compelling that they must "plead in the alternative," saying "in the first place, laws are irrelevant, and in the second place, even if they were relevant, they would be impossible to have." But in philosophy as in law, such a strategy often weakens one's overall argument, leaving the reader to believe that if one of your buckets held water it would not be necessary to point out a spare.

Even Charles Taylor himself seems to find it necessary, at the end of his article on interpretation, to resort to listing impossibility arguments, despite the fact that they have no discernible theoretical relationship to the underlying claim of irrelevance developed in the rest of his paper. Indeed, such a strategy merely tempts readers to disregard his carefully crafted argument that laws are irrelevant, given the better alternative of interpretation, once they have succeeded in refuting his claims about impossibility.

However, as mentioned earlier in this chapter, it would be a mistake to dismiss the interpretivist account simply because so many of its advocates have spuriously sought to support their claims with theories about impossibility. Remember here that the alternative reading of the interpretivist's claim about irrelevance, which does *not* rely on claims about the impossibility of social scientific laws, stands independently, and preserves the kernel of the interpretivist's argument that nomological inquiry is *irrelevant* to what we want to have explained in social science. This alternative reading of the argument from irrelevance makes an important charge against the usefulness of nomological explanation in social science in its own right and deserves to be considered on its merits.

How might we argue against it? Are laws so obviously irrelevant to the task of social scientific explanation? It is now time to evaluate the claim that social scientific laws are irrelevant to what we want to have explained about human action, irrespective of claims about their alleged impossibility, in light of the way that we have conceived of the subject matter and given the focus of our explanatory interests.

Fortunately for the defense of nomological social science, there are ample grounds upon which to critique the essential claim that stands behind the interpretivist argument for irrelevance. To start with, why is it that the ir-relevance (interpretivist) theorist's conception of what is explanatory in social science is so narrow? Why hold that there is only one level of de-scription and explanation (or categorization of social phenomena) at which it is legitimate to inquire into human affairs or at which we would desire explanation? Moreover, why think that there is only one thing that we want to know about human action? Surely there is more to the explanation of human action than the interpretivists have allowed.

Although the interpretive mode of explanation is itself legitimate, and reflects one important dimension of potential concern with human behav-ior, it is not exhaustive of our interest in human affairs and should not be taken to exclude all other levels of interest or explanatory accounts as ille-gitimate. Indeed, an important assumption behind the interpretivist's ar-gument is that human action is so rich and varied that the exclusive focus upon a single mode of explanation—the nomological—will likely miss important areas of interest. But why, then, tolerate this same exclusivity in the service of interpretivism itself? We ask, "why does it happen" in social affairs just as easily as we ask, "what does it mean?" So why think that only one of these questions is allowable and worthy of an explanation clas-sified as "social science"? Perhaps laws are irrelevant to inquiry about meaning, but is this *all* that we are concerned to know about in social sci-ence?

Here it is valuable to remember that the subject matter of social science is most basically *human behavior,* and not that behavior as captured by any particular theory or description of it.[17] If it is to be a live dispute, the debate about the status of laws in social science should be taken as more than just a disagreement about what is possible at one particular level of interest. The debate about whether there are laws in social science is certainly richer than just a "linguistic" dispute over the proper definition of "social sci-ence." Herein, we see the inherent narrowness of the interpretivist charge against laws due to its reliance on descriptivism. But in light of this, what is the status of social scientific laws?

Some, Carl Hempel for instance, have argued that one cannot have any explanation at all without causal laws; Hempel's view is that the kind of "empathetic understanding" sought in interpretive accounts is not really explanatory at all, but instead is just satisfying to our emotions and sense of familiarity with the phenomena being described.[18] "Meaning," it is held, is just an artifact of the causes at work, which is what our explanations should try to capture. So if we want to discover the fundamental causes behind our behavior, we must go beyond the level of description at which we concern ourselves solely with "meaning," and must instead try to ac-count for the phenomena nomologically.

Such a strong view, however, is not necessary for the defense of social scientific laws against the argument from irrelevance.[19] Instead, one might submit that we *are* legitimately interested in asking about the meaning of human action, and that we have a right to want "explanations" in terms of it. Moreover, one might concede that it is fruitless to argue over whether this qualifies as "social science." Indeed, the interpretive mode of analysis is an important one, and I do not mean for anything I say in this book to denigrate its value. What I *do* intend to dispute is the notion that we should be so impressed with the importance of interpretation that we think it is all there is to the explanation of human behavior.[20] Why should we be satisfied with a social science that made no attempt to discover causes?[21] Aren't we legitimately interested in knowing about them too?

Namely, many are also justifiably interested in studying human action at a level of description at which laws *are indeed relevant* to our explanatory interests; our questions about human behavior are often framed in such a way that a law-like account is sought as an answer to it.[22] Just as some will want to know about the *meaning* of some social event, others will not be satisfied unless they *subsume it under a law*—until they discover the causes that brought it about. And if available, many will hold that such a law would be perfectly explanatory and appropriate, given the nature of their interests. Given this, how can we rule out laws as irrelevant without running the risk of parochializing social science?

Moreover, law-like explanation, if available (and remember that availability isn't the issue in the argument from irrelevance), might even *enrich* our understanding of the meaning of human action. After all, in order to understand the meaning of human action, we must attempt to put it in context, and at least part of the ideal context would include an account of the causes that led up to the event itself. The earlier example of interpreting the meaning of a film is instructive. Could one really be a film critic if one knew nothing about how films were made? That is, even if one were only concerned with understanding the "meaning" of a film as a "text" and only sought to give an interpretation of it in order to evaluate its quality, wouldn't one also have to know something about the causal genesis of film? Wouldn't one need to know about editing, producing, and sound direction? Are these really alien to the interpretation of a film's meaning? Surely we must care to know whether some of the subtleties in the final product were intentional—or whether they were just artifacts of the limits of the medium itself.

Perhaps the same is true for the interpretation of human action. Even if one professes to be concerned solely with interpreting the meaning of human action, there may still be a role for causal inquiry. One must know something about the prior events that led up to the action as well as how the decision to act was formulated. What were the factors that influenced the thoughts the agent had? Could he or she have acted differently? To what extent was the action a function of intentions versus constraints imposed by other "human" factors? Was the actor tired, desperate, or hungry—had he or she just had a fight with someone? How do people normally act under these circumstances?

Thus, one may conclude that the interpretive and nomological modes of explanation of human action need not exclude one another; although given their differing commitments to what it is most important to have explained about human behavior, they will inevitably be at odds with one another about the proper focus of our inquiry.[23] This is something different, however, than the result sought by proponents of the argument from irrelevance—which seeks to exclude nomological inquiry all together.

We must, therefore, learn to be more *pluralistic* in our tolerance of many levels of inquiry into human affairs.[24] We must not be so willing to rule out whole areas of potential interest simply because they do not jibe with our preconceived notions of what we *ought* to want to have explained about human behavior.[25] True, some will be disappointed by any attempt to redescribe human behavior at other levels of inquiry, using different categorizations of the phenomena. Others, however, will want to search for the causes of human behavior and will find it most fruitful to do so in the context of a search for social scientific laws.

Surely, it would be pointlessly restrictive to hold that such a search is destined to be fruitless or that no one would find such laws, even if they could be formulated, to be explanatory or interesting. Similarly, it seems hopeless merely to lament that such inquiry—even if possible—is not "social science." No one level of interest in human behavior should be taken to be exhaustive. Indeed, the interpretive approach to social science grew out of frustration with the exclusiveness of "positivist" modes of inquiry. We should be careful, therefore, not to repeat this error in the advocacy of our alternatives.

The interpretive mode of inquiry is an important one, in that it lets us know that laws are not all there is to the explanation of human behavior.[26] But laws, nonetheless, are an important part of it. The nomological ideal plays a crucial role in shaping our search for explanations of human action. Thus, the claim that laws are irrelevant to the investigation of human behavior must be rejected.

Physicalism: Relevance Reconsidered

One must also consider, however, an alternative view, which is equally opposed to social scientific laws, but which rejects the interpretivist's claim that laws are irrelevant to the explanation of human action. For the physicalist thinks that laws are indeed relevant to the explanation of our behavior, even while sharing interpretivism's belief that they are not forthcoming at the level at which we are interested in doing *social science*.[27]

That is, both interpretivism and physicalism reject the idea of using laws for "social" explanation, even though they disagree on the issue of whether laws are ultimately relevant to the explanation of human action, as captured at some other level of inquiry.

Here, however, the differences between the interpretivist and the physicalist become more apparent. Faced with the absence of "social scientific" laws (based on the common "diagnosis" offered by descriptivism—that one can have no laws using the privileged terms thought to be constitutive of the subject matter of social science), the interpretivist and the physicalist offer different "prescriptions" about how to proceed, based on their differing commitments to the relevance of laws for the explanation of human action. Whereas the interpretivist argues in favor of giving up on the search for laws, while continuing to engage in social scientific inquiry (using the descriptive terms that we find most efficacious), the physicalist counsels giving up doing social science (in some sense), in favor of looking for the laws that underlie human behavior at the physical level. Compelled by a commitment to descriptivism, along with a belief in the relevance of laws to the explanation of human action, the physicalist is left to look for the laws governing human action at another level of inquiry. That is, the physicalist rejects "social" descriptions as the only basis for the explanation of human behavior. He or she admits that the interpretivist is right that there cannot be laws at the level of social scientific inquiry, but instead of dropping the quest for nomological explanation, the exclusive reliance on social descriptions is dropped instead.

Physicalism, at base, is the idea that purely physical descriptions of human action can be derived by reducing "social" terms to their underlying neurophysiological counterparts, and that it is only these basic terms that admit of nomological explanation. The physicalist believes that the "natural kinds" used in social scientific inquiry are not the only ones available in the investigation of human action and are probably not the most efficacious in understanding it. True, if we insist on using social "kinds," we will produce no laws. However, if we are willing to give up social science as the only legitimate level of inquiry into human action, it is argued, we may do better in explaining our behavior by discovering laws that may only be expressed in terms of physical descriptions of human behavior. Thus, the physicalist agrees that we are now "changing the subject matter," but, for him or her, this is a good thing, given the poverty of the existing explanatory accounts in social science.[28] If we are committed to nomological explanation, the physicalist alternative to social science would seem to offer us better prospects for success.

Of course there are competing views about what to do with existing social scientific inquiry and its relationship to the physicalist mode of inquiry—ranging from the conservative to the radical. Donald Davidson, for instance, advocates continuing social inquiry using the terms that we find most appropriate, but he warns not to expect any correlation between the "explanations" we may there find compelling and the physicalist laws we hope to discover at other levels. Davidson is willing to accommodate existing social science, that is, so long as one resists the temptation to unify explanations across different levels of inquiry.[29] Alexander Rosenberg, on the other hand, hopes to "preempt" social science all together, in favor of the science of sociobiology; he seeks to replace "social" kinds with "biological" ones.[30] Yet others have suggested that all that is compelling about social scientific inquiry can be reduced to inquiry at the neuronal level, and that we can do away with social vocabulary completely.[31]

The point here is not that all of these thinkers share a common idea of which alternative science will ultimately be successful in expressing the laws that stand behind human action, in the wake of giving up on the search for laws in social science, or even that they will all agree in their musings on what to do with existing social inquiry. Rather, the point is that all of these views share in common the idea that it is important to continue searching for laws, while giving up the hope that they can be expressed at the social level. That is, the "physicalists" are "descriptivists" (they believe that *social* inquiry is constituted by a particular level of description, which, unfortunately, does not allow for laws), who nonetheless believe in the relevance of laws to the explanation of human action. Given this, however, they believe that such laws must be expressed outside the domain of traditional social science. The physicalist therefore concurs with the interpretivist that we are not going to be able to produce "social scientific" laws, even while disagreeing sharply on the normative implications that one should draw from this; for the physicalist, it is important to pursue laws anyway, even if it means retreating from social inquiry.

Schematically, the argument might look like this:

1. There is one correct level of description of human behavior at which we desire *social scientific* explanation.

2. No laws can be given at this level.

3". It is nonetheless important, however, to continue searching for the regularities that underlie human action.

4". Therefore, we must proceed in this search at other levels of inquiry and must give up the search for laws in social science.

Notice that this argument is deeply committed to descriptivism, as seen by its first step, which it shares with both readings of the schematic for the argument from irrelevance.[32] The physicalist, no less than the interpretivist, buys into the central claim of descriptivism: that the subject matter of social science is just constituted by a particular set of descriptive terms that frame our explanatory inquiry; that we just want *social* explanation to be given in terms of this vocabulary; and that to change these descriptions is tantamount to giving up doing social science. When coupled with the next step—the idea that there can be no laws given at this level of description— one draws the obvious conclusion, which is that one ought to give up the search for social scientific laws.[33]

Thus, in some sense, the interpretivist and the physicalist hold twin views—they are flip sides of the same coin. But although they agree that there are not going to be autonomous social scientific laws, their ideas for what to do in the face of this are very different, reflecting their dissenting views about the relevance of laws to the explanation of human behavior: one gives up the "search for laws" in favor of preserving social scientific inquiry at a level that is meaningfully social scientific, and the other gives up nomological expression in terms of "social science" in order to search for laws at other levels of description. They disagree, in other words, over whether "social" descriptions of human action are the only ones relevant for the explanation of human behavior—whether social science is the only game in town. Here their opposition to one another is radical. They are united in their opposition to the "naturalist," however, in their contention that we must make a choice between laws and social science—that there can be no autonomous social scientific laws.[34]

Now, it is important to realize that although there may be much to be learned from this attempt to root our social behavior in terms of nomological explanations expressed at a non-social level, the physicalist (along with the interpretivist) may have been too hasty in the rejection of the search for *social scientific* laws. That is, just as adherence to descriptivism led to the downfall of interpretivism through the narrowness of its rejection of social scientific laws as irrelevant, we now see that even if one embraces the relevance of laws to the explanation of human action, descriptivism nonetheless parochializes one's view of social science and artificially narrows the search for laws. It tempts one to give up too soon on the attempt to produce laws that are genuinely social scientific, due to the rigid belief that the subject matter of social science is framed by a privileged set of natural kinds. Thus, physicalism allows for redescription in the search for nomological explanations but denies that this could occur within the context of social scientific inquiry.

But we now want to ask, even if one thought that it *was* possible to produce laws at the physical level, why would it necessarily follow that this is the *only* legitimate level at which they are expressible or could be explanatory? Why insist on such a limited scope for nomological inquiry?[35] On these questions we may found the basis for our critique.

First, it is important to realize that the physicalist *could very well be wrong* in saying that there are no laws that could be given, even using the descriptive terms that are desired in social scientific inquiry. Certainly it is an empirical question whether there are laws employing "beliefs" and "desires," and the issue does not deserve to be settled on a priori grounds.[36] Second, and more important, the physicalist could *also* be wrong in so narrowly limiting the avenues of description available to nomological inquiry. Remember the problems that descriptivism produced for all of the earlier arguments examined in this book?[37] In light of this, why make the same mistake as interpretivism? Why limit our search only to one favored level of description of the phenomena or insist that if we do not, we are no longer doing social science? What possible explanatory purpose can it serve to limit social scientific investigation to a proscribed set of natural kinds and theories, which are thought to be incompatible with the search for law-like explanations? The physicalist view, like interpretivism, seems overly narrow in its conception of the methodological tools available to social science; whereas interpretivism gave up too soon on laws, physicalism gives up too soon on social science. So yes, we might here change our view of the scope of social scientific inquiry by being willing to give up the exclusive reliance on previously favored "social" descriptive terms. But if our goal is explanation, and not merely looking for relationships given some particular descriptive terms, what is wrong with this?

Now perhaps one might here wish to offer an objection. For it could be argued that the physicalist program may be seen as fulfilling *precisely* the call for "redescription" made throughout this book. That is, one might point out that the physicalist is pursuing "social" inquiry at another level of investigation in the pursuit of law-like explanations: that the physicalist is merely choosing to redescribe the social in terms of the physical, and that he or she is uncomfortable calling this "social science." But is this a fair characterization? Is there only a *semantic* difference between the claim that we ought to widen the scope of our descriptive terms in the search for social scientific laws, and the claim that we ought to pursue the explanation of human action at the physicalist level of description? Is it just a question of what we are willing to *call* "social science?"

This would not capture the full value of what is meant by "redescription." The program advocated by the physicalist, and that embraced by those who would search for autonomous laws in social science (the "naturalists"), although they are in some respects similar, reflect widely divergent conceptions of the explanatory goal behind the investigation of human behavior. Despite the fact that both in some sense use "redescription," the way in which each view respects the autonomy of social inquiry as well as the diversity of interests that stand behind the search for laws, splits the two. For the physicalist embraces redescription in the face of the absence of social scientific laws by *narrowing* our search to a level at which they are thought to be available. Our explanatory interests are reduced to the realm of the possible. The "naturalist," on the other hand, turns to re-description as a means of liberating our search for nomological explanations from the hegemony of the descriptive terms that have been taken to exhaust our interest in human affairs. The goal is to *broaden* our inquiry for the sake of our explanatory interests.

Physicalism, that is, does not respect the idea that one may be interested in searching for laws at one level, even while realizing that they may also be expressible (and even explanatory) at other levels; it does not appreciate the diversity of our explanatory interests. Hamstrung by a commitment to descriptivism, the physicalist gives up on nomological inquiry in social science, choosing to play in a much smaller field. Physicalism roots its search for laws in terms of the physical, as a retreat from nomological social science, because of its adherence to the parochial descriptivist claim that by "social science" we must mean inquiry using only a given set of descriptive terms. Thus, even though physicalism abandons social science, its commitment to descriptivism *about* social science limits the scope of its search for laws. The naturalist's search for autonomous laws, on the other hand, is meant to widen our scope—to accommodate our interests by allowing for nomological inquiry at more than one level based on different descriptions of one and the same social event.

Moreover, it is noteworthy that the physicalist also seems guilty of assuming that his or her own nomological inquiry proceeds at the only legitimate level of investigation into human affairs and employs the proper natural kinds that characterize the very engine behind human nature. So beyond its hubris in supposing that the social sciences could never generate autonomous law-like explanations, descriptivism here leads to the additional oversight of ratifying the belief that only through physicalist inquiry will we gain insight into the true causal mechanism by which human action is generated. But here it would be wise to borrow a page from natural scientific inquiry and realize that we must be more flexible than this in our categorization into kinds, and the development of new theories, in the search for scientific explanations. For one reality may support perhaps an infinite variety of descriptions of it. And since science is based on our *descriptions* of reality, it is premature to suppose that there is a single privileged level that supports nomological explanation. That is, even if we believe that there is one level of causation behind human affairs, nomological explanation may proceed at many different levels of inquiry, reflecting the many different ways of describing the same reality.

Of course, on my view it is certainly conceivable that there may be a relationship between the search for laws at different levels (just as my earlier definition of social science allowed for both the interpretation of meaning and nomological explanation), and there is nothing in the position I am advocating that excludes this. One may argue that there is nothing wrong with permitting the search for laws at both the physicalist and the social scientific level (and indeed even in believing that there may be a legitimate theoretical relationship between them). But even while allowing for physicalism as a legitimate level of inquiry in its own right, we must reject the descriptivist assumption it smuggles into our conception of social science that works against such pluralism. For it may indeed be that just as there is a naturalistic dependency between the phenomena studied in chemistry and physics, the relationship between social science and physicalism is one where relationships in the former are grounded in relationships in the latter. Just as in chemistry, however, this does not mean that there is no legitimate secondary inquiry or that it is fruitless to pursue nomological explanations in terms that are uniquely meaningful to the secondary science. Even if one admits such naturalistic dependence, it still must be allowed that we may search for *autonomous* laws, given the diverse interests which motivate our inquiry. Explanation, we here realize, does not require a single level of inquiry. Laws, even if ultimately thought to be grounded in one level of causation, allow for many different expressions based on alternative characterizations of the underlying referents and depending on our explanatory interests.[38]

Recall here our finding in Chapter 4, that phenomena are explained only as captured by a given level of description—that laws are of the phenomena "as described." So if one is willing to allow for diverse descriptions of the same "social" event, reflecting our various interests in the subject matter, why *not* think that laws could exist at many different levels of inquiry and even that we could conduct nomological inquiry at many levels simultaneously? Why rule out a priori the possibility that there may be a genuine theoretical relationship between them? Indeed, wouldn't the abandonment of descriptivism serve precisely the explanatory goal that the diversity of our interests in social affairs requires? And doesn't the search for *social scientific* laws appropriately satisfy many practitioners' desire for the explanation of social events? Thus, we see that pluralism in our interests ratifies the search for autonomous laws and speaks against the descriptivist assumption that would so severely and artificially limit our inquiry. We need not here reject "physicalism", then, but just the argument that has been thought to motivate it, which focuses exclusively on a single level of inquiry and denigrates the search for autonomous social scientific laws. Although it is a legitimate level of inquiry into human behavior, physicalism (like interpretivism) is not the only game in town.

Conclusion

We can now see that there are problems with both interpretivism and physicalism in their prescriptions for social science due to the parochializing influence of their mutual commitment to descriptivism. For descriptivism is behind each view's rejection of the search for autonomous social scientific laws (whether it is because one believes they would be irrelevant or that they would be impossible) and overshadows even their disagreement on the relevance of laws to the explanation of human action.

The interpretivist claims that no laws are relevant to the explanation of human action, but that we must continue to pursue non-nomological social science. The physicalist holds that laws are relevant, but that they cannot be expressed in terms of social science. Although each has a different idea of where to go in the face of descriptivism (and the belief that no laws are forthcoming), neither allows for the continued pursuit of autonomous social scientific laws.[39] Both, on this point, are in favor of narrowing the scope of our inquiry.

In this chapter, however, I have shown that there are grounds for rejecting the descriptivist assumption that lies behind *both* the argument from irrelevance and physicalism. We have now seen that the claim it makes against laws is rooted in a quite narrow conception of social scientific explanation, and a very limited domain of concern with human affairs.

Along the way, I hope to have moved us toward a better understanding of the role of laws in social scientific explanation as well as the potential use and value of redescription in finding them. This was initiated in Chapter 4, by showing that there is an analogy between the barriers faced in social and natural science, and that the natural sciences make use of redescription in their own search for law-like explanations and the theories that may support them. In the first part of this chapter I continued with this task by pointing out the problems with the underlying "descriptivist" assumption implicit in the claim that no such analogy is appropriate, given the alleged irrelevance of laws to the type of understanding we seek in social science.

But the argument from irrelevance failed to show that non-nomological forms of inquiry are *all there is* to the explanation of human behavior, or that the search for laws would systematically fail to meet *any* of our most basic explanatory interests. To refute the argument from irrelevance, this is all that one need show. The nomological ideal survives intact.

Similarly, we saw that there are also drawbacks to a conception of "social" inquiry that insists that laws, if they could be given, could not be expressed within the domain of social science. Here the descriptivist assumption is no less damaging, for, as was the case with the argument from irrelevance, it also limits the scope of our inquiry, giving up on the search for autonomous social scientific laws and basing our concern with human behavior within a very limited explanatory context. Indeed, as was clear from the case made earlier for interpretivism, we often do want explanations that are recognizably social scientific. And interpretivism notwithstanding, many will wish to have such explanations in nomological terms. So just as we earlier made the point against interpretation that we *do* just want explanation in nomological terms, it is important to point out here in opposition to physicalism that we *do* just want explanation at the *social* level as well. No single level of inquiry will accommodate all of our interests in human affairs.

What sort of metaphysics might support these methodological conclusions? In the next chapter, I will sketch out a metaphysical program that defends such a wider view of social scientific explanation and supports the search for autonomous social scientific laws. Beyond the barrier of descriptivism, we run into a constellation of metaphysical issues that are important for the methodology of social scientific explanation, which we will turn to next.

Notes

1. That is, as in Chapter 2, where I show that social scientific laws are not impossible, and in Chapter 3, where I suggest that they are not impractical, here I aim to show that laws are not irrelevant—that the arguments for irrelevance fail.

2. I owe this point to David Anderson.

3. For instance, "belief," "desire," "intend," "want," and so on.

4. I have discussed this argument previously in Chapters 3 and 4 of this book.

5. The claim that the proper subject matter of social science is human intentions can be used to motivate arguments about both the possibility and relevance of laws. At some level, such arguments are probably related. Here, however, my focus is on claims about irrelevance. Cf. the typology of arguments given in Chapter 1 of this book.

6. I thank Larry Sklar for pointing out that the first version of the argument from irrelevance relies implicitly on a possibility claim.

One might think of the basic difference between the two versions of the argument as a dispute concerning whether laws would be explanatory at the level of description we desired, if in fact they could be given.

7. Cf. here the matrix given on p. 120.

8. Whether the arguments in favor of the impossibility of social scientific laws succeed isn't the point here. Surely, such arguments *could* fail (and I think I have provided grounds in Chapter 2 for thinking that they indeed do fail). But the point is that even if, for the sake of charity, we grant the success of such impossibility arguments, there is *still* room to attack the descriptivist/irrelevance argument. This is what I set out to do in the remainder of this section.

9. A good example of this is Charles Taylor, "Interpretation and the Sciences of Man," *The Review of Metaphysics*, Vol. 25, No. 1 (September, 1971), pp. 3–51. It is important to point out here that some of the impossibility arguments used may be ones that we have not heretofore considered. I hope to have demonstrated the general point in Chapter 2, however, that all a priori arguments for the impossibility of social scientific laws are suspect.

10. R. G. Collingwood, *The Idea of History* (London: Oxford University Press, 1967), p. 214.

11. Collingwood, *The Idea of History, passim.* A good example of this in practice can be seen in the works of Clifford Geertz, especially his *The Interpretation of Cultures* (New York: Basic Books, 1973).

12. Collingwood's thoughts about the methodology of inquiry proper to history can be read as providing the first proto-interpretive methodology for the social sciences. Charles Taylor's work, especially, owes much to Collingwood.

13. Citation in note 9 above.

14. Taylor, "Interpretation," p. 3.

15. Paul Rabinow and William M. Sullivan, eds., *Interpretive Social Science: A Reader* (Berkeley: The University of California Press, 1979), p. 13.

16. Cf. William Dray, *Laws and Explanation in History* (Oxford: Oxford University Press, 1957); and Collingwood, *The Idea of History, passim.*

17. This idea was brought to my attention in conversation with Mary Williams.

18. Carl G. Hempel, "The Function of General Laws in History" reprinted in *Aspects of Scientific Explanation* (New York: The Free Press, 1965), pp. 231–243.

19. All that is needed here is to show that the argument from irrelevance fails, which is something different from showing that laws are indeed relevant to social scientific explanation. This is an important area of further research, but it is beyond the scope of the present book.

20. Cf. Brian Fay and J. Donald Moon, "What Would an Adequate Philosophy of Social Science Look Like?" *Philosophy of the Social Sciences,* Vol. 7 (1977), pp. 209–227. On page 214 they write, "impressed by the elegance and penetration of interpretive theories, humanist philosophers of social science have assumed or argued that interpretation is all there is. They have gone from the correct observation that social theories must be interpretive, to the incorrect conclusion that they can *only* be interpretive."

21. Hempel argues that insofar as we aim at explanations that are causal, we will find it necessary to employ nomological models. See Hempel, "Function," *passim.*

22. Think, for example, of the experiments done in social psychology cited in the last chapter.

23. An interesting discussion of this point is made throughout Fay and Moon's article, cited in note 20 above.

24. But Rabinow and Sullivan, at least, in the introduction to the second edition of their anthology *Interpretive Social Science,* seem uncomfortable with this kind of pluralism. They write: "Interpretation has too often been accepted by practitioners of the human sciences as merely one methodological option among a growing number of available investigation tools. For us, this view displaces the significance of the interpretive turn and ultimately empties it of its capacity to challenge the practices of knowing in our culture." *Interpretive Social Science: A Second Look* (Berkeley: University of California Press, 1987), p. 2.

But isn't this point of view just the kind of hubris that Fay and Moon were warning against?—that in the interpretivist challenge to naturalistic methods one ends up with a very proscribed view of social science?

25. This does not mean, however, that "anything goes" in social science. There must be standards employed, drawn from both inside and outside the explanatory account examined, which help us to adjudicate between models that are explanatory, testable, and consistent, and those that are not.

26. A valuable discussion of this point can be found in Harold Kincaid's "Confirmation, Complexity, and Social Laws," *PSA 1988*, Vol. 2 (East Lansing, Mich.: The Philosophy of Science Association, 1989), pp. 299–307.

27. The physicalist, that is, thinks laws are *unavailable* using the natural kinds proper to social inquiry.

28. The physicalist would tend to agree with Hempel that interpretation is not *explanatory* (though, ultimately, they part company over the question of whether reductionist strategies are the only ones appropriate in the search for scientific modes of analysis of human behavior).

29. Donald Davidson, "Psychology as Philosophy," in *Essays on Actions and Events* (Oxford: Clarendon Press, 1980), pp. 229–244. Davidson's views have received a generous amount of attention and have generated much controversy in the literature. This is probably due to the novelty of the set of beliefs he holds consistent: that there can be no laws of "belief" and "desire," that we should yet continue traditional social scientific inquiry despite our recognition that its explanations will be non-nomological, that there *are* laws governing human phenomena that are expressible at the physical level of description (and which support the phenomena at other levels), but that there is no satisfactory way in which these relationships can be translated into the vocabulary used in social science. Despite the cleverness of this account, however, it is obvious that Davidson's views suffer strongly from "descriptivism." Is social science entirely exhausted by inquiry into beliefs and desires? Why not support the idea that redescriptions of the subject matter of social science—which is "human behavior"—are legitimately open to nomological social inquiry? And indeed how can we even be sure that there cannot be laws employing the terms "belief" and "desire"?

30. Alexander Rosenberg, *Sociobiology and the Preemption of Social Science* (Baltimore: The Johns Hopkins University Press, 1980).

31. An interesting discussion of this topic is provided in Paul Churchland, "Eliminative Materialism and the Propositional Attitudes," in R. Boyd et al., eds., *The Philosophy of Science* (Cambridge: The MIT Press, 1991).

32. Note also its commitment to the unavailability of laws in its second step, which it shares with the first reading of the argument from irrelevance.

33. Although for the physicalist this is because the laws are thought to be *unavailable*, and not because they would be irrelevant. Cf. note 27 above. There may be some extracurricular dispute here over whether it is better to say that the physicalist thinks social scientific laws don't exist at all, or that they are merely unexplanatory (because they are not given at the level at which causation occurs). But in any case, the physicalist does indeed believe that there are no laws forthcoming in social science.

34. One might usefully think of the difference between interpretivism and physicalism here as one of whether they critique the position I am defending from the "left" or the "right." Namely, the interpretivist is hostile to the whole idea of law-like explanation of human action and counsels giving up on it completely. The

physicalist, however, believes that laws are important to the explanation of human action but is just not very sanguine about their availability in social science; the naturalist is on the right track, this view holds, but just does not go far enough. It is important to note, however, that despite this basic disagreement both views are irretrievably "descriptivist." They are both committed to the idea that *social* inquiry must be carried out at a privileged level of description, using specific natural kinds that are taken to constitute the very subject matter of social science. Thus, just as in the political arena, even the far left and the far right hold certain immoderate beliefs in common.

35. These questions highlight the physicalist's parallel commitment to "reductionism," which along with descriptivism defines the physicalist's views about the proper level of explanation open for nomological inquiry into human behavior. A full account of reductionism and its relationship to descriptivism is offered in Chapter 6.

36. It is important to remember, however, that the physicalist is *looking* for such laws and does not think, along with the interpretivist, that they would be incoherent. The physicalist does not buy the interpretivist idea that if they *could* be produced, social scientific laws would be irrelevant. My point, however, is that even if there could *not* be laws using these terms, this should not close the question of nomologicality in social science.

37. Recall here the point that descriptivism causes problems for explanation in *both* natural and social science.

38. For a dissenting view, see Jaegwon Kim's "Mechanism, Purpose, and Explanatory Exclusion," in J. Tomberlin, ed., *Philosophical Perspectives,* Vol. 3 (Atascadero, Calif.: Ridgeview, 1989), pp. 77–109. Kim's view is that there is a single level of description that is appropriate for the explanation of human behavior because there is only one level at which causation occurs. My own view, however, is that this is far too narrow a conception of explanation. It is better to support pluralism of explanatory stances and argue that there are many alternative descriptions of the same event. That is, that there is not just one explanation, but many because there are many potential descriptions. See the argument given in Chapter 6.

39. Or for that matter, each other. The interpretivist intends to exclude both physicalism and naturalism as misdirected, given their nomological focus. Likewise, the physicalist regards interpretation as "quaint" but not particularly explanatory.

6

Metaphysical Interlude

I [once] claimed that much important work in the philosophy of science is indepen-
dent … and that [it] could neither be accepted nor rejected on the strength of alterna-
tive answers to fundamental questions in philosophy. This is a belief of which I have
repented. … While I still believe that findings about the actual practice of scientists
can decide no fundamental metaphysical or epistemological issues, I now hold that
the sides one takes on these issues must decisively determine the character of strate-
gies of research in the natural and social sciences. … All the chief answers to the
question about differences among natural and social sciences make … strong [meta-
physical and epistemological] assumptions.

—Alexander Rosenberg

It may by now have occurred to the reader that the methodological program that I have been defending in the last several chapters holds implicit
certain metaphysical commitments. If one hopes to uphold the legitimacy
of social scientific laws, what sort of ontology might be presupposed? In
this chapter, I will sketch out a metaphysical framework that supports the
methodological views I have been advocating about the importance of social scientific laws.

First, it is important to be clear that the laws I hope to defend here are
autonomous, genuine laws of social science. We saw in the last chapter the
problems associated with physicalism and its idea of narrowing the focus
of our explanatory inquiry through a commitment to descriptivism. I want
to suggest here that we do away with such reductionist explanatory strategies in social science (to the extent that they encourage us to narrow our
explanatory focus to a single level of inquiry) and instead advocate the
pursuit of many different levels of inquiry, including the search for autonomous laws.[1] Thus, I will defend the idea that we can have nomological
inquiry without reduction; for even where reduction is in principle possible, it does not exhaust our explanatory desiderata. But if one hopes to
find autonomous social scientific laws, I think it is by now clear that one
will need to use redescription and reject the belief that we can rely on discovering one perfect level of description, which will allegedly capture all

143

of our interests and observations about social phenomena; one will need to be flexible in the categorization into kinds that precedes scientific explanation.

But can one do this even within a "naturalist" account of metaphysics? Can one admit that the relationships as described at the social level are ontologically dependent upon relationships as conceived at a more "basic" level of organization without falling into the descriptivist trap that threatens reductive explanation? That is the challenge of this chapter—to develop a metaphysical view that allows for the ontological primacy of the physical, while still allowing for autonomous nomological social explanations; to defend a naturalist ontology that is shorn of reductionism, and which therefore supports the methodological conclusions about the search for autonomous social scientific explanations that I have developed elsewhere in this book.

Naturalism Without Reductionism

At the outset, it is important to be clear about what we mean here by "naturalism." Naturalism, in the metaphysical sense, is a view about ontological dependence between phenomena at different levels of organization.[2] It is a hierarchical view about the dependency and determinative relationships that hold between things "as such," where relationships at secondary levels of organization, for instance, are dependent upon relationships at the primary level. An example might be seen in the relationship between the normative and the descriptive in ethics, or the mental and the physical in the philosophy of mind, where each change at the secondary level is materially dependent upon a corresponding change at the primary level. Thus, naturalism is a rather strong metaphysical thesis about what exists and the ontological relationships between the phenomena that reality supports.

Indeed, it is probably out of this sense of dependency and determination between phenomena at different levels of organization that we get the threat of reductive explanation. The idea here is that it would serve our explanatory purposes to reduce explanations of phenomena to their most basic causal components—that we should get our epistemology to follow the metaphysics as closely as possible, so that our explanations are a mirror of reality. And indeed there is a healthy tie between naturalism as a metaphysical view, and descriptivism and reductionism about explanation, where we wish our explanation to proceed at one privileged level of description, which we hold to be ontologically fundamental.

It has often been thought that a naturalist ontology must carry within it a desire for reductive explanation. If we indeed are naturalists (and therefore believe in an ontological connection between, say, natural and social phenomena), then certainly, it is assumed, we will think that the best type of explanation we might offer for social phenomena is to show how they are a function of regularities at a more basic level. After all, doesn't the naturalist propose to tell us that social scientific facts are ontologically dependent upon physical ones?[3] Yes—and if so, the argument runs, one will naturally wish to frame our explanatory accounts of social phenomena in terms of these non-social relationships. Once we have bought into the naturalist ontology, it is assumed that the best explanation we can have, and the one we will aspire to, will be one that shows how the phenomena at the "higher" or "secondary" level are really a function of regularities at the "basic" or "primary" level. That is, it is assumed that we will want to reduce one level of inquiry to another that is recognized as more fundamental. Thus, we see how reductionism purports to further the naturalist's explanatory goal.

Yet while there certainly are cases where reductive explanation is a well-warranted methodological tool, there are also those areas in which its appropriateness is more controversial. In his account of reductionism given in *The Structure of Science*,[4] Ernest Nagel has highlighted the relevant issues. According to Nagel,

> Reduction ... is the explanation of a theory or a set of experimental laws established in one area of inquiry, by a theory usually though not invariably formulated for some other domain. For the sake of brevity, we shall call the set of theories or experimental laws that is reduced to another the 'secondary science,' and the theory to which the reduction is effected or proposed the 'primary science.'[5]

Nagel then goes on to point out, however, that reduction is not always an unqualified success, and indeed that,

> [In problematic cases] the distinctive traits that are the subject matter of the secondary science fall into the province of a theory that may have been initially designed for handling qualitatively different materials and that does not even include some of the characteristic descriptive terms of the secondary science in its own set of theoretical distinctions. The primary science thus seems to wipe out familiar distinctions as spurious, and appears to maintain that what are *prima facie* indisputably different traits of things are really identical.[6]

Thus, we can begin to see that there are certain cases where reductionism may run *contrary* to our desire for explanation by distorting the very regularities that we desire to have explained; it will gloss over secondary distinctions that we find it meaningful to have explained, and which may form the very backbone of our explanatory inquiry.

But is this a possible admission by a naturalist? Yes. It is perfectly appropriate to be a thoroughgoing naturalist and yet reject reductive explanation. To see this, it is significant to realize that naturalism is a *metaphysical* view about what exists, but that explanation is an *epistemological* one relative to how we have described it. And as a metaphysical view about the nature of the phenomena *as such*, why should a naturalist ontology so closely constrain our beliefs about the epistemology that will best help us to capture the phenomena *as described*, which forms the basis for our explanations? It is, after all, the phenomena as described that we hope to account for in our explanations. And it is only after we have captured the phenomena in terms of a certain description that regularities begin to emerge. Ontology alone does not dictate the terms of our explanations, but also the level of description that we have used to characterize the nature of any regularities arising out of metaphysical dependency. So why should the mere fact that one is a naturalist cause us to prejudge the issue of which *descriptions* of the phenomena, supported by ontological dependency, we will find most compelling and in need of explanation? Even given certain metaphysical relationships, there are a variety of questions we might ask about the phenomena under investigation and the regularities that they support.

One reality, that is, may support a multitude of descriptions—and therefore explanations—of it. In matters of explanation we should thereby be free to pursue the phenomena at many different levels of description, corresponding to our interests. It is important to remember that even a strong metaphysical connection between different sets of phenomena need not fully determine the epistemology that we should use to study the regularities that may arise out of these ontological connections, expressed at different levels of organization. This is to say that even if we believe in a *single ontological reality* (which must constrain our scientific inquiry by ruling out those accounts that are inconsistent with it), this still may support an infinite number of different levels of description of the connections that arise out of it. Different patterns, that is, emerge at different levels of description; thus we see how one reality may support a multiplicity of sciences based on alternative accounts of the regularities supported within it. And since scientific explanation is relative to our *descriptions* of reality, it is perfectly appropriate to contend that we ought to pursue the regularities that arise out of these ontological dependencies at many different levels of explanation based on alternative accounts of the phenomena in question and our diverse explanatory interests. There is more than one way to conduct nomological inquiry. So we see how even a naturalist may support a wide range of descriptions of the same phenomena, given our diverse interests and explanatory goals.

It is unfortunately the case, however, that many advocates of naturalism have underestimated these considerations and have instead fallen into the *descriptivist* trap of supposing there is a single privileged level of description that captures all facets of a given ontological relationship, and that our explanations must suitably mirror this ontology. This, however, is to read an epistemological moral in what is at base a metaphysical story. For how can we be so sure that we have ever *discovered* this perfect level of description, or that it would capture all that we want to know about the phenomena in question? No description, I contend, can hope to capture all facets of reality. We therefore should pursue many levels of explanation of the phenomena nature presents us, corresponding to various descriptions of the regularities that are supported by underlying ontological dependency.

Reduction, therefore, even where it is in principle possible, may not exhaust our interest in scientific explanation, and indeed in some cases may run contrary to our explanatory goals. For often we want explanation of phenomena as captured at a certain level of description. Phenomena exhibit different regularities at different levels of organization. Laws, after all, are accounts of regularities in the phenomena as described, not merely as such. Indeed, patterns emerge at the secondary level precisely because it's not just the phenomena that make up the subject of our study, but the phenomena as described. Thus, interactions at the primary level may only take shape as *regularities* when captured by the concepts and theories that are employed at the secondary level of investigation. So even if reduction is in principle possible (because we believe in materialism about relationships between primary and secondary levels of organization), this may not be all there is to explanation—we may want autonomous explanations of regularities that emerge only at secondary levels of description. We find it explanatorily relevant to pursue description of the phenomena at secondary levels and to explain the regularities we find there in terms of conceptual distinctions that are meaningful at the secondary level. Thus, a naturalist ontology need not compel the abandonment of nomological inquiry at secondary levels, in favor of reductive explanation, even when we admit that secondary regularities may be supported by more basic ontological relationships; for it is more than just the bare bones of ontology that we find in need of explanation, but often why, at certain levels of description, we see regularities that vanish at other levels.

A good example here may be drawn from the actual practice of science in the relationship between chemistry and physics.[7] Chemical regularities are ontologically dependent upon underlying physical relationships. And yet there are certain phenomena that emerge only at the chemical level of description and require explanations in terms that are meaningful to that science. Take, for example, the phenomenon of liquidity. There is nothing controversial in the claim that the properties of a liquid depend on the physical relationships of its molecular structure. And yet the properties of a liquid that are most interesting to the chemist—its surface tension, clarity, viscosity, index of refraction, and boiling point—emerge only at the level of description at which we are dealing with the behavior of molecules at the macro level. The phenomena may admit of descriptions at other levels of interest, but the chemist wants explanations of the phenomena in terms that are useful to the theories, concepts, and distinctions that are basic to this science. Thus, we legitimately want autonomous explanation of chemical phenomena as described in chemical terms, even though we admit that they are dependent upon relationships that are instantiated at the micro-physical level. Chemical laws may at base be dependent upon phenomena that can also be captured at some other level of description (although perhaps not nomologically), and yet we find them explanatory nonetheless. Thus, it seems perfectly appropriate to reject reductionism in these instances and to preserve the chemical terms and distinctions that ratify explanation at the secondary level despite our commitment to naturalism. Even while admitting that all chemical phenomena are ontologically dependent upon physical relationships, we eschew the reduction of chemistry to physics. For in chemistry we wish to study relationships that seem "epistemologically emergent" from the more basic ontological relationships, and which are only accountable through inquiry at the secondary level.

Such epistemological emergence, it is important to point out, is emphatically *not* a claim—at least it need not be—that certain phenomena are ontologically emergent as well. We need not appeal here to "supernatural" or other "metaphysical" conceptions of a breakdown in ontological dependency in order to back up the general point about explanatory autonomy.[8] Rather, the idea here is one of emergence relative to the patterns and regularities we seek when engaging in scientific inquiry. What then is epistemological emergence? It is the claim that certain patterns and regularities "emerge" as a function of the way that we have organized the data of our experience. The world itself does not fully provide the regularities that we study in our scientific investigation. Instead, these laws and patterns are partially characterized by the descriptions and concepts we employ, the regularities and organization we discern, the patterns that we find interesting, and the theories that we have at each particular level of inquiry. Emergence, therefore, is not relative to the phenomena as such, but is rather dependent upon the phenomena as described and organized in a particular way. Thus, the laws that are the fruit of our inquiry are not only a function of the nature of ontological dependency but also importantly depend upon our contributions to the study of it, which forms our epistemological point of view.

The world is composed of a package of loose and separate events.[9] Of course, there are certain ontological dependencies that exist between some of these events (and indeed any scientific inquiry seems founded on some version of this minimal "realist" premise). But the "subject matter" of any science consists of more than just this primitive "stuff" of the world; the "subject matter" of any science is just "matter" before we begin to analyze it. It is the character of those dependencies that we find puzzling and problematic, however, that shapes and frames our inquiry, and thus out of the myriad connections of the world a "subject" first arises.

This is not to argue that we impose all regularities upon the world—rather it is merely to note that there are so many possible connections between the phenomena with which we are presented that our investigation must necessarily be selective. To make this idea more concrete, let's examine an analogy. Think of a vast mosaic tile floor.[10] There is a definite, determinate relationship between each tile and those adjacent to it. This relationship is capturable in a complex account of the placement of each relative to its neighbors. But it is also true that there are certain patterns that emerge only at a distance, and even that different people will see different correlations at the same or further distances. The same "real world" geometric relationship between the tiles may support perhaps thousands of possible perceived patterns in it. The design I see, therefore, seems dependent not merely upon the "real world" arrangement of the tiles next to one another, but also on the level or character of my point of view. Our interests and perceptions, that is, make a contribution to our experience of the pattern that we will see, and we may choose to describe it in unique terms. Different observers may thus describe the same design in divergent though equally accurate ways. One mosaic may support many different descriptions of it. The relation of the tiles underdetermines our experience of it and the way that we will attempt to account for the patterns that we see in it.

We seem to carve up the ontological data of the world differently, that is, at different levels of inquiry relative to our concepts, theories, descriptions, and the questions we are interested in asking. Some of the connections we observe seem to us to need an explanation, and some do not (and indeed many we may never notice). Thus, our investigation is shaped both by the dependencies in the world and the conceptual tools that we use to examine them. The world provides us with the data that constitute our experience, but it is up to us to arrange this into a meaningful pattern that will be the subject of scientific investigation. In short, patterns do emerge at secondary levels of investigation because it's not just the phenomena as such that make up the subject of our study, but the phenomena as described; interactions at the primary level may only take shape as regularities when captured by the concepts and theories employed at the secondary level. It comes as no surprise, therefore, that we seek pluralistic modes of description and investigation in seeking to explain the patterns we perceive in nature.

This all comes down to the idea that one ought to be skeptical that there are "natural kinds" that structure our experience and, in turn, our scientific investigation. True, there may be real ontological connections that support the phenomena we observe, but the nature of those connections must be captured in a description before it is suitable as a subject for scientific treatment. Nature alone underdetermines the categorization of our experience, which is necessary before we can offer an explanation. For there are many different ways of describing the same reality, and we will notice different correlations depending on the groupings that we use. There are no brute law-like relationships. Laws are a function of the world *as described* in a certain theoretical vocabulary. One reality, therefore, may support a plethora of different explanations of it because there are so many different possible categorizations of the phenomena it supports.[11] Thus, one may believe in the reality of the ontological connections that underlie the phenomena, while being a skeptic about the reality of the descriptive terms that we have used to capture them in our explanations. One may be a realist, that is, about ontology, but a "nominalist" about the terms that we have used to understand it. After all, is it the phenomena that are real, or the phenomena as described in a certain way? If we want to maintain the flexibility in scientific inquiry necessary in order to find laws, surely it is better to prefer the former view. We should therefore be free to *redescribe* the phenomena we observe in terms that are most efficacious to our inquiry, when the descriptive terms that we have been using yield correlations that are unsatisfactory.

Thus, we may now see how it would be useful to reject reductive explanation in favor of autonomous inquiry at secondary levels of description, even if one is a metaphysical naturalist and believes that nomological correlations are supported by the underlying ontology of nature. One can believe in the search for laws at secondary levels of description, that is, even if one also believes that the phenomena can be covered by descriptions given at other levels (which may or may not be law-like). Likewise, one can believe that there are objective metaphysical connections, without necessarily believing that there is a single best way to describe the phenomena they support, or that explanation of these regularities must proceed at one single level. Thus, we can now see that it is best to reject reductive explanation because it provides too strong a view about the level at which the phenomena we desire to have explained would have to be described before they would admit of scientific treatment. It may "run the risk of wiping out familiar distinctions," as Nagel warned, and thus would stifle rather than enhance our explanatory goals. For such descriptions, even if they could be given, may miss precisely those distinctions we desire to have explained.

The difficulties we would face in reducing the concepts and descriptions that constitute the patterns at the secondary level would therefore be compounded as we attempted to give an explanation of these regularities at the primary level, for an explanation at the secondary level contributes to our understanding of the patterns in question in a way that one at the primary level would not—to offer a reductive explanation would require that we effect a perfect description of the regularity without the requisite concepts available at the secondary level. But this, I argue, would hopelessly frustrate the adequacy of the reduced explanatory account. The concepts and theories employed at the secondary level cannot be so easily eliminated without remainder, and thus the terms in which one might hope to give a primary account of secondary phenomena would likely be impoverished. This problem with reductive explanation is seen in two points.

Nicholas Sturgeon has argued, following Richard Boyd, that we should take note of the fact that the metaphysical notion of ontological dependence is separate from that of explanation.[12] Thus, even if there are "any continuous physical parameters, then there are continuum many physical states of the world, but there are at most countably many predicates in any language, including that of even ideal physics; so there are more physical properties than there are physical expressions to represent them."[13] The issue is crucial for explanation: even if there indeed do exist connections at the primary level (that mirror the relationships we are studying at the secondary level), this is no guarantee that these secondary phenomena are capable of any—not to mention nomological—expression at the primary level. And in a related capacity, Ernest Nagel here adds the observation that in some sense it is misleading even to ask whether the "properties" of one science are reducible to another given the fact that the "nature of things" is not amenable to direct inspection, but rather is a function of the theoretical framework that we are employing.[14] In short, Nagel builds upon Sturgeon's point by highlighting the fact that correlative predicates may not exist at the primary level because the properties that are under investigation may not even be meaningful there. For reduction, Nagel points out, is theory dependent.[15]

To carry this argument further, it is important to note that some secondary phenomena would not even be interesting at the primary level, because it is only at the secondary level that we notice the "emergence" of specific law-like regularities. So it seems appropriate that we seek explanation at the secondary level. Indeed, the way that we conceive of any regularity will have a significant impact on what we will find adequate as an explanation of it. This, of course, is not to argue that the basic ontological connections between properties may not be expressed at other levels (although even so they may not be law-like), but is merely to note that the explanation we seek should fulfill our epistemological goals. Even if a connection exists at other levels of description, it may not be meaningful there. Remember that the regularities and relationships—the "laws"—that are the subject of our inquiry seem to be epistemologically emergent. And as we noted before, a few ontological connections can support an infinite array of perceptual arrangements; ontological connections alone underdetermine the subject matter of any science. The inquirer must also make a contribution before a subject matter, and regularities, begin to emerge. Explanation, that is, presupposes a description before it can answer a question. Thus, as Sturgeon notes, it seems implausible that explanations at the secondary level can be paraphrased at the primary level without explanatory loss.[16] For our explanations seem to mirror not merely the way that the world is "really" divided, but must correspond to the way that we have chosen to divide it at each level of investigation, given our theories and descriptions.

This now brings us to the considerations that will frame my second point. At this juncture a critical reader might object that in the examples just given I have not shown that we could not offer reductive explanations of a naturalistic relationship, nor have I pointed out why one might not insist that, the problems so far raised notwithstanding, we still ought to aim at reductive explanation as our ideal. And indeed there is some sting in this observation—although, I will argue, not much. The critic is right to point out that the choice of the level of inquiry engaged in is in some sense arbitrary in that it depends upon what we happen to find interesting, and therefore we have not upset the reductionist enterprise. A committed reductionist might therefore claim that he or she does not find an explanation adequate unless it goes to the very root of the dependency between the levels to uncover the basis of the ontological dependency. And isn't this what all explanations should aim at? Certainly we *may* be satisfied by a non-reductive explanation, but have we really then given a full account? How can one deal with such criticism?

First, it is important to point out that nothing in my earlier account required that we abandon reductionism in those regions where we find it useful. Instead, I argued that there seem to be certain cases in which we want to maintain our naturalism even though we recognize that reductive explanation is not adequate, precisely because we would not in some instances find it explanatory. But what to do about the person who finds *only* reductive explanation adequate? We are here forced to depart from simple examples and note that there are several instances where, although we suspect that there is indeed an interesting naturalistic relationship between two levels of phenomena, we may not yet know what it is. To say that we believe that the nature of ontological dependency supports reduction in principle is something very different than to say that it is available for our explanations. Therefore, to require that we pursue only reductive explanations may in many cases be tantamount to stopping all inquiry.

A relevant example here is the relationship between mental and physiological states. Certainly in its full detail this is a perplexing problem, but the general point of concern for our discussion is that even though we may recognize that each mental state has a specific physiological state behind it, we may have no way of knowing right now what that relationship is. Fodor has pointed out that identical mental states would seem to require identical physiological states—yet we lack access to the causal laws that would allow us to articulate the nature of this dependency. That is, we do not yet (and some have argued that we can never) know the "bridge laws" that would be required to connect these two realms and thus provide us with the mechanism that would help to explain psycho-physical causation.[17] So should we stop all secondary inquiry?

Clearly, we should not. For it is often only via the secondary science that we later find out what the bridge laws may be and thus become capable of expressing the original relationship in terms of the primary science. So, if for no other reason, one might wish to eschew an exclusively reductionist explanatory framework for heuristic reasons as well as those concerning the adequacy of explanation. It may well be that research at the secondary level will aid research at the primary level and will prove fruitful for our inquiry there. Thus, if we ever hope to reduce mental states to physiological ones, to return to our immediate example, we had better continue our pursuit of law-like patterns at both levels of inquiry; we should persist in trying to account for the phenomena at both levels of description.[18]

Second, and more importantly, one should note that there seems to be a conceptual confusion at the root of this desire to forego explanation at all of these other levels of description (in favor of the pursuit of reductive explanation), so that we can get to the heart of ontological dependency. For even reductive explanations are dependent upon our *descriptions* of reality and are theory dependent. How then can we hope to get to the root of ontological dependency by using reductive explanations? Mustn't it be true that there is more than one way of characterizing such relationships, and therefore that there may even be many *competing* reductive explanations? The goal of reducing all explanations to a single foundational account of ontological dependency is a myth. The descriptivist assumption is just as false when we are aiming at reductive explanations as when we are offering autonomous ones. For there is no single objective vocabulary we can use to capture ontological dependency. Our explanations of metaphysical relationships must always be mediated by an imperfect and incomplete language. Thus, even if one is a committed naturalist who believes only in reductive explanations, we can never hope to escape the fact that there are many different ways of describing the same reality, which may form the basis of alternative explanations. There is always going to be a break between the world as such and the words that we use to describe it (which are the basis for our explanatory accounts). Descriptivism, that is, is false precisely because once we realize that our knowledge of ontology is necessarily filtered through linguistic categorizations of the phenomena, it becomes clear that there are many alternative descriptions of one and the same reality, and so there must be many possible ways of explaining it as well.

Where are we left, then, in our consideration of reduction, and what is the point of our analysis for the social sciences? So far there have been three general points of interest for our argument that one can legitimately sever naturalist metaphysics from reductive explanation. First, we have noted that reductionism is not always consistent with our goal of explanation. Often we would find reductive explanation inadequate precisely because the very regularities we are seeking to explain do not exist at the primary level, and also because, even if they did exist, we would probably not find them as interesting or meaningful as the original patterns.[19] Second, it seems clear that even if what we are aiming at is a fully reductive account, we will probably only get there by recognizing the useful role of autonomous inquiry. Third, it becomes clear that there are deep epistemological problems with the attempt to single out reductive explanation as free from the descriptive difficulties that are a part of offering scientific explanations.

How are these points tied to social science? Simply by noting that in social inquiry they all find more particular methodological expression in the support of autonomous nomological investigation. If it is true to say that the naturalist perspective in chemistry does not interfere with the chemist's investigation at a legitimately autonomous level of inquiry, then why should we suppose that the case should be otherwise for the naturalist in social science?[20] If we do not advocate the abandonment of nomological inquiry in chemistry in favor of reduction to physics, why should we suppose that physicalism would be an adequate replacement for the search for social scientific laws? Certainly, we may admit that social facts seem dependent upon physical ones (just as the chemist realizes that his or her subject finds its basic dependencies at the physical level), yet this is no argument in favor of reductive *explanation*. Social scientific phenomena, I contend, are epistemologically emergent in just the same way as are certain phenomena in chemistry. Moreover, the laws that relate these phenomena might be emergent as well. The phenomena seem interesting to us at the secondary level, and so we choose to seek our explanation in terms that seem appropriate to autonomous investigation. We develop theories, concepts, and distinctions that are unique to such secondary inquiry. And it seems clear that social inquiry has even more in common with the example of psycho-physical investigation than it does with chemistry and physics. In some sense it is not just that we find social scientific phenomena interesting in their own terms, but that we do not yet know how the relationships that emerge at that level of investigation might be better explained at any other level of description. Explanation is more than just a matter of capturing ontology; we must account for why we see the regularities that we do, given the descriptive categories we have chosen.

The point, then, is that naturalism and reductionism are separate issues—just as are ontology and explanation; metaphysics and epistemology. Ontological dependencies may influence our epistemology, but so do the questions that we bring to our inquiry. Thus, inquiry must not be taken to be perfectly determined by the dependency relationships that exist at the ontological level, but is rather shaped by the interrelation between this ontology and the epistemology that we bring to its study. For it is only when filtered through our descriptive categorizations that the phenomena admit of any kind of explanation at all. Naturalism is a commitment to the idea that there is an ontological dependency between phenomena at different levels of organization, but it does not dictate a single type of explanation that may illuminate these connections. Moreover, it does not fix the descriptive terms we will need to use in order to pursue an explanation in the first place. We have thus moved beyond reductive explanation in the social sciences.

Supervenience

I have now shown that it is possible to defend a view of naturalism that is consistent with autonomous, non-reductive inquiry in the social sciences. But what kind of a naturalist account might support this viewpoint? Some have suggested supervenience.

Supervenience seems to have originated in the field of ethics; indeed, we can trace the idea back to G. E. Moore.[21] Jaegwon Kim notes that although Moore did not himself use the term "supervenience," he nevertheless recognized its metaphysical force. Moore writes, "if a given thing possesses any kind of intrinsic value in a certain degree, then not only must that same thing possess it, under all circumstances, in the same degree, but also anything *exactly like it,* must, under all circumstances, possess it in exactly the same degree."[22] The idea here is one of consistency based upon the ontological dependence of sets of properties on relationships at other levels of organization. Kim has characterized supervenience as,

> belonging in that class of relations, including causation, that have philosophical importance because they represent ways in which objects, properties, facts, events, and the like enter into dependency relationships with one another, creating a system of interconnections that give structure to the world and our experience of it.[23]

Yet it is here that Kim stops to consider the difference between two different types of supervenience relationships: weak and strong.[24]

Although both weak and strong supervenience share the notion of recognizing the dependency relationships between sets of properties, we note that weak supervenience does not imply the full sense of property-to-property entailment that strong supervenience does. Weak supervenience, as exemplified in the passage by Moore, rather stops short of such direct entailment, calling our attention instead to the partial dependency relationship that is required for consistency. Kim writes, "weak supervenience ... only requires that any two things having the same natural properties must be either both good or both not good. This is surely not enough for saying that a thing's being good 'follows' from its having the natural properties it has."[25] We see, then, that weak supervenience does not imply the stronger metaphysical thesis that the set of natural properties, for instance, fully fixes the set of social (or moral, or aesthetic, etc.) properties at the secondary level; rather it merely implies a "consistency requirement"—namely, that if we are going to say that two properties are equivalent in all natural respects, then we must also say that they are going to be equivalent in all social (or other secondary) respects. Thus, what strong supervenience implies that weak supervenience does not is "world-to-world" consistency— the idea that the secondary properties *follow* from the primary ones in a deterministic way.

Strong supervenience, on the other hand, *does* imply the kind of property-to-property entailment across possible worlds that weak supervenience does not, such that when we have fixed what Kim calls the "base" properties, we have also fixed the "family" properties that are supervenient upon them. That is, since the family properties are held *in virtue of* the base properties, once we have fixed the natural properties, the social properties will fall out of them necessarily.[26]

To capture this distinction more concretely, let's consider an example. Suppose that I am grading the final exams for my class in philosophy. I finish assigning point values and note that five of the exams are in the low 90s, five are in the low 80s, five are in the low 70s, and so on. Based on my desire to spread the grades out more or less evenly across the class, I decide on a curve by which 90 and above is an *A*; 80 and above is a *B*; 70 and above is a *C*, and so on. Later, I run across three exams that I forgot to grade. I do so and notice that the point values are 72, 89, and 89. After giving the 72 a *C*, I am in a quandary about what to do. I do not want to give more than six *A*s in the class, but since I have already decided on five *A*s, I am presented with the problem of what to do with the two exams that are 89 points. Clearly, I must treat like cases alike; if I am going to give one an *A*, I must do so for the other. Finally, I decide to stick to my original plan of giving all exams in the 80s a *B*. In this instance, one might say that the grade of *B* weakly supervenes on the fact that the exam had 89 points, for any other exam that had 89 points must be assigned the same grade as this one. But this is certainly less than saying that the exam is a *B in virtue of* the fact that it had 89 points, for I was free to change the curve and decide that both deserved an *A*. To say that I must treat like cases alike is *not* to say that the fact that a particular exam got a *B* was *determined* by the fact that it had 89 points, for it is clear that in other circumstances (for instance, if there were no exams in the 90s, or even if there had been only *one* with an 89), I may well have given it an *A*. We thus begin to see the distinction between weak and strong supervenience.

But what work does this distinction do for us in our search for an ontology that supports the non-reductive conclusions we came to in the last section? I hope to show that both weak and strong supervenience can provide the framework for which we are looking—that each can be squared with both naturalism *and* autonomy—and specifically, despite skepticism to the contrary, that even strong supervenience can support non-reductive explanation.

First, it is important to note that both supervenience relationships are true to the ontological dependency between primary and secondary properties that is required of naturalism. Surely strong supervenience, with its sense of full entailment, is consistent with this outlook; and even weak supervenience, with its consistency requirement, points out that secondary properties are partially dependent upon primary ones as well.[27] It should be clear, then, that both types of supervenience relationships do not compromise our commitment to naturalistic connections between social and natural phenomena, for both uphold the notion that phenomena at secondary levels of organization are dependent upon those at primary levels. That is, whether relationships at the primary level are thought to determine, or merely to influence, those at the secondary level, it is clear that we have not compromised our commitment to metaphysical dependence. But do both views support the non-reductive epistemology that I have outlined?—I hope to show that they do.

Starting with weak supervenience, it seems clear that its sense of partial dependency (free from full determination) supports the conclusion that our social scientific explanations must do something more than simply mimic the specific property-to-property connections between natural and social phenomena; for with weak supervenience we are not proposing that there necessarily *are* any such connections! Remember that with weak supervenience we are endorsing a partial dependency requirement between phenomena at different levels of organization (that is, the relationships at the secondary level will also depend on other factors, for instance, what is held constant in this world). And with this, we are denying the existence of stronger metaphysical connections (needed to support bridge laws between the two levels) that are necessary for reduction. Thus, one is here constrained to argue that a reductive explanation of social phenomena, set in terms of natural relationships, would be fundamentally frustrated by the lack of complete ontological (and nomological) connections *between* the two levels of organization.[28] We may know that changes at the primary level result in changes at the secondary level, but this does not guarantee that the causal mechanism by which this takes place is available for our explanations, nor does it highlight which other factors may be influential.[29]

Thus, as Kim notes, many would find weak supervenience to be quite attractive if our desire is to support autonomous explanation, for it "acknowledges the primacy of [natural properties] without committing us to the strong claims of … reductionism."[30] The dual implications of ontological dependency wedded to the viability of autonomous (non-reductive) explanation lends weak supervenience a powerful endorsement as a candidate in our search; it provides us with the delicate duality that is needed, for freedom from full entailment liberates us from the need for reductive explanation.

But to carry the point about supervenience even further, one can argue that *strong* supervenience is *also* consistent with the epistemological virtues of autonomous non-reductive social scientific explanation. Now it may, at first glance, appear that strong supervenience could not be squared with the non-reductive conclusions that we have just considered. After all, the account that has been given of strong supervenience points out that there do seem to exist the strict property-to-property connections here that result from full entailment, which are a prerequisite for reductive explanation. That is, if we allow that the primary properties "fix" (determine) the secondary ones necessarily, we have left the door open for an epistemology that will exploit the nature of these ontological connections in its explanations. Reduction "in principle" now becomes possible. And in fact, there has been some heated debate in the literature over whether strong supervenience implies reductionism and hence that it is hostile to autonomous explanation. In fact, some have said that the supervenience relationship itself is just disguised reduction![31]

But there are problems with this view, and it is clear that we needn't go this far. Indeed, whether such claims are compelling even on their own terms (and there is growing evidence that they are not),[32] it seems that such a strong view about the inevitability of reduction is motivated by *additional epistemological commitments* about the nature of explanation, which are not themselves implicit within the metaphysics of supervenience.[33] And it is within these commitments that we can identify the roots of the mistaken characterization of strong supervenience.

First, it is important to realize that although reductionism may be *permitted* by the ontological assumptions of strong supervenience, this does not show that reductionism is *implied* by it. Indeed, quite the contrary. Reductive explanations may be possible in some cases but with one qualification—we have to know what the ontological connections are before we can hope to fashion explanations that reflect them and, more importantly, we will need to be sure that the phenomena we are attempting to explain are not epistemologically emergent, such that the type of explanations we are seeking will be those that we would find satisfactory in a reductionist context. I will argue that it is hard enough to satisfy the first condition, let alone the second—and here lies the epistemological point.

Following Kim, we should here note that it is one thing to say that the connections implied by strong supervenience *exist*, but it is quite another to say that they are *available* for reductive explanation.[34] For there is no guarantee that our epistemology will be able to follow our ontology this closely.[35] Kim writes,

> strong supervenience ... says nothing about how successful we shall be in identifying causes and framing causal explanations; it is also silent on how successful we shall be in discovering causal laws. Explanation is an epistemological affair. ... The thesis that a given domain supervenes on another is a metaphysical thesis about an objectively existent dependency relation between the two domains; it says nothing about whether or how details of the dependency relation will become known so as to enable us to formulate explanations [or] reductions.[36]

Thus, it is clear that the claim that there are dependency connections between two sets of properties exemplified in causal laws is separate from having in hand those "bridge laws" that would make reduction possible.[37] We just may not be in a position to make explanatory use of even our strongest intuitions about these relationships.

This is not to deny, however, that the bridge laws connecting these two realms may exist (and thus that the possibility of "local" reductions in the future is closed), but is merely to point out that we have no way to measure our future *access* to these bridge laws, even if we think they exist, and thus find that autonomous inquiry is the only kind that is now available in many disciplines. This, of course, matches our earlier reflections about the heuristic value of non-reductive explanations in the absence of connecting data. Here we can appreciate the perhaps fully determinate relationships that may exist between natural and social phenomena yet recognize that our lack of epistemological access to these ontological connections requires agnosticism about the viability of reductive explanation in these fields. This lack of access thereby recommends the pursuit of non-reductive alternatives in the interim. It is wise to pursue pluralistic modes of investigation in the face of our ignorance. Supervenience thus is consistent with the epistemological autonomy of social scientific inquiry even when it is interpreted "strongly."

Moreover, why think that even if reduction in principle were possible, this would imply that we must desire it? Remember that there is an important break between metaphysics and epistemology.[38] Supervenience is a metaphysical thesis about ontological dependency—it refers to relations in the phenomena *as such,* not as described; but reduction is an *epistemological* view about *explanation.* We will remember that explanation, however, depends not just on the ontology of nature, but is also relative to the phenomena *as described,* and what we are interested in knowing about them. And why assume that there is only *one* legitimate description of any given ontological relationship, which must be captured through reductive explanation? Indeed, what guarantee do we have that reductive explanation will be able to effect an adequate description of the relationship in question such that we will be able to offer a satisfactory explanation, even supposing that there is an objectively existent ontological relationship? Just because supervenience may allow for the minimum requirement of ontological dependency necessary for reductive explanation, this does not ensure that we will desire reductive explanations, or that we will find them explanatory. Nor should it compel us to give up on the pursuit of explanatory inquiry at other levels of description. Supervenience does not entail reduction because *descriptions* mediate our transition from ontological dependency to explanation. And this is an epistemological matter that is extracurricular to the metaphysical commitments of supervenience.

We may now realize, then, that even if access to bridge laws were possible, it still may be a difficult issue to identify those phenomena which we would find it explanatory to reduce. Even supposing that we had a genuine ontological connection, why think that it would be a trivial matter to describe it, or that there is only one way that we could possibly *want* it described? The epistemological emergence of social scientific phenomena, for instance, may require the pursuit of autonomous (non-reductive) inquiry even in those cases where we perhaps do know the precise nature of ontological dependence. That is, strong supervenience may be strong enough to guarantee full entailment metaphysically, but it is not strong enough to insure that the "laws" or "patterns" that seem to emerge at the secondary level will also reflect meaningful relationships that are present at the primary level. Entailment *between* two levels does not guarantee that the patterns we desire to have explained *at* one level are capable of nomological (or perhaps any other interesting kind of) explanation at another level of description. Reductive explanation is not our only option. It is a myth, therefore, that naturalism about ontology compels us toward reduction, for we now see that there can be many different explanations of things, depending on our descriptions of the underlying ontological relationships. Explanation is more than just a matter of mirroring ontology. This is why it is wrong to say that supervenience is just disguised reduction.

Recall here the earlier example drawn from chemistry. We may rightfully hold that whether a compound is in a liquid state is strongly supervenient upon its physical disposition, and yet we may understandably choose not to undertake a reductive explanation of regularities that we take to be most interesting at the chemical level. Just because reduction is possible does not mean that we must or should pursue it in order to give an adequate explanation; for knowledge of ontological dependence does not insure explanatory merit.

In the end, therefore, it is not at all clear that supervenience must lead us toward reductive explanations. Thus, our reflections on supervenience may be reconciled with our earlier hopes for a more sophisticated understanding of naturalism. For we now see that it is possible to be a naturalist about ontology without believing in the necessity of reductive explanation. It is clear that the ontological thesis behind naturalism is fundamentally separate from the methodological or epistemological question of the possibility or desirability of giving reductive explanations. Supervenience may allow for the *possibility* of reduction in principle (if desired) by underwriting our confidence in the ontological dependencies necessary for it, but it does not say that we must buy into the additional epistemological commitments— like descriptivism—necessary to embrace reductive explanation as the sole legitimate account that is consistent with naturalist ontology. It therefore seems appropriate to interpret supervenience (both weak and strong) as a naturalist metaphysical commitment that nonetheless sanctions our search for autonomous non-reductive explanations.

We have thus found a metaphysical framework that is beyond descriptivism, and which may back up our methodological commitments about the search for autonomous social scientific laws. Properly understood, supervenience allows for redescription and the search for explanations of regularities at secondary levels, even while admitting that the patterns here supported may be dependent upon ontological relationships at other levels of organization. Supervenience thus supports our commitment to the pluralism of explanatory stances and to the search for laws in the social sciences.

Notes

1. It is all right to use reduction to "unify," that is, but not to exclude.

2. Note the distinction between the metaphysical sense of "naturalism" given here and the methodological one, given in Chapter 1.

3. It is sometimes argued that this dependency thesis requires that social facts are "nothing but" natural ones. But such a claim is ambiguous for, when discussing *conceptual* emergence it is false. I wish to interpret naturalistic dependence broadly enough so that it will allow for conceptual emergence and thus reject the strong version of the "nothing but" claim.

4. Ernest Nagel, *The Structure of Science* (New York: Harcourt, Brace, and World, 1961).

5. Nagel, *Structure*, p. 338. Throughout this chapter I will follow Nagel's usage of the terms "primary" and "secondary."

6. Ibid., p. 340.

7. Peter Railton has used this example to make a similar point in his "Explanations Involving Rationality," (manuscript).

8. One does not need to argue here that the "whole is greater than the sum of its parts," or that there is some non-natural entity that emerges only at certain levels. I point this out because the literature on "spontaneous orders" sometimes is confused on the point of whether the emergence of patterns at higher levels of organization is due to ontological or epistemological emergence.

9. Cf. David Hume's argument about the problem of induction in *An Enquiry Concerning Human Understanding* (Indianapolis: Hackett, 1977).

10. One could easily imagine other examples to make this same point, for instance, abstract painting, the interpretation of ink blots in the Rorschach test, and so on. This particular example is borrowed from Peter Railton's lectures on the philosophy of science, given at the University of Michigan, Winter, 1985.

11. Indeed, one may even support the idea that there can be many differing *nomological* explanations of the same event. For a dissenting view cf. Jaegwon Kim's "Mechanism, Purpose, and Explanatory Exclusion," in J. Tomberlin, ed., *Philosophical Perspectives*, Vol. 3 (Atascadero, Calif.: Ridgeview, 1989), pp. 77–108.

12. Nicholas Sturgeon, "Moral Explanations" in Copp and Zimmerman, eds., *Morality, Reason, and Truth* (Totowa, N.J.: Rowman and Allanheld, 1985), p. 59. Sturgeon writes, "what I deny … is that from this metaphysical doctrine about what sort of facts moral facts are, anything follows about the possibility of reduction. …"

13. Ibid., p. 60.

14. Nagel, *Structure*, p. 364.

15. Ibid., pp. 364–366.

16. Sturgeon, "Moral Explanations," p. 62.

17. For discussion of this point see Donald Davidson, *Essays on Actions and Events* (Oxford: The Clarendon Press, 1982); and Jaegwon Kim, "Psychophysical Laws" in E. LePore and B. McLaughlin, eds., *Actions and Events: Perspectives in the Philosophy of Donald Davidson* (Oxford: Basil Blackwell, 1985).

18. Sturgeon, "Moral Explanations," p. 62.

19. Also, we should note here Sturgeon's point—it may be terribly difficult to find a way to express the original regularities at another level because we do not have an adequate language in hand. See text accompanying note 13.

20. Cf. David Thomas, *Naturalism and Social Science: A Post-Empiricist Philosophy of Social Science* (Cambridge: Cambridge University Press, 1979). Another good example of the same point is winetasting. Surely all would agree that the "balance," "taste," and "integrity" of a wine is naturalistically dependent upon its physical composition, and yet no winetaster would hold that a merely chemical analysis of each glass of wine could replace the job of the taster.

21. Jaegwon Kim, "Concepts of Supervenience," *Philosophy and Phenomenological Research*, Vol. 45, No. 2 (December 1984), p. 154.

22. Quoted in Kim, "Concepts of Supervenience," p. 154.

23. Ibid., p. 154.

24. In his later work Kim adds the concept of "global" supervenience and explores its relationship to strong supervenience. For our present purposes, however, the fine points of this relationship can be ignored.

25. Ibid., p. 161.

26. Ibid., p. 160.

27. Indeed, weak supervenience is all that naturalism requires. The naturalist need only argue that social scientific properties are dependent upon natural ones in this world, not that we need to specify across all possible worlds what the connections in fact might be.

28. The claim is that we not only may not know the relationships, but also that weak supervenience does not require that such rigid ontological connections exist.

29. Cf. Kim, "Concepts of Supervenience," p. 161. See also note 17 above.

30. Ibid., p. 156.

31. Paul Teller, "Is Supervenience Just Disguised Reduction?" *Southern Journal of Philosophy*, Vol. 23, No. 1 (1985), pp. 93–99; Harold Kincaid, "Supervenience Doesn't Entail Reducibility," *Southern Journal of Philosophy*, Vol. 25, No. 3 (1987), pp. 343–356; Harold Kincaid, "Supervenience and Explanation," *Synthese*, Vol. 77 (1988), pp. 251–281.

32. In addition to Kincaid's work cited above, see also Geoffrey Hellman and Frank Thompson, "Physicalism: Ontology, Determination, and Reduction," *Journal of Philosophy*, Vol. 72 (1975), pp. 551–564.

33. For instance, descriptivism, which leads to the idea of explanatory exclusion. But why think that there is just one description that is adequate? Shouldn't we believe that there are many possible explanations precisely because there are so many possible descriptions?

34. Kim, "Concepts of Supervenience," p. 173. Kim writes, "Reduction, explanation, and the like are epistemic activities, and the mere fact that such equivalence or biconditionals 'exist' is no guarantee that they are, or will ever become *available* for reductive or explanatory uses."

35. Despite Kim's recognition that supervenience is a metaphysical relationship (and that there is a break between metaphysics and epistemology), his views about *explanation* are quite remarkable. Kim seems to believe that although supervenience doesn't *imply* reductionism, there *is* only one level of explanation that is adequate to capture material relationships. That is, like Davidson, Fay, Scriven, and so many others, Kim is a *descriptivist*, who is against the idea of pursuing different explanations of the same phenomena (cf. here his paper "Mechanism, Purpose, and Explanatory Exclusion"). Kim seems to have broadly *physicalist* explanatory commitments; even though he realizes that strong supervenience *by itself* cannot ensure reductionism, he nonetheless finds the reductionist's case compelling for other reasons. He assumes, that is, that there is a single ideal language for describing social reality, which forms the basis for our explanations. See here Kim's paper, "The Myth of Non-Reductive Materialism," *Proceedings of the APA*, Vol. 63, No. 3, pp. 31–47. Harold Kincaid has some relevant things to say about Kim's recognition that supervenience does not entail reducibility in his "Supervenience Doesn't Entail Reducibility," at p. 355, note 9.

36. Kim, "Concepts of Supervenience," p. 175.

37. Bridge laws are epistemological; they concern the relationship between the phenomena as described. Although they depend on ontological connections between the two levels, the bridge laws themselves are epistemological.

38. In his "Supervenience, Determination, and Reduction," *Journal of Philosophy*, Vol. 82 (1985), pp. 616–618, Jaegwon Kim writes, "[there is] a distinction between the ontology of dependency and the epistemology of reduction and explanation."

7

Prospects and Limitations
of a Nomological Social Science

It is agreeable to think that what is unknown to us in our day and generation is also unknowable. The advance of knowledge has, however, constantly shown how false such an assumption might have been in the past: forewarned by this, we should be wise to presume that this assumption is not less dubious now.

—Barbara Wootton

In light of the analysis of the last six chapters of this book, we are now in a position to draw some conclusions about the status of laws in the explanation of human behavior—the prospects and limitations of a nomological social science. So far, in Chapters 2 through 6, we have examined those arguments that have purported to show that social scientific laws are either impossible, impractical, or irrelevant in light of the intractability of the subject matter of social science and what we desire to know about it. We have seen, however, just how hard it is to motivate such claims, and I have shown that each of the arguments examined in service of these goals fails to support the rejection of social scientific laws. Moreover, in view of the continuity between the kinds of problems generated by the subject matters of natural and social science, I have suggested that there is an important methodological analogy to be drawn between the types of explanation used in natural and social science; to the extent that natural science has overcome an "intractable" subject matter, so may we have confidence in the ability of social science to do so as well. Finally, I have suggested that the search for social scientific laws may legitimately be carried out at an autonomous level of inquiry.

But we now face some very difficult questions. For if all of these things are true, why is it that after two centuries of largely positivistic social scientific inquiry, we have yet to produce any unequivocal examples of social scientific laws?[1] If social scientific laws are not impossible, impractical, or irrelevant, then why are they not actual? Below, I will sketch out my reasons for thinking that we have been prevented from discovering social scientific laws up until now, but I will also provide reason for being optimistic about their future prospects for the explanation of human behavior.

First, it is important to remember our earlier discovery in Chapter 4 that one may be expecting social science to live up to a standard of nomologicality that could not even be met in natural science. The notion that a social scientific law would have to be exceptionless and reflect a necessary connection, for instance, reveals adherence to an idealized standard of nomologicality that is out of touch with the actual practice of scientific explanation. That is, it may well be possible to have social scientific regularities that could live up to the expected standards of nomologicality when confronting a complex subject matter (as compared, for example, to that in volcanology or meteorology), but in social science we have just been unwilling to do the work necessary to refine them into law-like form or to think of them as potential laws. Compared to what we are willing to think of as candidates for law-like explanation in some of the natural sciences, and our willingness to continue searching for ever more accurate generalizations even in the face of vast practical barriers, what we do in social science may not compare so unfavorably.[2] That is, even if we are not there yet, in volcanology or in social science, there is often a difference in *attitude* toward the appropriateness of the nomological ideal in shaping our explanations across these disciplines that, if one looks at the criteria used and the barriers faced, seems inappropriate. The issue is *not*, however, that if only we were willing to lower our standards, social scientific "laws" would become available. Rather, the idea is that we have suffered from a regrettably "honorific" definition of nomologicality drawn from an idealized view of natural science. But if it is supposed to be an *empirical* issue whether or not there are laws in social science, we must be fair in saying what we are willing to *count* as a law in social science, as compared to natural science, by setting out realistic criteria by which to judge them.

A second point, however, is even more compelling. In concert with Mary Williams' findings in the philosophy of evolutionary biology, we must realize that even if laws are ultimately possible, we cannot expect to find them right away—or at all—unless we are prepared to do the conceptual work necessary for their formulation.[3] Several factors stand in the way of our task. Williams argues that without the proper vocabulary and theory, we will be unable to recognize the referents of any laws and so will be led falsely into thinking that they do not exist or could not be discovered. As has been the case in evolutionary biology, Williams suggests, the underlying presence of law-like regularities has been obscured by improper identification of the "natural kinds" embedded in the theory and an unwillingness to entertain any changes in the way that we conceive of the phenomena (i.e., descriptivism). But if we hope to find laws, she argues, we must be ready to do the conceptual work necessary to find the better theories and vocabulary, which will be needed for their recognition. Thus, in social science, one might argue, the conviction that we *already have* the proper descriptive terms in hand may be what is standing behind our inability to find any social scientific laws.

Here it is important to realize that what are later thought to be "simple" regularities often only seem so once we have in hand the theoretical apparatus that allows us to identify the proper nomological referents. But without the natural kinds and theoretical vocabulary already in place—especially when dealing with "complex" phenomena—recognition of even straightforward laws can be delayed indefinitely. Consequently, even those practical difficulties that may ultimately yield in the face of scientific refinement can be made to seem insurmountable if we are not willing to be flexible in our descriptions of the phenomena under investigation in the service of ferreting out the underlying law-like connections. In natural science as in social science, "descriptivism" stands as a barrier to the recognition of laws.[4] The process of scientific explanation only succeeds when we are flexible in our descriptions and theories because we are adamant in our commitment to the nomological ideal.[5]

But what might lie behind this unwillingness on the part of some philosophers and social scientists to allow the development of the proper theories and vocabulary for investigating social phenomena, which are necessary for the formulation of social scientific laws? We have just seen that one barrier might be the false analogy with an idealized view of natural science, where we expect that the search for social scientific laws should go as smoothly as we (in retrospect) imagine it went for the discovery of the simplest laws of physics. Such a commitment might lead us to believe that scientific procedures have no place in those areas of inquiry that it has not already conquered. Yet an even more daunting impediment might be the fact that we may well not *want* to discover any laws in social science.[6]

Often, the closer a subject matter is to us the more threatened we are by the idea that there are laws governing it. The idea that there may be laws governing human behavior is seen by many to threaten our dignity and autonomy, to degrade our status as humans, and potentially to give rise to horrible moral and political consequences.[7] There is indeed a longstanding undercurrent in the literature that recounts essential limitations on nomological social science that it is a good thing that laws are impossible because their realization would be so dangerous.[8] Hence, we cannot ignore the possibility that much of the literature purporting to place the blame for social science's inability to arrive at suitable laws on its intractable subject matter is actually rooted not in the belief that the subject matter of social science is unsuitable, but to a prior commitment to some essential difference between humans and nature.[9]

But such fears and prejudices, I argue, have no place in deciding what are straightforwardly methodological matters. Indeed, as Williams points out, such resistance often impedes scientific progress in legitimate areas of inquiry, and may itself stand behind the long delay in admitting that there are laws in evolutionary biology. And unfortunately, since the investigation of social phenomena is even closer to home, the search for laws here will be even more volatile and controversial, and we can expect the resistance to employment of nomological modes of explanation to be proportionately greater. Thus, one might submit that the ease with which people are willing to blame the subject matter of social science for the absence of social scientific laws masks their deep-seated fear that our behavior may indeed be law-governed. If this were true, of course, it would not necessarily mean that all of the arguments against social scientific laws made on the basis of the intractability of its subject matter were therefore wrong. Yet the point of this book has been to show just how problematic some of those arguments in fact are. And in the hope of advancing the debate—and improving the outlook for a nomological social science—I am here considering the question of why they have nevertheless remained so popular, by unearthing some of the misconceptions behind the arguments against laws.

The search for laws, even when we have a comparatively simple subject matter and no psychological resistance, can take a long time. And the lesson to be learned from Williams is that laws can be held off almost indefinitely if we will not do the work necessary to find them. In the meantime, there are plenty of culprits to blame for their absence; unlike some of the simpler regularities in astronomy (which were resisted in their own time too, one should add), we are not compelled by the gradual collection of overwhelming and easily accessible evidence to admit that they exist. The extent to which social scientific regularities are deeply embedded in "non-human-sized" theories is just one factor that can be expected to delay their recognition. Likewise, the belief that there is only one level of conceptualization and description appropriate to the investigation of social phenomena only makes matters worse. Thus, we now come to understand why it may be that we have not yet discovered any social scientific laws.[10]

In order to find social scientific laws we must give up the notion that if laws are present, somehow we would already have discovered them, and must instead think more in terms of how to bring about the conditions necessary for their realization. The formulation of social scientific laws requires the right theory, natural kinds, and vocabulary (as well as the willingness to look for them) coupled with the proper view of what a law would entail (i.e., it would only have to live up to the standards of nomologicality fulfilled in actual natural scientific practice). Moreover, one must be willing to employ a rigorous attitude toward testing the theories that one is considering.[11] But most important is the requirement that we be motivated to do the work necessary to develop better theories and alternative categorizations of social phenomena, evidenced by a more open attitude toward the value of redescription. All of this must precede the task of learning how to ameliorate some of the practical barriers standing in the way of laws provided by the subject matter, which can only be arrived at through the process of science itself. But are such barriers insurmountable? Or, do we still have reason to be hopeful about the possibility of a nomological social science?

What I hope to have shown in this book is that it *is* worthwhile to look for social scientific laws—that we shouldn't be so anxious to close the debate about their availability or usefulness in social inquiry in light of the problems with the arguments against them and their relevance to some of our most basic explanatory interests. True, it is easy to despair about the prospects for social scientific laws and to blame their absence solely on the intractability of the subject matter. After all, it is often our inability to overcome some of the practical problems generated by the subject matter (at some particular level of description), that is the immediate barrier to the formulation of laws. But, we have seen throughout our analysis that the uniqueness of the subject matter of social science cannot account fully for the absence of laws—for complexity, openness, limitations on our ability to perform controlled experiments, and other such problems are also present in the subject matter of much of natural science and would preempt the discovery of laws there as well.[12] We must not misunderstand the reason for the success of natural science. The ability of natural science to find laws is not due to the fact that the subject matter it studies is simple or repetitive, or that it allows for controlled experimentation, but that our approach to the subject matter is one that allows for flexibility in the description of the phenomena and the development of new theories in the search for laws, which allows us to ameliorate those barriers the subject matter provides. So when we face a subject matter in social science that seems disanalogous to the one in natural science, we must not be so ready to blame the difficulty in obtaining laws merely on the alleged intractability of the subject matter and thus conclude that laws are here unattainable. Instead, we must realize that there are problems unique to all of the subject matters that are studied by science—each provides its own unique set of challenges. But the issue is whether the problems faced in social science are sufficient to prevent nomological explanation because they are not open to scientific treatment. I hope to have given reason for thinking that such widespread pessimism is unwarranted.

Moreover, it should also be clear that despite the refrain that we want something different explained *about* human behavior, which laws cannot give us, this does not show that laws are irrelevant to all forms of inquiry into human behavior. Nor, we should remember, were the arguments made by the physicalist any more compelling, who—despite the claim that laws *are* relevant to the explanation of human behavior—would have us give up the search for social scientific laws by narrowing our search to a level of description that is felt to be more efficacious. The underlying commitment to descriptivism that motivates *both* of these alternatives to nomological social science may cause us to be too hasty in our abandonment of the search for laws in social science. We must learn, however, to be more tolerant in the face of our diverse explanatory interests.

We are thereby drawn to the conclusion that many of the barriers to the formulation of social scientific laws are conceptual and provide no essential barriers manifested through the uniqueness of the subject matter of social science, which would require abandonment of the nomological ideal, or which would suggest a fundamental methodological split between natural and social science. Indeed, we would do well here to emulate the attitude taken in natural science when faced with what appear to be intractable barriers in the subject matter, by being willing to redescribe the phenomena we are investigating in the hope of ameliorating some of the barriers to law-like explanation. For at base, it is not the subject matter that keeps us from finding laws, but rather our unwillingness to think of the subject matter in other terms (or to amend our theories about it) in search of law-like regularities. Indeed, laws are not of the phenomena as such, but as described by a particular level of inquiry. Thus, the prospect of redescription holds out the possibility of social scientific laws.

Of course, this does not amount to a full blown *defense* of laws in the explanation of human behavior. I have not here produced any laws, offered any new social theories, or even given any redescriptions. Rather, I have tried to move us *toward* a defense of social scientific laws by engaging in the important conceptual and a priori work that serves as a prelude to the empirical work necessary to actually produce a nomological social science: to identify those areas of inquiry where we desire nomological explanation and to come up with the means for ameliorating some of the practical barriers standing in the way of their formulation by identifying the proper theories, categorizations, and vocabulary. The latter task, of course, cannot be solved through philosophical analysis, but requires the process of scientific investigation itself. This scientific scrutiny, however, cannot begin unless we are clear about the epistemological status of our subject. I hope to have moved us toward a better understanding of this point.

In this book, I have tried to vindicate the *search* for social scientific laws—the nomological ideal—even while recognizing the important barriers that remain in the way of their realization. I have tried to do this by showing that the arguments against social scientific laws fall short, and by showing that there is reason to be optimistic about finding them in light of continuity with the situation faced in the development of laws in natural science. I am not, then, dealing with the issue of whether there are now social scientific laws, or even with what they would look like if we had them. Rather,

I am defending their potential existence from those who think that there are arguments that preempt their value in social inquiry.

In the end, of course, it is—just as in natural science—an empirical question under what conditions we can expect to find laws in the social sciences, and when we would find them to be explanatory. And as in natural science, we must look at each instance on a case-by-case basis. In any event, though, we need to stay away from the temptation of providing sweeping generalizations about what is or is not ultimately possible in social science in an attempt to close the debate prematurely and to dismiss nomological explanation as unworthy of further consideration. We cannot afford the luxury of such a hasty decision; the potential role of laws in illuminating the causes of some of the most longstanding social dilemmas facing social science should persuade us to keep this path open.

In a way, then, one might think of this work as a long promissory note for the explanatory value of the search for social scientific laws that can only be cashed out empirically by future social scientists. I hope, however, to have made an important contribution to the future realization of laws simply by providing a more complete understanding of the conditions surrounding their potential development. To sweep away spurious objections and to put the debate about the status of laws on better philosophical footing would be to have made progress.

This is not to say that the discovery of social scientific laws will be easy, nor do I mean to underestimate the magnitude of the task that lies ahead; in addition to the difficulty of identifying the proper natural kinds, vocabulary, and theory there are indeed enormous practical barriers provided by the subject matter we are investigating in social science, which we do not yet know how to overcome. But, the point is that such barriers do not divide neatly along disciplinary lines, nor do they uniquely implicate factors found only in social science. And most important, the problem of figuring out how to ameliorate these difficulties is a perfectly appropriate job for science itself. It is true that there are problems facing the discovery of laws in the social sciences, just as there are in natural science. But the problems confronted, although they must be taken seriously, do not counsel abandonment of the nomological ideal in social science. And I hope to have demonstrated that it is not so easy to generalize about what these limitations might be. We have yet to confront a difference in the subject matter of natural and social science that would necessitate an essential difference in the methodology of explanation. Indeed, many of the barriers to the pursuit of laws in social science are of the same type as those that have been faced (and overcome) in the development of laws in natural science.

At high levels of description, such as those routinely confronted in meteorology and evolutionary biology, complexity and openness provide practical barriers to the pursuit of laws. But we do not here give up on the search for laws in the face of such barriers, despite the qualifications they must sometimes put on our immediate success. The present question for social science is whether we have reason to think that such barriers could not be handled by the methods of science.[13] Throughout this work, I have tried to show that the case for such a pessimistic conclusion is not compelling. We must learn to look for laws despite the practical limitations sometimes placed on our inquiry by its subject matter.

What advice, then, might be given to a working social scientist? Do not give up on the nomological ideal merely because the descriptive terms you are currently using are not yielding law-like regularities. It is important not to be wedded to the theoretical terms you have used to describe reality when better alternatives are potentially available. The attitude that fosters "descriptivism" must be avoided. For the subject matter of social science is human behavior, and not that behavior as captured by some particular theory or vocabulary. Second, recognize the power of experimentation, insofar as it is currently available. There are areas of social science that are open to experimentation, and which may yield explanations that surprise us (witness those described in Chapter 4). The willingness to treat our behavior as the subject of legitimate scientific investigation, which may tell us things we did not expect, and to reject the hubris that merely because we are human beings we already basically understand the causes of human action, are the first steps to the discovery of social scientific laws.

As in natural science, we must therefore continue to search for ways to ameliorate such obstacles; we must allow social scientific investigation the same freedom to redescribe the phenomena, and to develop new theories and categorizations, that has allowed natural science to succeed in the face of what were once thought to be insurmountable barriers to nomological explanation. In short, we must resolve not to hamstring the process of scientific inquiry by wedding the investigation of human behavior to one particular level of description and explanation—for science works only when we have the freedom to pursue regularity wherever it may lead, even if it requires the redescription of the phenomena we seek to have explained.[14] Of course, in social science we must probably start out with what will be initially unsatisfying explanations.[15] But the difficulty of figuring out how to improve them should not prompt us to suppose that we can do no better. The course of natural science in its development of laws may here provide us with general grounds for encouragement about the future of social scientific laws. At the very least it tells us this: One cannot find laws unless one is willing to do the conceptual work necessary for their discovery.[16]

Perhaps it is too soon to know whether such a task will ultimately be successful. But it is similarly too early to know that it will not be. In light of the important role laws have played in the history of natural scientific explanation, we must admonish ourselves to tolerate many levels of inquiry until it is clear which way things will turn out. In the interim we should not be so anxious to *close the debate* about the role of laws in the explanation of human behavior by hoping to account for the absence of social scientific laws through some essential deficiency in its subject matter. We must remain comfortable in our ignorance for at least awhile longer. The nomological ideal has proven robust in structuring our explanations throughout the corpus of science, even in those cases in which we are still seeking fully satisfactory nomological accounts. But there must be in social science, as there is in natural science, a presumption in favor of laws and a willingness to abide by the methodological dictates necessary for their search until it can be shown that they would be of no further use in structuring our explanations of human behavior.[17]

Of course, to some it seems clear that the day has already arrived when we may dismiss laws as having no legitimate role in the explanatory task faced by social science. But to follow the route of the critics of the nomological ideal is to run the risk of deciding prematurely the single most important issue in the philosophy of social science. The alternative, to some, may appear equally unpromising. But to withhold our judgement is distinct from forever giving up hope.

Throughout this book we have found reason to be optimistic about the future of social scientific laws, despite the limitations imposed on it by its subject matter and the nature of our interests, in light of (1) the failure of the arguments from complexity and openness to show that social scientific laws are either impossible or impractical, (2) the narrowness of the claim that social scientific laws are irrelevant to the task of explanation in social science, and (3) the strength of the analogy between the methodological situation faced by natural and social science. We may remain hopeful, therefore, about the prospects for a nomological social science, even though we recognize that the search for those laws that may explain human behavior cannot proceed without facing the practical barriers imposed by its subject matter—for in this way, as in others, social science reveals itself to be just like natural science.

Notes

1. Of course, this is something of an embarrassment for social science. But it should be noted that depending on what we mean by a law, it is debatable whether or not "unequivocal" laws have been achieved even in natural science. See Carl Hempel's discussion of the problems surrounding his notion of an "explanation sketch," in his "The Function of General Laws in History," *Aspects of Scientific Explanation* (New York: The Free Press, 1965), p. 238. One might argue that the present issue, however, is why social science hasn't been able to live up to even the more qualified standards.

2. The point is that despite barriers to laws in natural science, we do not give up on the nomological ideal.

3. This is not the old line about the "youth" of social science. Without the proper theories, one could well be patient forever. Rather, the issue is not the youth of social science per se, but its youth relative to a well-codified theory. Think here of the parallel situation faced in evolutionary biology.

4. Imagine a case in which you were using the wrong natural kinds, which you just thought were constitutive of the phenomena you were studying; even if there were underlying laws, you would be hard-pressed to find them. Science needs the flexibility to evolve new vocabularies and to develop new theories to deal with the barriers that come up in the search for laws. No single level of description can be privileged—if it does not yield law-like regularities, we must be willing to change it. See note 14 below.

5. The idea here is that the search for laws is *primary*, and that the other goals of inquiry are in service of this. This may be true even if we could never hope to reach a fully law-like description of an event. In these cases one might think of the nomological ideal as a "useful fiction" in structuring our explanations. Think here of how the nomological ideal is used in meteorology, where our theories can get asymptotically close to law-like regularity, even while they in practice never quite achieve the ideal of flawless prediction.

6. In his *Reason and Nature: An Essay on the Meaning of Scientific Method* (Glencoe, Ill.: The Free Press, 1931), pp. 348–349, Morris Cohen cites a paraphrase of a statement by Bertrand Russell, "the reason social scientists do not more often arrive at the truth is that they frequently do not want to."

7. Rollo Handy, *Methodology of the Behavioral Sciences: Problems and Controversies* (Springfield, Ill.: Charles C. Thomas, 1964), p. 126. Such claims have also been made about determinism, evolutionary theory, and sociobiology.

8. This suggestion is seen throughout the literature that recounts essential limitations, perhaps most pointedly in Hayek, whose fear of a planned economy goes hand-in-hand with his attempt to show that the laws necessary to build one are impossible.

9. Handy, *Methodology*, p. 170.

10. And yet a critic might continue to press, doesn't it at least count against the prospects for a nomological social science that this program has been tried before and failed? Doesn't the similarity of the argument to that made by the logical positivists undermine the nomological status of social science in light of the positivists' failure to establish a unified science? But the answer to this is no. The logical positivists tried to bring social science up to the impossibly high standards that allegedly framed natural scientific inquiry. But the last thirty years of the philosophy of science has led to a reevaluation of our understanding of those standards. On a more realistic view, we may see how much natural and social science had in common all along. Thus, the failure of the logical positivists to achieve unification at such an idealized level is irrelevant to the prospects for success of the current program.

11. Rigorous testing, however, will never be enough, especially when one is facing a complex subject matter. It is my view that far too much confidence has

been placed on testability as the arbiter for good scientific theories. For in social science, it is not so easy to come up with theories that are worth testing in the first place. Of course, testing is important, but one must also admit, with Mary Williams, that proper theory *development* should also be emphasized. When facing the prejudice of descriptivism and the barriers of complexity and openness, it is harder to come up with good theories than one might imagine.

12. Of course, one might try to argue here that there is an important difference in the degree to which each discipline suffers from such problems. But the important issue to note for social science is that even in those areas of natural science that arguably face phenomena just as complex, where we are just as inhibited from performing controlled experiments, and so on, we do not give up searching for laws.

13. Harold Kincaid, "Defending Laws in the Social Sciences," *Philosophy of the Social Sciences,* Vol. 20, No. 1 (March 1990), pp. 56–83.

14. Throughout the history of natural science, there have been many examples of the abandonment of certain descriptions of natural phenomena, which were not yielding satisfying law-like regularities. Think, for instance, of the debate surrounding "phlogiston" or "caloric," or the medieval use of "the four humors." Imagine our dilemma if later scientists had insisted that those terms were "natural kinds," which were just constitutive of the phenomena under investigation. The search for laws would have been radically impeded.

15. Barbara Wootton, *Testament for Social Science: An Essay in the Application of Scientific Method to Human Problems* (London: George Allen and Unwin, 1950).

16. Some have argued that there are in fact no laws in natural science either. But as I have pointed out before, although this is an interesting issue, it does not detract from my argument here. My point has been a comparative one—that whatever method of explanation is used in natural science (that has heretofore gone under the name of "nomological"), there are no essential barriers preventing us from employing this methodology in the explanation of human behavior. Whether one chooses to call this mode of explanation "nomological" is a separate issue.

17. For instance, if it could be shown that humans do indeed have free will, this might be a strike against laws. And yet even then one might hold out for the search for regularity on pragmatic grounds. For if we indeed have free will, then why do we act so regular and make such poor use of our freedom? A nomological social science might continue to be useful and liberating even if it turned out that the nomological ideal was only a useful fiction. On the other hand, if we do *not* have free will, it would seem important to investigate the causes behind our action and the constraints under which human action proceeds.

Bibliography

Achinstein, Peter. *Law and Explanation: An Essay in the Philosophy of Science*. Oxford: The Clarendon Press, 1971.

Adelstein, Richard P. "Institutional Function and Evolution in the Criminal Process," *Northwestern University Law Review*, Vol. 76, No. 1 (March 1981), pp. 1–99.

Adorno, Theodor, et al. *The Positivist Dispute in German Sociology*. New York: Harper and Row, 1969.

Apel, Karl Otto. "Types of Social Science in the Light of Human Interests of Knowledge," *Social Research*, Vol. 44 (1977), pp. 425–470.

———. *Understanding and Explanation: A Transcendental-Pragmatic Perspective*. Georgia Warnke, trans. Cambridge: The MIT Press, 1984.

Armstrong, D. M. *What Is a Law of Nature?* Cambridge: Cambridge University Press, 1983.

Aronson, J. L. "Explanation Without Laws," *The Journal of Philosophy*, Vol. 66, No. 17 (September 1969), pp. 541–557.

Ayala, F. J. and T. Dobzhansky, eds. *Studies in the Philosophy of Biology: Reduction and Related Problems*. Berkeley: University of California Press, 1974.

Ayer, A. J. "What Is a Law of Nature?" *The Concept of a Person*. New York: St. Martin's Press, 1963.

Beck, Lewis White. "The 'Natural Science Ideal' in the Social Sciences," *The Scientific Monthly*, Vol. 68 (June 1949), pp. 386–394.

Bell, Daniel. *The Social Sciences Since the Second World War*. New Brunswick, N.J.: Transaction Books, 1982.

Berelson, Bernard and Gary Steiner. *Human Behavior: An Inventory of Scientific Findings*. New York: Harcourt, Brace, and World, 1964.

Bergner, Jeffrey. *The Origins of Formalism in Social Science*. Chicago: University of Chicago Press, 1981.

Bernstein, Richard. *Praxis and Action: Contemporary Philosophies of Human Action*. Philadelphia: University of Pennsylvania Press, 1971.

———. *The Restructuring of Social and Political Theory*. New York: Harcourt, Brace, Jovanovich, 1976.

Blalock, Hubert M. *Causal Inferences in Nonexperimental Research*. Chapel Hill: The University of North Carolina Press, 1964.

———. *Basic Dilemmas in the Social Sciences*. Beverly Hills: Sage Publications, 1984.

Bohman, James. *New Philosophy of Social Science: Problems of Indeterminacy*. Cambridge: The MIT Press, 1991.

Borger, Robert and Frank Cioffi, eds. *Explanations in the Behavioral Sciences*. Cambridge: Cambridge University Press, 1970.

Boulding, Kenneth. *Beyond Economics: Essays on Society, Religion, and Ethics.* Ann Arbor: The University of Michigan Press, 1968.

Braithwaite, Richard. *Scientific Explanation: A Study of the Function of Theory, Probability and Law in Science.* Cambridge: Cambridge University Press, 1968.

Braybrooke, David. *Philosophical Problems of the Social Sciences.* London: MacMillan, 1965.

———. *Philosophy of Social Science.* Englewood Cliffs, N.J.: Prentice-Hall, 1987.

Brock, Timothy and Lester Grant. "Dissonance, Awareness, and Motivation," *Journal of Abnormal and Social Psychology,* Vol. 67, No. 1 (1963), pp. 53–60.

Brock, Timothy. "Dissonance Without Awareness," in R. Abelson, ed. *Theories of Cognitive Consistency: A Sourcebook.* Chicago: Rand McNally, 1968, pp. 408–416.

Brodbeck, May. "On the Philosophy of the Social Sciences," in E. C. Harwood, ed. *Reconstruction of Economics.* Great Barrington, Mass.: American Institute for Economic Research, 1955.

———, ed. *Readings in the Philosophy of the Social Sciences.* New York: MacMillan, 1968.

———. "Explanation, Prediction, and 'Imperfect' Knowledge," in May Brodbeck, ed. *Readings in the Philosophy of the Social Sciences.* New York: MacMillan, 1968, pp. 363–398.

———. "Methodological Individualisms: Definition and Reduction," in May Brodbeck, ed. *Readings in the Philosophy of the Social Sciences.* New York: MacMillan, 1968, pp. 280–303.

Bronowski, J. *The Identity of Man.* London: Heinemann, 1965.

Brookings Institute. *Essays on Research in the Social Sciences.* Washington D.C.: The Brookings Institute, 1931.

Brown, Lee. "The Sufficiency of Nomological Subsumption for the Explanation of Events" (Ph.D. dissertation, University of Michigan, 1986).

Brown, Robert. "Explanation By Laws in Social Science," *Philosophy of Science,* Vol. 21 (1954), pp. 25–32.

———. *Explanation in Social Science.* London: Routledge and Kegan Paul, 1963.

———. *The Nature of Social Laws.* Cambridge: Cambridge University Press, 1984.

Brown, S. C., ed. *Philosophical Disputes in the Social Sciences.* Sussex: The Harvester Press, 1979.

Bryson, Lyman. *Science and Freedom.* New York: Columbia University Press, 1947.

Buck, Roger C. "Reflexive Predictions," in May Brodbeck, ed. *Readings in the Philosophy of the Social Sciences.* New York: MacMillan, 1968, pp. 436–447.

Cartwright, Nancy. *How the Laws of Physics Lie.* Oxford: The Clarendon Press, 1983.

Chase, Stuart. *The Proper Study of Mankind: An Inquiry into the Science of Human Relations.* New York: Harper and Bros., 1948.

Cohen, Morris R. *Reason and Nature: An Essay on the Meaning of Scientific Method.* Glencoe, Ill.: The Free Press, 1931.

Collingwood, R. G. *The Idea of History.* Oxford: Oxford University Press, 1946.

Dallmayr, Fred and Thomas McCarthy, eds. *Understanding and Social Inquiry.* Notre Dame: University of Notre Dame Press, 1977.

Danto, Arthur. *Narration and Knowledge.* New York: Columbia University Press, 1985.

Davidson, Donald. *Essays on Actions and Events.* Oxford: The Clarendon Press, 1980.

————. "Mental Events," in *Essays on Actions and Events*. Oxford: Oxford University Press, 1980.

————. "Psychology as Philosophy," in *Essays on Actions and Events*. Oxford: Oxford University Press, 1980.

Dennett, Daniel. *Brainstorms*. Cambridge: The MIT Press, 1978.

Donagan, Alan. "Are the Social Sciences Really Historical?" in Bernard Baumrin, ed. *Philosophy of Science: The Delaware Seminar, Vol. 1, (1961–1962)*. New York: Interscience Publishers, 1963.

Doyal, Len and Roger Harris. *Empiricism, Explanation, and Rationality: An Introduction to the Philosophy of the Social Sciences*. London: Routledge and Kegan Paul, 1986.

Dray, William. *Laws and Explanation in History*. Oxford: The Clarendon Press, 1957.

Dreyfus, Hubert. "Why Current Studies of Human Capacities Can Never Be Scientific," *Berkeley Cognitive Science Report No. 11*, (January 1984).

Durkheim, Emile. *The Rules of Sociological Method*. Glencoe, Ill.: The Free Press, 1965.

Dyke, Charles. *The Evolutionary Dynamics of Complex Systems: A Study in Biosocial Complexity*. Oxford: Oxford University Press, 1988.

Earman, John. *A Primer on Determinism*. Dordrecht, Netherlands: D. Reidel Publishing Co., 1986.

Emmet, Dorothy and Alasdair MacIntyre, eds. *Sociological Theory and Philosophical Analysis*. New York: MacMillan, 1970.

Fay, Brian. *Social Theory and Political Practice*. London: George Allen and Unwin, 1975.

Fay, Brian and J. Donald Moon. "What Would An Adequate Philosophy of Social Science Look Like?" *Philosophy of Social Science*, Vol. 7 (1977), pp. 209–227.

Fay, Brian. "General Laws and Explaining Human Behavior," appears as Chapter 5 in Daniel R. Sabia, Jr. and Jerald Wallulis, eds. *Changing Social Science*. Albany, N.Y.: SUNY Press, 1983, pp. 103–128.

————. "Naturalism as a Philosophy of Social Science," *Philosophy of Social Science*, Vol. 14 (1984), pp. 529–542.

————. *Critical Social Science: Liberation and its Limits*. Ithaca, N.Y.: Cornell University Press, 1987.

Feyerabend, Paul. *Problems of Empiricism: Philosophical Papers Volume 2*. Cambridge: Cambridge University Press, 1981.

Flanagan, Owen. *The Science of the Mind*. Cambridge: The MIT Press, 1984.

Flew, Anthony. *Thinking About Social Thinking: The Philosophy of the Social Sciences*. Oxford: Basil Blackwell, 1985.

Fodor, Jerry. *Representations: Philosophical Essays on the Foundations of Cognitive Science*. Cambridge: The MIT Press, 1981.

French, P., Vahling, T., and H. Wettstein, eds. *Midwest Studies in Philosophy, Vol. 15: The Philosophy of the Human Sciences*. Notre Dame: University of Notre Dame Press, 1990.

Friedman, Milton. "The Methodology of Positive Economics," in May Brodbeck, ed. *Readings in the Philosophy of the Social Sciences*. New York: MacMillan, 1968, pp. 508–528.

Gaffron, Hans. *Resistance to Knowledge*. San Diego: The Salk Institute for Biological Studies, 1970.

Garfinkel, Alan. *Forms of Explanation*. New Haven, Conn.: Yale University Press, 1981.

Geertz, Clifford. *The Interpretation of Cultures*. New York: Basic Books, 1973.

Gergen, Kenneth J. "Social Psychology as History," *Journal of Personality and Social Psychology*, Vol. 26, No. 2 (1973), pp. 309–320.

Gergen, Kenneth and Mary Gergen. *Social Psychology*. New York: Harcourt, Brace, Jovanovich, 1981.

Gewirth, Alan. "Can Men Change Laws of Social Science?" *Philosophy of Science*, Vol. 21 (1954), pp. 229–241.

Gibbard, Allan and Hal R. Varian. "Economic Models," *The Journal of Philosophy*, Vol. 75 (1978), pp. 664–677.

Gibson, Quentin. *The Logic of Social Enquiry*. London: Routledge and Kegan Paul, 1960.

Gleick, James. *Chaos: Making a New Science*. New York: Viking, 1987.

Gleitman, Henry. *Psychology*. New York: W.W. Norton, 1981.

Goldman, Alvin. "Actions, Predictions, and Books of Life," *American Philosophical Quarterly*, Vol. 5, No. 3 (July 1968), pp. 135–151.

Goodman, Nelson and W.V.O. Quine. "Steps Towards a Constructive Nominalism," *The Journal of Symbolic Logic*, Vol. 12, No. 4 (December 1947), pp. 105–122.

Goodman, Nelson. *Fact, Fiction, and Forecast*. Cambridge: Harvard University Press, 1955.

Gordon, Scott. *Social Science and Modern Man*. Toronto: University of Toronto Press, 1970.

Gould, Stephen J. "Dollo On Dollo's Law: Irreversibility and the Status of Evolutionary Laws," *Journal of the History of Biology*, Vol. 3, No. 2 (Fall 1970), pp. 189–212.

Greenwald, Anthony and David Ronis. "Twenty Years of Cognitive Dissonance: Case Study of the Evolution of a Theory," *Psychological Review*, Vol. 85, No. 1 (1978), pp. 53–57.

Grunberg, Emile. "'Complexity' and 'Open Systems' in Economic Discourse," *Journal of Economic Issues*, Vol. 12, No. 3 (September 1978), pp.541–560.

Handy, Rollo. *Methodology of the Behavioral Sciences: Problems and Controversies*. Springfield, Ill.: Charles C. Thomas, 1964.

Handy, Rollo and Paul Kurtz. *A Current Appraisal of the Behavioral Sciences*. Great Barrington, Mass.: Behavioral Research Council, 1964.

Harrod, Roy. *Sociology, Morals, and Mystery*. London: MacMillan, 1971.

Harwood, E. C., ed. *Reconstruction in Economics*. Great Barrington, Mass.: American Institute for Economic Research, 1955.

Hausman, Daniel, ed. *The Philosophy of Economics*. Cambridge: Cambridge University Press, 1984.

Hayek, F. A. "The Use of Knowledge in Society," *The American Economic Review*, Vol. 35, No. 4 (September 1945), pp. 519–530.

———. *Studies in Philosophy, Politics and Economics*. Chicago: The University of Chicago Press, 1967.

———. "Degrees of Explanation," in *Studies in Philosophy, Politics and Economics*. Chicago: The University of Chicago Press, 1967.

———. "The Theory of Complex Phenomena," in *Studies in Philosophy, Politics and Economics*. Chicago: The University of Chicago Press, 1967.

———. "The Results of Human Action But Not of Human Design," in *Studies in Philosophy, Politics and Economics*. Chicago: The University of Chicago Press, 1967.

———. "The Pretence of Knowledge," *Swedish Journal of Economics*, Vol. 77 (December 1975), pp. 433–442.

———. *The Counter-Revolution of Science: Studies on the Abuse of Reason*. Indianapolis: Liberty Press, 1979.

Hempel, Carl G. "Explanation in Science and in History" in R. G. Colodny, ed. *Frontiers of Science and Philosophy*. Pittsburgh: University of Pittsburgh Press, 1962, pp. 9–33.

———. "Explanation and Prediction by Covering Laws," in Bernard Baumrin, ed. *Philosophy of Science: The Delaware Seminar, Vol. 1, (1961–1962)*. New York: Interscience Publishers, 1963.

———. *Aspects of Scientific Explanation and Other Essays in the Philosophy of Science*. New York: The Free Press, 1965.

———. "The Function of General Laws in History," in *Aspects of Scientific Explanation and Other Essays in the Philosophy of Science*. New York: The Free Press, 1965.

Hempel, Carl G. and Paul Oppenheim. "Studies in the Logic of Explanation," in *Aspects of Scientific Explanation and Other Essays in the Philosophy of Science*. New York: The Free Press, 1965.

Hempel, Carl G. *Philosophy of Natural Science*. Englewood Cliffs, N.J.: Prentice-Hall, 1966.

———. "Logical Positivism and the Social Sciences," in Achinstein and Barker, eds. *The Legacy of Logical Positivism*. Baltimore: The Johns Hopkins University Press, 1969, pp. 163–194.

Henderson, David K. *Interpretation and Explanation in the Human Sciences*. Albany, N.Y.: SUNY Press, 1993.

Hendrick, Clyde. "Social Psychology as Historical and as Traditional Science: An Appraisal," *PSPB*, No. 2 (1976), pp. 392–403.

Hindess, Barry. *Philosophy and Methodology in the Social Sciences*. Sussex: The Harvester Press, 1977.

Hollis, Martin. *The Philosophy of Social Science: An Introduction*. Cambridge: Cambridge University Press, 1994.

Homans, George C. *The Nature of Social Science*. New York: Harcourt, Brace, and World, 1967.

———. *Social Behavioral: Its Elementary Forms*. New York: Harcourt, Brace, and World, 1981.

Hookway, C. and P. Pettit, eds. *Action and Interpretation: Studies in the Philosophy of the Social Sciences*. Cambridge: Cambridge University Press, 1978.

Hoy, David, ed. *The Critical Circle*. Los Angeles: University of California Press, 1982.

Hughes, John. *The Philosophy of Social Research*. London: Longman Group, 1980.

Hull, David. *Philosophy and Biological Science*. Englewood Cliffs, N.J.: Prentice-Hall, 1974.

Kaplan, Abraham. *The Conduct of Inquiry: Methodology for Behavioral Science*. San Francisco: Chandler Publishing, 1964.

Kaufmann, Felix. *Methodology of the Social Sciences.* New York: The Humanities Press, 1958.

Keat, Russell. "Positivism, Naturalism, and Anti-Naturalism in the Social Sciences," *Journal for the Theory of Social Behaviour,* Vol. 1, pp. 3–17.

Kim, Jaegwon. "Supervenience and Nomological Incommensurables," *American Philosophical Quarterly,* Vol. 15, No. 2 (April 1978), pp. 149–156.

———. "Psychophysical Supervenience," *Philosophical Studies,* Vol. 41 (1982), pp. 51–70.

———. "Psychophysical Laws," in E. LePore and B. McLaughlin, eds. *Actions and Events: Perspectives in the Philosophy of Donald Davidson.* New York: Basil Blackwell, 1985, pp. 369–386.

———. "Concepts of Supervenience," *Philosophy and Phenomenological Research,* Vol. 45, No. 2 (December 1989), pp. 153–176.

Kincaid, Harold. "Confirmation, Complexity, and Social Laws," *PSA 1988,* Vol. 2. East Lansing, Mich.: Philosophy of Science Association, 1988, pp. 299–307.

———. "Defending Laws in the Social Sciences," *Philosophy of the Social Sciences,* Vol. 20, No. 1 (March 1990), pp. 56–83.

———. "Quine, Meaning, and the Social Sciences," (manuscript).

Kitcher, Phillip and Wesley Salmon, eds. *Scientific Explanation: Minnesota Studies in the Philosophy of Science, Volume 13.* Minneapolis: University of Minnesota Press, 1989.

Krimerman, Leonard I., ed. *The Nature and Scope of Social Science: A Critical Anthology.* New York: Appleton-Century-Crofts, 1969.

Kuhn, Thomas. *The Structure of Scientific Revolutions.* Chicago: The University of Chicago Press, 1962.

Lessnoff, Michael. *The Structure of Social Science: A Philosophical Introduction.* New York: International Publications Service, 1975.

Little, Daniel. *Varieties of Social Explanation.* Boulder, Colo.: Westview Press, 1990.

———. "On the Scope and Limits of Generalizations in the Social Sciences," *Synthese,* Vol. 97, No. 2 (November 1993), pp. 183–208.

Louch, A. R. *Explanation and Human Action.* Berkeley: University of California Press, 1966.

Lundberg, George. "Alleged Obstacles to Social Science," *The Scientific Monthly,* (May 1950), pp. 229–305.

———. *Can Science Save Us?* New York: Longmans, Green, 1961.

Lynd, Robert S. *Knowledge for What? The Place of Social Science in American Culture.* Princeton: Princeton University Press, 1939.

Machlup, Fritz. *Methodology of Economics and Other Social Sciences.* New York: Academic Press, 1978.

———. "Are the Social Sciences Really Inferior?" in *Methodology of Economics and Other Social Sciences.* New York: Academic Press, 1978, pp. 345–367.

———. "Friedrich Hayek on Scientific and Scientistic Attitudes," in *Methodology of Economics and Other Social Sciences.* New York: The Academic Press, 1978.

———. "If Matter Could Talk," in *Methodology of Economics and Other Social Sciences.* New York: The Academic Press, 1978, pp. 309–332.

———. "The Inferiority Complex of the Social Sciences," in *Methodology of Economics and Other Social Sciences.* New York: The Academic Press, 1978, pp. 333–344.

MacIntyre, Alasdair. *Against the Self-Images of the Age: Essays on Ideology and Philosophy*. New York: Schocken Books, 1971.

———. *After Virtue: A Study in Moral Theory*. Notre Dame: University of Notre Dame Press, 1981.

MacIver, A. M. "Levels of Explanation in History," in May Brodbeck, ed. *Readings in the Philosophy of the Social Sciences*. New York: MacMillan, 1968, pp. 304–316.

Manicas, Peter. *A History and Philosophy of the Social Sciences*. New York: Basil Blackwell, 1987.

Martin, Michael. "Explanation in Social Science: Some Recent Work," *Philosophy of the Social Sciences*, Vol. 2 (1972), pp. 66–81.

———. *Social Science and Philosophical Analysis: Essays in Philosophy of the Social Sciences*. Washington D.C.: University Press of America, 1978.

———. "Geertz and the Interpretive Approach in Anthropology," *Synthese*, Vol. 97, No. 2 (November 1993), pp. 269–286.

Martin, Michael and Lee McIntyre, eds. *Readings in the Philosophy of Social Science*. Cambridge: The MIT Press, 1994.

Mayr, Ernst. *The Growth of Biological Thought: Diversity, Evolution, and Inheritance*. Cambridge: The Belknap Press of Harvard University, 1982.

———. *Towards a New Philosophy of Biology: Observations of an Evolutionist*. Cambridge: The Belknap Press of Harvard University, 1988.

McIntyre, Lee. "Complexity and Social Scientific Laws," *Synthese*, Vol. 97, No. 2 (November 1993), pp. 209–227.

Meehan, Eugene. *Explanation in Social Science: A System Paradigm*. Homewood, Ill.: The Dorsey Press, 1968.

Michalos, Alex. "Philosophy of Social Science," in P. D. Asquith and H. E. Kyburg, Jr., eds. *Current Research in Philosophy of Science*. East Lansing, Mich.: Philosophy of Science Association, 1979, pp. 463–502.

Mill, J. S. *A System of Logic*. London: Longmans, 1961.

Miller, Richard. *Fact and Method*. Princeton: Princeton University Press, 1987.

———. "Fact and Method in the Social Sciences," appears as Chapter 4 in Daniel R. Sabia, Jr. and Jerald Wallulis, eds. *Changing Social Science*. Albany, N.Y.: SUNY Press, 1983, pp. 73–101.

Minkoff, Eli C. *Evolutionary Biology*. Reading, Mass.: Addison-Wesley Publishing, 1983.

Monod, Jacques. *Chance and Necessity: An Essay on the Natural Philosophy of Modern Biology*. New York: Knopf, 1971.

Moon, J. Donald. "The Logic of Political Inquiry: A Synthesis of Opposed Perspectives," in F. Greenstein, ed. *Handbook of Political Science*, Vol. 1. Reading, Mass.: Addison-Wesley, 1974.

Mukerjee, Radhakamal. *The Philosophy of Social Science*. London: MacMillan, 1960.

Nagel, Ernest. *The Structure of Science: Problems in the Logic of Scientific Explanation*. New York: Harcourt, Brace, and World, 1961.

Natanson, Maurice, ed. *Philosophy of the Social Sciences: A Reader*. New York: Random House, 1963.

Neurath, Otto. *Foundations of the Social Sciences*. Chicago: The University of Chicago Press, 1944.

Nicholson, Michael. *The Scientific Analysis of Social Behaviour: A Defence of Empiricism in Social Science*. London: Frances Pinter Publishers, 1983.

Nisbett, R. and T. Wilson. "Telling More Than We Can Know: Verbal Reports on Mental Processes," *Psychological Review*, Vol. 84 (1977), pp. 231–259.

Outhwaite, William. *Understanding Social Life*. London: George Allen and Unwin, 1975.

Papineau, David. *For Science in the Social Sciences*. London: MacMillan, 1978.

Phillips, D. C. *Philosophy, Science and Social Inquiry: Contemporary Methodological Controversies in Social Science and Related Applied Fields of Research*. Oxford: Permagon Press, 1987.

Popper, Karl R. *The Logic of Scientific Discovery*. New York: Harper Torchbooks, 1959.

———. *The Poverty of Historicism*. New York: Harper Torchbooks, 1961.

———. *The Open Society and Its Enemies, Volumes 1 and 2*. Princeton: Princeton University Press, 1962.

———. *Conjectures and Refutations: The Growth of Scientific Knowledge*. New York: Harper Torchbooks, 1965.

———. "Prediction and Prophecy in the Social Sciences," in *Conjectures and Refutations: The Growth of Scientific Knowledge*. New York: Harper Torchbooks, 1965, pp. 336–346.

———. "The Logic of the Social Sciences," in *The Positivist Dispute in German Sociology*. London: Heinemann Educational Books, 1976.

———. *The Open Universe: An Argment for Indeterminism*. Totowa, N.J.: Rowman and Littlefield, 1982.

Porpora, Douglas. "On the Prospects for a Nomothetic Theory of Social Structure," *Journal for the Theory of Social Behaviour*, Vol. 13 (1983), pp. 243–264.

Pratt, Vernon. *The Philosophy of the Social Sciences*. London: Methuen, 1978.

Prigogine, Ilya. *From Being to Becoming: Time and Complexity in the Physical Sciences*. San Francisco: W. H. Freeman, 1980.

———. *Order Out of Chaos: Man's New Dialogue with Nature*. London: New Science Library, 1984.

Prigogine, Ilya and Nicolis Gregoier. *Exploring Complexity: An Introduction*. New York: Freeman, 1989.

Rabinow, Paul and William Sullivan, eds. *Interpretive Social Science: A Reader*. Berkeley: University of California Press, 1979.

———, eds. *Interpretive Social Science: A Second Look*. Berkeley: University of California Press, 1987.

Radcliffe-Brown, A. R. *A Natural Science of Society*. Glencoe, Ill.: The Free Press, 1957.

Railton, Peter. "A Deductive-Nomological Model of Probabilistic Explanation," *Philosophy of Science*, Vol. 45 (1978), pp. 206–226.

———. "Explaining Explanation: A Realist Account of Scientific Explanation and Understanding" (Ph.D. dissertation, Princeton University, 1980).

———. "Probability, Explanation, and Information," *Synthese*, Vol. 48 (1981), pp. 233–256.

———. "Explanation and Metaphysical Controversy" in P. Kitcher and W. Salmon, eds. *Scientific Explanation: Minnesota Studies in the Philosophy of Science, Vol. 13*. Minneapolis: University of Minnesota Press, 1989, pp. 220–252.

———. "Explanations Involving Rationality," (manuscript).
Rensch, Bernhard. "The Laws of Evolution," in S. Tax, ed. *Evolution After Darwin: The University of Chicago Centennial*. Chicago: The University of Chicago Press, 1960, pp. 95–116.
———. *Biophilosophy*. C.A.M. Sym, trans. New York: Columbia University Press, 1971.
———. *Biophilosophical Implications of Inorganic and Organismic Evolution*. Verlag die blaue eule, 1985.
Rickman, H. P. *Understanding and the Human Studies*. London: Heinemann, 1967.
Robinson, James Harvey. *The Mind in the Making: The Relation of Intelligence to Social Reform*. New York: Harper and Bros., 1921.
———. *The Humanizing of Knowledge*. New York: George H. Doran, 1923.
Root, Michael. *Philosophy of Social Science*. Oxford: Blackwell, 1993.
Rose, Arnold M. *Theory and Method in the Social Sciences*. Minneapolis: The University of Minnesota Press, 1954.
Rosenberg, Alexander. *Microeconomic Laws: A Philosophical Analysis*. Pittsburgh: The University of Pittsburgh Press, 1976.
———. *Sociobiology and the Preemption of Social Science*. Baltimore: The Johns Hopkins University Press, 1980.
———. *The Structure of Biological Science*. Cambridge: Cambridge University Press, 1985.
———. *The Philosophy of Social Science*. Boulder, Colo.: Westview Press, 1988.
———. *Economics—Mathematical Politics or Science of Diminishing Returns?* Chicago: University of Chicago Press, 1992.
———. "Scientific Innovation and the Limits of Social Scientific Prediction," *Synthese*, Vol. 97, No. 2 (November 1993), pp. 161–182.
———. *Instrumental Biology or the Disunity of Science*. Chicago: University of Chicago Press, 1994
Roth, Paul A. *Meaning and Method in the Social Sciences: A Case for Methodological Pluralism*. Ithaca, N.Y.: Cornell University Press, 1987.
Rothbard, Murray. *Individualism and the Philosophy of the Social Sciences*. San Francisco: Cato Institute, 1979.
Ruben, David-Hillel. *The Metaphysics of the Social World*. London: Routledge and Kegan Paul, 1985.
Rudner, Richard S. "Philosophy and Social Science," in E. C. Harwood, ed. *Reconstruction of Economics*. Great Barrington, Mass.: American Institute for Economic Research, 1955.
———. *Philosophy of Social Science*. Englewood Cliffs, N.J.: Prentice-Hall, 1966.
Runciman, W. G. *Social Science and Political Theory*. Cambridge: Cambridge University Press, 1963.
Ruse, Michael. "Are There Laws in Biology?" *Australasian Journal of Philosophy*, Vol. 48, No. 2 (August 1970), pp. 234–246.
———. *The Philosophy of Biology*. London: Hutchinson University Library, 1973.
Ryan, Alan. *The Philosophy of the Social Sciences*. New York: Pantheon Books, 1970.
———, ed. *The Philosophy of Social Explanation*. Oxford: Oxford University Press, 1973.

Sabia, Daniel R. and Jerald Wallulis, eds. *Changing Social Science*. Albany, N.Y.: SUNY Press, 1983.

Salmon, Merrilee. *Philosophy and Archaeology*. New York: Academic Press, 1982.

———. "Explanation in the Social Sciences," in P. Kitcher and W. Salmon, eds. *Scientific Explanation: Minnesota Studies in the Philosophy of Science, Vol. 13*. Minneapolis: University of Minnesota Press, 1989, pp. 384–409.

———. "Reasoning in the Social Sciences," *Synthese*, Vol. 97, No. 2 (November 1993), pp. 249–268.

Salmon, Wesley. "Four Decades of Scientific Explanation," in P. Kitcher and W. Salmon, eds. *Scientific Explanation: Minnesota Studies in the Philosophy of Science, Vol. 13*. Minneapolis: University of Minnesota Press, 1989, pp. 3–219.

Sayer, Andrew. *Method in Social Science: A Realist Approach*. London: Hutchinson, 1984.

Scheffler, Israel. *The Anatomy of Inquiry: Philosophical Studies in the Theory of Science*. New York: Knopf, 1963.

Schlenker, Barry R. "Social Psychology and Science," *Journal of Personality and Social Psychology*, Vol. 27, No. 1 (1974), pp. 1–15.

Scriven, Michael. "A Possible Distinction Between Traditional Scientific Disciplines and the Study of Human Behavior," in *Minnesota Studies in the Philosophy of Science*, Vol. 1. Minneapolis: University of Minnesota Press, 1956, pp. 330–339.

———. "Truisms as the Grounds for Historical Explanations," in P. Gardiner, ed. *Theories of History*. Glencoe, Ill.: The Free Press, 1959, pp. 443–471.

———. "Explanation and Prediction in Evolutionary Theory," *Science*, Vol. 130, No. 3374 (August 28, 1959), pp. 477–482.

———. "Explanations, Predictions, and Laws," in H. Feigl and G. Maxwell, eds. *Minnesota Studies in the Philosophy of Science*, Vol. 3. Minneapolis: University of Minnesota Press, 1962, pp. 170–230.

———. "The Temporal Asymmetry of Explanations and Predictions," in Bernard Baumrin, ed. *Philosophy of Science: The Delaware Seminar, Vol. 1, (1961–1962)*. New York: Interscience Publishers, 1963.

———. "Views of Human Nature," in T. W. Wann, ed. *Behaviorism and Phenomenology: Contrasting Bases for Modern Psychology*. Chicago: The University of Chicago Press, 1964.

———. "Explanation in the Biological Sciences," *Journal of the History of Biology*, Vol. 2 (1969), pp. 187–198.

Simon, Herbert. "Bandwagon and Underdog Effects of Election Predictions," *Public Opinion Quarterly*, Vol. 18 (1954), pp. 245–253.

Simon, Michael. *Understanding Human Action: Social Explanation and the Vision of Social Science*. Albany, N.Y.: SUNY Press, 1982.

Smart, J.J.C. *Philosophy and Scientific Realism*. London: Routledge and Kegan Paul, 1963.

Sober, Elliott, ed. *Conceptual Issues in Evolutionary Biology: An Anthology*. Cambridge: The MIT Press, 1984.

Studdert-Kennedy, Gerald. *Evidence and Explanation in Social Science: An Interdisciplinary Approach*. London: Routledge and Kegan Paul, 1975.

Taylor, Charles. *The Explanation of Behaviour*. London: Routledge and Kegan Paul, 1964.

————. "Interpretation and the Sciences of Man," *Review of Metaphysics*, Vol. 25, No. 1 (September 1971), pp. 3–51.

————. *Philosophy and the Human Sciences: Philosophical Paper 2*. Cambridge: Cambridge University Press, 1985.

Thomas, David. *Naturalism and Social Science: A Post-Empiricist Philosophy of Social Science*. Cambridge: Cambridge University Press, 1979.

Trigg, Roger. *Understanding Social Science*. London: Blackwell, 1985.

Truzzi, Marcelo, ed. *Verstehen*. Reading, Mass.: Addison-Wesley, 1974.

Van Fraassen, Bas. *The Scientific Image*. Oxford: The Clarendon Press, 1980.

————. *Laws and Symmetry*. Oxford: Oxford University Press, 1989.

Van Parijs, Philippe. *Evolutionary Explanation in the Social Sciences*. Totowa, N.J.: Rowman and Littlefield, 1981.

Vetterling, Mary. "Social Science Prediction" (Ph.D. dissertation, Boston University, 1976).

Von Wright, George I⁻. *Explanation and Understanding*. Ithaca, N.Y.: Cornell University Press, 1971.

Wallace, Walter. *The Logic of Science in Sociology*. New York: Aldine Publishing, 1971.

Wann, T. W., ed. *Behaviorism and Phenomenology: Contrasting Bases for Modern Psychology*. Chicago: The University of Chicago Press, 1964.

Weber, Max. *The Methodology of the Social Sciences*. New York: MacMillan, 1950.

White, Morton. *Foundations of Historical Knowledge*. New York: Harper and Row, 1965.

Williams, Mary. "Deducing the Consequences of Evolution: A Mathematical Model," *Journal of Theoretical Biology*, Vol. 29 (1970), pp. 343–385.

————. "Falsifiable Predictions of Evolutionary Theory," *Philosophy of Science*, Vol. 40, No. 4 (December 1973), pp. 518–537.

————. "Similarities and Differences Between Evolutionary Theory and the Theories of Physics," *PSA 1980*, Vol. 2. East Lansing, Mich.: Philosophy of Science Association, 1980, pp. 385–396.

————. "Is Biology a Different Type of Science?" in Sumner, Slater, and Wilson, eds. *Pragmatism and Purpose: Essays Presented to Thomas A. Goudge*. Toronto: University of Toronto Press, 1981, pp. 278–289.

————. "The Importance of Prediction Testing in Evolutionary Biology," *Erkenntnis*, (1982), pp. 291–306.

————. "Species are Individuals: Theoretical Foundations for the Claim," *Philosophy of Science*, Vol. 52 (1985), pp. 578–590.

Wilson, Bryan, ed. *Rationality*. Oxford: Basil Blackwell, 1979.

Wimsatt, William C. "Complexity and Organization," in Kenneth F. Schaffner and Robert S. Cohen, eds. *PSA 1972*. East Lansing, Mich.: Philosophy of Science Association, 1972, pp. 67–86.

————. "Reductionism, Levels of Organization, and the Mind-Body Problem," in G. G. Globus, G. Maxwell, and I. Savodnik, eds. *Consciousness and the Brain: A Scientific and Philosophical Inquiry*. New York: Plenum Press, 1976, pp. 199–267.

Winch, Peter. *The Idea of a Social Science: and its Relation to Philosophy*. London: Routledge and Kegan Paul, 1958.

Wisdom, J. O. *Philosophy of the Social Sciences I: A Metascientific Introduction*. London: Averbury, 1987.

————. *Philosophy of the Social Sciences II: Schemata.* London: Averbury, 1987.
Wootton, Barbara. *Testament for Social Science: An Essay in the Application of Scientific Method to Human Problems.* New York: W.W. Norton, 1950.

About the Book and Author

The first full-length defense of social scientific laws to appear in the last twenty years, this book upholds the prospect of the nomological explanation of human behavior against those who maintain that this approach is impossible, impractical, or irrelevant. By pursuing an analogy with the natural sciences, McIntyre shows that the barriers to nomological inquiry within the social sciences are not generated by factors unique to social inquiry, but arise from a largely common set of problems that face any scientific endeavor.

All of the most widely supported arguments against social scientific laws have failed largely due to adherence to a highly idealized conception of nomologicality (allegedly drawn from the natural sciences themselves) and the limited doctrine of "descriptivism." Basing his arguments upon a more realistic view of scientific theorizing that emphasizes the pivotal role of "redescription" in aiding the search for scientific laws, McIntyre is optimistic about attaining useful law-like explanations of human behavior.

Lee C. McIntyre is assistant professor of philosophy at Colgate University.

Index

and the Study of Human
    Behavior," 25, 57–59
"Views of Human Nature," 25, 56–
    57, 103
second law of thermodynamics, 115–
    116n.33
"self-fulfilling prophecy," 42
self-understanding. *See* consciousness;
    intentionality; meaning and
    purpose
Simon, Herbert, 52n.76
Skinner, B. F., 52n.77
social science. *See also* description; law;
    natural science
  absence of laws in, 109–110, 165–166
  analogous to natural science, 76–77,
    77–78n.6–7, 110–113, 120, 137
  autonomous explanation in, 154–
    155, 158 (*see also* law, autono-
    mous)
  conceptual work necessary for laws
    in, 29–30, 45, 166–167, 168–169,
    170, 172
  as different "in kind" from natural
    science, 15–16, 26–27, 33, 67
  disciplines of, 11n.1
  and the empirical question of law,
    76, 81n.45, 171
  and idealized standards of nomo-
    logicality, 94–97, 111–113, 166,
    167, 174n.10
  impossibility and impracticality of
    laws in, 8–9, 11 (*see also* complex
    ity; openness, of systems)
  and intractability of subject matter,
    1, 2, 7, 13n.25, 40–41, 46, 76, 121–
    122, 167–168 (*see also* subject
    matter)
  irrelevance of laws in, 7–8, 9,
    13n.24, 169–170
  lessons for, from evolutionary
    theory, 30, 33, 77n.6, 103–113,
    166–167
  levels of description in, 60–61, 63–
    64, 68, 71–73, 79–80n.31, 104–113,
    168–169 (*see also* description)

nomological "bad luck" of, 25–26,
    29–30
and the nomological threat to
    human dignity, 167–168
ontological dependence of on
    natural science, 144–145, 150–152
and physicalism, 169–170 (*see also*
    physicalism)
primitive terms in, 110, 166–167, 168
and the role of laws, 1–11, 168–173
sociobiology, 109, 132
Sturgeon, Nicholas: "Moral Explana-
    tions," 151, 152
subject matter, 22, 30–31, 48n.16, 54–55,
    148–149. *See also* description;
    social science, intractability of
    subject matter in
supervenience, 155–161
  and ontological dependency, 157
    (*see also* ontological dependence)
  and reductive explanation, 157–161
    (*see also* reductionism)
  strong, 156–157, 158–159
  weak, 156–157

Taylor, Charles, 37–44, 64–65, 69, 125
  "Interpretation and the Sciences of
    Man," 39–44, 126
testability, of theories, 82n.54, 168, 174–
    175n.11. *See also* experimentation
theoretical entities, 96–102
theory, "size" of, 96–102
truism. *See* description, and truism

variables, in complex systems, 44–45,
    58
verstehen, 9–10, 125, 128
volcanology, 30, 31–32, 166. See also
    "fringe" natural science
voting, as reflexive activity, 51n.59,
    52n.76

winetasting, 162n.20
Wisdom, J. O.: *Philosophy of Social
    Science*, 30